WASHINGTON
ENGINEERED

VINCENT LEE-THORP

Noble House

A Division of American Literary Press

Washington Engineered

Library of Congress
Cataloging-in-Publication Data
ISBN 1-56167-940-2

Library of Congress Card Catalog Number:
2006902358

Published by

8019 Belair Road, Suite 10
Baltimore, Maryland 21236

Manufactured in the United States of America

TABLE OF CONTENTS

1 . . . What is an Engineer?

This is the story of a city—Washington, D.C. It is for everyone who is curious about how the town of Washington began in open pastures and a forest of hardwood trees, oaks and hickories, and in little more than two hundred years grew into a city that is now the capital of the United States of America. Much has been written about the great leaders of the new republic whose influence guided us to where we are, and of the grand static monuments and edifices created to serve and honor these men and women. This story does not dwell on them.

Instead, this book tells the story of the inventions and creations that were born to serve the people of this new nation, and of the men and women who were behind these creations. It is the story of the provision of potable water, sanitation, manufacturing, transportation, means of communication and other systems that have led to a society that is safer, healthier, richer in ideas, art and financial wealth, and able to bring help in so many ways to other parts of the globe that are beginning the march to economic success.

This story is also for everyone who gets up in the morning, turns on an electric light, runs the water till it's hot, showers, listens to the television news, gets dressed, makes coffee and toast, glances at the newspaper and drives to work in traffic that is beyond what a person should have to endure, yet never gives much thought to the process except for the traffic. Every step taken that morning is the product of an engineer, except the traffic jams. The traffic is the product of government, taxation, activists, and economic success.

The reality is that almost every convenience in your life that separates you from the colonists of the 1600s happened because of engineering. Science discovered the principles; engineering took those principles and through a developed vision called "invention" created products that make our lives longer, safer, healthier, more comfortable and more efficient, giving us time to relax and enjoy ourselves. Who can remember the poem about a ploughman who worked from dawn to dusk, six days a week—a seventy-hour week with no baseball on television, no refrigerator, no hot shower, no toilet, no heating in the winter, just the words of a poet?

> "The curfew tolls the knell of parting day,
> The lowing herd winds slowly o'er the lea.
> The ploughman homeward plods his weary way;
> And leaves the world to darkness and to me." (1)

The grandest edifices in the world are beautiful to behold in the bright sunlight, but lose much of their grandeur unless there is sufficient light to bring out the color, texture and relief. In darkness they disappear. The castles of the kings of the realm were cold, smelly, drafty backdrops to lives of intrigue and power for the anointed, and places of service and misery to the serfs. But engineering has changed most of it, except the power and the intrigue. Engineering has given to people better standards of living through the harnessing of heat energy—in the form of steam to begin with, then electricity, fossil fuels and nuclear power. People are able to produce more in a day with modern technology than their forefathers ever dreamed of.

And yet, those of us who are lucky enough to visit Paris or London, gaze at the palaces in wonder; marvel at the Sacre Coeur or the Houses of Parliament, usually give little thought to the jet aircraft that got us across the Atlantic. Our concerns generally include whether the flight is on schedule, the entertainment, the food, and our connections when we arrive safely in Paris or London. We tend to shy away from consideration of the aircraft as a complex combination of systems of communication, controls and computers managing the engines, the airframe and a myriad of subsystems in a safe and productive manner. We seldom face the reality that it is our or our parents' productivity, enhanced by engineering, that allows us to afford the luxury of a European adventure in the first place.

But to feel an emotional sense of pleasure from a huge jet airliner requires some serious thought about the dynamics of the aircraft. Said another way, to feel something good in one's heart about a Boeing 777, one has to feel good about things in *motion*; physical *forces* that are acting on the plane; *energy* being expended; myriad *systems working in harmony* together, a little like the human body. This internal awareness of the energy produced or expended by a piece of art is what defines the engineer from the painter, the weaver, the architect or the sculptor. "Ah," one might say, "does this mean that a safe bridge or building is not a piece of engineering art? It is after all very static." The answer is that it is engineering art, because of the forces captured and restrained in the structural members; the beams, columns and arches. The structure is not just sitting quietly without any engineering feeling, sensibly behaving itself. It is for the whole of its existence constantly resisting one or more of the forces of nature, like gravity.

Perhaps it is that we are creatures drawn by our animal instincts to static things; paintings, buildings, mountain scenes, or jewelry, because they are easier to comprehend and accept immediately as a whole. Perhaps it is the proportions of the building, the content of the painting, the peace and grandeur of the mountain scene that immediately resonates with a previous experience and causes our minds to fill with joy. It is said that, "Beauty is in the eye of the beholder." This is easy to understand and accept. Not so easy is the premise that, "Engineering leads from the mind to the heart."

Many of us are drawn to a new automobile by the "design" of the exterior bodywork; the manufacturers have learned how quickly we associate with static art, and how some buyers will make a decision based primarily on the appearance of the vehicle. Most buyers, however, will take the car for a test run and get a sense for the handling, steering, braking and overall "feel" of the machine before making a decision, and in so doing, classically demonstrate the difference between the easy acceptance of static art and the more involved process of understanding dynamic art.

To appreciate the difference between the sculptor and the engineer, one must look at what propels each to do what they do. The similarities are easy to understand. Each is creative, a loner, seeking to release what lies pent up in the brain; challenged sometimes to a point of despair, and joyful when the result emerges. Each has a solution in mind. The solution is unique; if it were not, it would be a case of repetition of some previous challenge, and therefore no challenge at all. Each has a message to convey to the viewer; to open a door to the viewer's mind, thereby expanding the living experience.

The differences lie in what is created and the meaning and impact of the creation to the artist and society. The sculptor's story is built into the three dimensions of space that the sculpture occupies. To the artistically aware observer the statue of David shows a beautifully proportioned young man, handsome, carrying a sling, nude; so even if the story of Goliath is unknown to the viewer, there is a feeling of curiosity and awe. How could a chisel and hammer release this object from a block of marble? If the story of David is known to the observer, there is an immediate recognition and identification, the feeling one gets meeting a hero in the flesh.

The engineer's story is similar and is also about a piece of sculpture, evoking no great curiosity while it sits dormant on the floor or the table. It does not bring any grand feeling to the viewer until it is turned "on" to do the thing it was designed to do. To the casual, distracted observer, it is but another gadget; the world is full of them. But to the thinker, here is what the technical journey was all about.

Consider for example the little device that sits on the bedside table in your hotel room in London. It does very little for your vacation until the buttons are pushed in the right sequence and you hear a voice: you recognize your mother's voice and you begin to share your experiences and love with someone thousands of miles away on another continent. If the invention can produce a usable product or service, and a feeling of accomplishment, then it has communicated not only to the creator but also to the user, who is of necessity, an astute observer.

Said another way, "The painter touches our minds with the skill of his hands; the engineer brings a living system to actually touch our hands and then our minds."

So, then, what is an engineer? *He or she is someone who thinks, who relates to the body of science surrounding the problem, and applies a rational methodology to the solution.*

Some have suggested that to be an engineer one has to be able to visualize the solution in arithmetic, mathematics, sketch, diagram, word description or computer code, or a combination of some of the foregoing. Certainly the reduction of a mechanical problem to a sketch is basic. The inventor visualizes a device that has never existed in the human domain. A doorbell, a corkscrew, a typewriter or a door hinge. The thought is then reduced to a two- or three-dimensional picture or sketch. The solution may lie in a simple modification of the original sketch. Or it may lie in the verbal definition of the problem, after considerable investigation, the reduction of the definition to relevant equations, and the testing of the solution by theoretical analysis. Once the solution has been proven to be sound, it can be reduced to diagrams, and the diagrams transformed into the finished model; an engine; a washing machine; a steam turbine; a calculator or any "thing." A study on how to approach the energy needs of the United States with minimum impact on the environment and conserving depletable resources is engineering.

Engineering, when viewed as creations in motion, goes back to the Roman era, with the building of aqueducts to bring water to remote cities: sewers, buildings with under-floor heating, wheeled carriages, arches and bridges. However the practice of science and engineering really begins after the end of the Dark Ages in the 13th century, with the onset of the Renaissance in Europe.

Before the awakening to the power of energy, in the Industrial Revolution, the people of Europe moved through the Renaissance, which taught them *to think; to evaluate; to choose* and *to believe*, not only in a creator of the universe, but in themselves. This self-belief led to the possibility of self-analysis, and then to the analysis of the external world.

The classic proof of this process is the development of mathematics, which is *logical argument*, and physics, which began to introduce us to the *meaning of the world around us*. It started with simple truths and moved, step by step, to the theoretical understanding of the elements of engineering; motion, force, pressure, temperature, and a host of other variables that make up the physical world.

The word "analysis" has several related meanings and is used here to mean the break-ing of the problem into its major parts. Then the breaking of those parts into ever smaller parts (elements) until we are able to look at, evaluate and understand each element; then by putting the elements back together we are finally able to understand the whole problem. This process, called "The Scientific Method," is one of the most powerful and widely used techniques for solving and understanding the issues and problems that challenge people. And it was this approach that the early practitioners of engineering learned to use.

It was the rigorous application of science that began to slowly define the difference between the students at Colbert's Academie Royale d'Architecture in Paris in 1666. There were those more drawn to the form and appearance of a canal or building design, defined by the long-practiced static rules of proportion and decoration. And then there were oth-ers more concerned with the velocity of the water in the canal or the size of a column defined by the bearing strength of the material; and these differences gradually led to the specialization of the professions so apparent today. The key to understanding the differ-ence between the two kinds of art is to recognize that the painter, architect and sculptor are defining their message in a visual picture in the mind of the beholder, whereas the engineer paints a picture of motion, force and energy. Both are valid. Both are art. All are the outcome of the incredible breakthroughs in man's mental capacity, which started in the Renaissance.

It is curious but not surprising that the National Gallery of Art in Washington contains a world class collection of paintings and sculpture but no works of science or engineering. The latter are reserved in various museums. Perhaps if painters, sculptors, architects, engineers and art critics could spend more time learning about each other's specialty and spreading the information to the public at large, they would bring people closer together in our understanding of each other and the complex world we live in.

Washington Engineered is the story of how engineering embraced the various new advances of science, which began in England and the continent of Europe about the year 1280, and were gradually brought to the New World by the settlers of the 1600s, and how they were used in the building of the city of Washington. The story begins in France and England, where the fruits of the Renaissance were amplified and put to practical, as well as academic, breakthroughs. The rise of the academic institutions in France started the training of generations of *theoretical* engineers, while in England, the emphasis was on the *practical* execution of manufacturing technique. In time, mainly after the Revolution in America, both schools of learning were brought to Washington and the rest of the new United States of America. There were almost no engineers in the whole country in 1776.

The story that follows is a journey with the people and the events that shaped and produced, by the year 2000, a metropolitan complex of five million inhabitants. Obviously these events did not begin with the selection of the site for the new capital in 1789. They have their origins in the end of the Middle Ages in England, when the fruits of the Age of Enlightenment began to nourish men's minds with the nectar of free thought and analytic ability. The age of exploration of the oceans and lands beyond began in the 1400s, leading to the arrival of the Colonists in North America in the early 1600s.

The Revolution has come and gone. The British have been defeated and the Colonists are no longer beholden to a king. The land stretches to the horizon and beyond. The Constitution has defined the limits of the federal government, and the states have the responsibility of meeting the needs of the citizens. The site for the future capital of the nation has been selected, and President Washington has the authority to begin the task of turning rural countryside into the center of government. To do this he will need surveyors, masons, carpenters, blacksmiths, stone cutters; and the French Military Engineers who helped win the War of Independence. What follows is what George Washington and others did to make this country what it is.

But before we start our journey with George Washington we need to go back in time some 500 years to collect and view the events that caused Western society to emerge from the Dark Ages and start the *process* of the gradual development of engineering technology.

2 . . . The Early years in England and France
1280 - 1600

Clearly the beginning of the settlement of people in the New World had its origin in Europe and England. There for several hundred years, the French and Germans had pursued theoretical research into the laws of nature and the application of mathematics to the solution of philosophical challenges. In contrast to the Europeans, the English, on the other side of the Channel, pursued primarily the practical art of making things out of the materials available at that time, while developing their universities to become places of higher learning.

England

Initially England lagged behind Europe in the Age of Enlightenment, perhaps because of its history. The Celtic nation first overwhelmed by the Saxons from Northern Germany in the 600s, then the Danes and Vikings, and finally the Normans from France in 1066—all ferocious warriors and seafaring men not much given to the intellectual or artistic, but driven to impose their will on the island.

As these newcomers began to mellow, there emerged in the Medieval period a strong commitment to religion. The church formed the focal point of people's lives, providing the meaning of life and the rules by which behavior on earth should be conducted. Coupled with a strong central government, headed by a king, English society relied heavily on the teachings of the church and the edicts of the ruling monarchy; the result was a stable nation of workers and aristocrats, mutually supportive, if not socially equal.

A curious but vital development of this closed society was the emphasis on the manufacture of fine tools and their use in creating various unique products, some for warfare and others for improving daily chores, such as the baking of bread. And, through an unknown flash of genius, the invention of the mechanical clock occurred about the year 1280. With small gears, all hand cut, and precision weights that powered the mechanism, here for the first time it was possible to tell the time in the village. The first reference to the manufacture of a time machine occurred in 1286, followed by the installation of larger clocks in church steeples in the 1300s, which became the daily authority on when to rise, to worship, to eat and to sleep for those within earshot of the bells.

By the 1500s the art of clock-making had advanced with the invention of the spring as a means of storing energy for longer periods of time, which spawned the invention of the first pocket-watches worn by fashionable men. The precision and dedication of these artists resulted in the formation of a powerful guild of superior craftsmen, capable of improving and extending one invention to the next. So by the time the Industrial Age began to emerge, England had a supply of skilled workers capable of bringing their expertise to waterwheel drives and, later, to the construction of textile spinning machines.

A second and critical factor in the rise of England as a leading industrial power was the beginning of university education. Students gathered around cathedrals and began to learn the philosophies of the Greeks and Romans, and by the late-1300s a university system of education had been formed, organized around institutions consisting of four departments. The first department offered instruction in the arts, consisting of the study of seven discrete subjects; grammar, rhetoric, logic, music, geometry, arithmetic and astronomy. (2, Page 44)

Upon completion and oral examination in each of the seven subjects, the student was then considered to be ready to embrace one of three professions: law, divinity or medicine. This system formed a nucleus of thinkers, different from their counterparts of the Renaissance, but equipped to begin the process of an analytical approach to the challenges and inventions of the day. Married with the superior craftsmen of the clock and instrument industry, these academic thinkers were able to move into the development and production of mechanical devices.

Critical to the growth and success of Western European culture was the accommodation between religion, on one hand, and the growth of technology on the other. The students of new universities sought to understand both the religious scripture and the newfound philosophical theories without creating a conflict between them, which may have negated the validity of one or the other. Christianity, in retrospect, was able to accept the new theories and technologies while maintaining its original teachings essentially unchanged, and it this mutuality that allowed our deeply religious forefathers to practice their religion and their chosen profession without fear or criticism from the government or the church.

By the 1500s England had settled down to a succession of kings, a queen, relative peace and, as an island nation, a firm commitment to the sea and discovery. And then, over a number of years, arrived Shakespeare and Bacon, displaying genius and artistic intellect, closely followed by the likes of Halley, Boyle, Hooke and Wren, all thinkers and inventors who brought maturity to an industry of watchmakers, craftsmen, instrument makers and writers. With the founding of Cambridge University in 1440, England had its first institution devoted to the theories of philosophy. Little emphasis was placed on the development of engineering principles.

The British, in the seventeenth and eighteenth centuries, had no schools of theoretical engineering, yet there was an increase in the manufacture of technical products that was not matched anywhere else in the world. The leaders of this new "engineering" class were the graduates of the first department of the universities; men with an education in the classics and an exposure to logical and mathematical thinking, and an ability to extrapolate from one success to the next, learning quickly from their failures.

There developed, by the 1700s, a class of professionals, skilled in the art of roads, canals, bridges and buildings, who began to meet in formal surroundings for the exchange of experiences. These were the beginnings of the professional societies we know today.

There also developed a rigorous apprenticeship system, where the art of making products and constructing buildings, both from a practical and theoretical perspective, was passed on to entrants to the trade. A man's worth was determined by his known accomplishments among a relatively small audience.

During this time the Europeans, mainly the Germans and French, made substantial strides in the application of mathematical theory to the construction of buildings, canals and bridges. The quality of their designs were in most respects ahead of their British counterparts, but they had not been able to improve the efficiency of manual labor. Ironwork was all hammered by hand. Stone was cut with a mallet and chisel, and mines pumped by hand.

On the other side of the Channel, experimentation was occurring on the use of "coke," as opposed to charcoal, in furnaces used for the production of iron. With the higher temperatures achieved in a coke furnace, the quality of the metal castings was refined to the point that things could be "fitted" together, with greater precision than ever before. (2, Page 110)

France

French engineering had its beginnings in the sixteenth and seventeenth centuries under powerful and centralized monarchies, with their ability to collect taxes from all parts of the economy, thereby generating the money to support a large military establishment which, in turn, provided employment for military engineers. Explosives, mainly in the form of black powder, were becoming popular, and the architecture of cast brass and cast iron cannons was improving, based largely on the skill of carvers and blacksmiths. Military tactics were also undergoing a revolution with the spreading use of the musket—using black gunpowder and lead shot—and the development of defensive moves, as opposed to the rather wild behavior of mass charges and hand-to hand combat. The building of both temporary and permanent fortifications became common, and the need for trained engineers to build these earth works and the roads began to increase.

The men who knew how to build roads and forts were mainly the aristocratic and intellectual class. They had no interest in moving on to the field of battle, so it soon became obvious to the French minister of war, that a trained cadre of educated military personnel was needed to join the troops and build the installations. In 1676 a special branch of the army was created, called the *Corps du Genie* (Corps of Engineers), who would be skilled in military engineering, primarily fortifications and roads. Leading thinkers in France were assembled, a curriculum outlined, and by 1683 the Corps was staffed with 130 of the brightest minds in the Army. Thirty years would pass before the government realized that the Corps du genie needed to be supported by a field staff capable of performing the survey and planning for a nationwide system of roads and canals with capacity to move the army to any point in the country. So the *Corps des Ponts et Chaussees* (Corps of Bridges and Roads) emerged in 1719, and was given the responsibility for the engineering and architectural construction of these facilities. (2, Page 182)

The demand for technically trained craftsmen for all types of buildings, as well as those able to design fortifications and roads, increased toward the end of the 1700s, culminating in the founding of *Ecole Polytechnique* in Paris in 1794. This institution attracted the brightest of the middle class and lower echelons of the nobility to the study of mathematics, philosophy, science, and the theory of military and civil engineering. Nurtured and supported by the state, these engineers were exposed to all manner of construction and provided their expertise to towns throughout France—in particular, the structural design of buildings which were getting taller and needed the integration of a new material called *cast-iron* into the floors and columns.

The distinction between engineering and architecture, so obvious in the twenty-first century, was not at all apparent in the seventeenth. When the French in 1719 started *Corps de Ponts et Chaussees,* it was under the command of an engineer-senior-architect and staffed with assistant engineers.

The Frenchman J.B. Colbert (1619-1683), a visionary bureaucrat who supported the theory that a successful economy had to produce fine materials, such as tapestries, porcelain and perfumes, founded the *Academie Royale des Sciences* in 1666 to study the techniques of their production and quality. He also believed that the nation needed a system of communication, by roads and canals, to foster the economy and enable the benefits to be brought to all parts of the country. Most engineers were in the military, designers and constructors of forts and machines of war, and Colbert realized that the techniques of building roads, buildings and bridges must be learned by a new breed of professionals. To this end, he established the *Academie Royale d'Architecture* to study and advise on the construction of buildings, bridges and other civil works. In France at that time there was no distinction between engineers and architects, and more often than not, they were one and the same. (2, Page 99)

Their similarity is exemplified by various technical treatises written by scientific scholars between 1737 and 1753, such as Bernard de Belidor's *Architecture Hydraulique*, which became a standard reference for the design of roads, bridges and buildings, as well as hydraulics. This similarity continued until the advancement of engineering technology gradually began to create a distinction between the artist concerned with the visual impact of design, and the artist concerned with functional impact of design.

Between 1802 and 1821 Jean-Nicolas-Louis Durand wrote a three-volume set concerning the practice of architecture as it was being taught at *l'Ecole Polytechnique* in Paris in the 1800s. He opened his treatise with the admonition that there is essentially no difference between the graduates of the institution, and that, "The architect is not the only designer of important buildings; the *Ingenieurs*, both Civil and Military may also do this." Reading on one finds that the practice of design of an "edifice" can be readily undertaken by anyone who has a good carpenter and is able to select which type of building is appropriate to the occasion, and by turning to the right page in one of the three volumes and selecting the plan grid and the right elevation, with towers, arch de triomphe, or colonnade. These documents disclose that the artist is a subtle balance between the politician, the student, the astute observer, and the accomplished creator, none of the traits being dominant, but all influencing the final product. (3)

The overall thrust of the treatise was to give the student a reverence for the power of construction creativity, with a solid grounding in the geometric and graphic rules that govern the proportions of buildings and related engineering works. Economics play no part in the treatise. It is curiously refreshing that the volumes make no mention of fortifications, canals or roads, leaving the reader with the impression that those subjects were not implicitly part of the curricular at l'Ecole.

The methods of construction of buildings had been handed down for generations of guild craftsmen who knew the strengths and limitations of their trade and could extrapolate from one building to the next without the need for drawings or "professional" advice. The dimensions and strength of arches had been learned through trial and error, and contributed to the form of the finished building. The styles of buildings, starting with the Romans, moved through several classic periods. Each had its rules and proportions, but with the same engineering concept of stone supporting stone to create walls, arches in compression to support upper floors in palaces and cathedrals, and stout wood beams for buildings of lesser quality. This method of building design was practiced by the master craftsman who led the design and provided the mountings for decorative stone carvings on both exterior and interior surfaces.

The trial and error method of design is no more apparent than in the age of cathedrals. The flying buttress so admired by tourists of a later age was not invented for aesthetic reasons, and there were no supporting calculations that determined the horizontal thrust necessary to stabilize the main walls of the chancel. It was done by trial and error.

Then came the age of enlightenment, the Renaissance, mathematics, and the arrival on the scene of the man with technical skill. A skill that had not been handed down for generations but had been conceived by an inventive mind based on an ever-growing body of knowledge. With the application of iron, and later steel, the form of the building could be radically altered, and this led to a dependence on technology for the safe design of structures.

Engineering, which for years was slanted toward the building of military and related national installations, was released to become the civil and structural branches of the technology that we know today. Colbert and his students achieved remarkable success, one of the most notable being the construction of the Canal du Midi—a 200-mile-long canal connecting Marseilles with Bordeaux, and containing 100 locks, lifting the ships more than 500 feet, and then down to the level of the Garonne River. The project, started in 1666 and completed in 1681, was considered the greatest feat of engineering since the Roman Aqueducts. It is still in good condition and a waterway for barges of all sizes. (2, Page 99)

One of the ironies of the success of Canal du Midi, when news of its marvelous performance spread through Europe, was the way in which foreigners visited the locks in order to copy them in their own countries. The British, in particular, learned a great deal about the engineering, which was readily applied in their own country. But it did raise the issue of protecting new inventions against theft. This protection lead to the patent laws.

Patents

Early inventors throughout Europe and England were faced with the dilemma of keeping their inventions secret. To put the product, usually developed over years of trial and endeavor, on the open market revealed the invention to all, with the result that competitors could copy the design and produce it for their own gain. The early English cotton industry, with the world's most modern spinning and weaving equipment, was carefully guarded and protected against theft and outside observation for many years.

The first patents were granted by kings to their favorite subjects, usually for a hefty bribe, but this method finally ended in England in 1624 with the passage of the Statute of Monopolies, which guaranteed to an inventor the sole monopoly to his invention for 22 years. While not doing much to prevent theft of intellectual property by foreigners, it did give the local inventor the opportunity for the first time to develop and market his invention, usually with the financial help of wealthy investors. The veritable explosion of invention that followed is credited to a large degree to the fact that original ideas and inventions were protected. They could therefore be discussed with academics and potential competitors in intellectual meetings, thereby spreading the technology, which could then be applied to an analogous invention without violating the original idea. The philosophical and scientific societies were a direct outgrowth of the patent laws because the leaders and interested parties could meet in an open forum and debate the scientific and engineering content of an idea. (2, Page 105)

In a dynamic society, rich in research and invention, the need to protect the inventor for a reasonable time became obvious. To enable the product to be developed and marketed over sufficient time for investors to recoup their outlays and make profit on their capital proved to be a good thing for society and one of the main driving forces which lead to the Industrial Revolution.

3 . . . THE INDUSTRIAL REVOLUTION IN ENGLAND

The emergence of the city of Washington as the capital of an industrial society has its roots in the transformation of England from an agrarian country into a dynamic "industrialized" nation. This transformation has become known as the Industrial Revolution. Since the United States of America did not exist in the Medieval era, its creation and growth occurred largely because of the economic forces generated in Europe by the introduction of technology. For example, the pressure of a growing population in England, a direct result of the Industrial Revolution, produced the men and women willing to leave their homelands and settle in the New World.

The term "Industrial Revolution," coined in 1880 by Arnold Toynbee (1852-1883), a professor of Political Economics at Oxford University, highlights the events of some two hundred years in England, during which time the culture and economic practices of the Medieval era came to an end and the world of competitive manufacturing began. With the first settlements by the English in the New World beginning in Virginia in 1607, clearly the town of Washington has no medieval history, and all of the subsequent development is based on the events that became known as the Industrial Revolution.

These events, which occurred roughly between 1624, with the passage of the Patents Monopoly Law by the British Parliament, and the application of electric power around 1880, incorporate a number of separate but interlocking revolutions, which when taken together form the Industrial Revolution.

These revolutions include:
> The appearance of newspapers and an encyclopedia
> The rapid increase in population
> The reduction in commonland caused by enclosure laws
> The change from home weaving to factories
> The improvements in agriculture
> The invention of the heat engine

The passage of the patent laws and the protection that they offered to *inventors and investors* meant that for the first time in history it was possible to persuade an individual with capital assets to lend money to an inventor, and if successful, reap financial gain, while protected from competition for a number of years. This fortuitous marriage between enlightened invention and uncovering the hitherto concealed stores of wealth provided the initial thrust that propelled many thinkers to seek solutions to the problems of society. These thinkers were not confined to the production of mechanical systems that became the trademark of the revolution, but included breakthroughs in the fields of banking, medicine, philosophy, economics, and many others.

Newspapers and Journals

One effect of the Patent Laws enabled all manner of people to begin public dialogues on the effects of the newly invented products and institutions on their daily lives. This was new. Up to this time most of the discussions were held in private forums or in secret. The myriad of opinions led to the foundation of journalism and the publication of newspapers in Europe and England. The *London Gazette* first appeared in 1666, followed by England's first daily newspaper in 1702. Here for the first time in history, *information* was showered on the common man, who, for all time before, had to rely on the word of mouth of his neighbor. The truth was hard to come by.

With information from the daily news, supported by the publication in 1704 of a *Universal Dictionary of Arts and Science,* it was now possible for technical and engineering information to be available to the nation as a whole. The effect was stunning. All manner of invention followed, giving solid proof that a revolution was occurring. (2, Page 106)

The Enclosure Laws

In medieval times there were few large cities or towns of significant magnitude, and the population survived in villages, each an economic entity supporting the inhabitants through farming, the raising of live stock, home industries that produced woolen cloth and garments, and the hand working of wood and metal. Communication between towns and villages occurred primarily through riders on horseback. Roads were virtually impassable. There were as yet no canals. Rivers formed the major arteries between centers of population.

The land surrounding the villages was known as "commonland," inasmuch as the yeoman farmers had access to the fields and pastures from generation to generation while paying a small annual rent to the landowner, who was the Lord of the Manor, with title to the land in a grant from the king. Each piece of commonland included three cultivated pastures, shared by the farmers, and ploughed individually in small parcels, with the same crops every year. One third of the land lay fallow on a rotating basis and the other two thirds were sewn with barley or wheat. The balance of the commonland was given to the open fields on which the farmers raised cattle, carefully dividing the acreage based on the age of the farmer and the number of years he had been farming. The cultivated pastures seldom received fertilizer, while the animal waste remained in the fields, doing little good and contributing to pollution of the streams.

The original enclosure laws allowing the landlord to occupy a portion of the commonland for his sole use date from the thirteenth century, in particular the Statute of Westminster in 1285. From that time on, there was a gradual reduction in commonland available to the yeoman farmers, and a corresponding growth in land farmed by the landlord and the farmers in his employ. The result was quite unpredictable. Instead of the total volume of produce facing a gradual decline, the reverse occurred. Because of poor farming practices the production on the yeoman farmers' commonland gradually decreased, whereas the yield of the land controlled by the landlord increased out of all expectation. The increase happened because of *new farming methods*, in particular the invention of the beneficial effects of crop rotation, the introduction of potatoes, turnips and grasses for feeding cattle, and the use of all cattle droppings as manure dug into the pastures. Potatoes, in particular, proved to be a stroke of genius, because they provided a means of reconstituting the soil and provided a new and major food source for the general population. According to Arnold Toynbee, the population of England in 1696 included some 5,500,000 persons, of whom 75 percent, or 4,100,000, occupied villages and hamlets; with 870,000 living in market towns and 530,000 in the city of London. (4)

The practice of enclosure had several consequences, some bad but most good. One bad feature turned out to be the reduction of population on the commonland. Better farming methods reduced the number of farmers and farmhands needed to produce an ever-increasing volume of farm products, with the result that people gravitated to the cities. Many villages disappeared, with the skilled weavers and metalworkers migrating with the farmers. It was this population redistribution that provided the pressure in growing towns and cities to encourage people to leave their homeland for the New World. For many families the future in the towns of England looked very grim, whereas the possibilities of land grants in America and elsewhere provided hope for a successful future. It was this hope in thousands of poor city dwellers that caused them to leave and become a necessary element to populate the Colonies.

The positive effects of enclosure included the emphasis on scientific agriculture, and the introduction of the turnip, not only as a food for humans but as a food for sheep in winter. The immediate results were a rapid increase in sheep farming, increased weight as well as numbers of animals, and an increase in the available wool harvest, which moved from an average of three pounds of fleece per animal in 1700 to nine pounds in 1800. Cattle, in the same period, showed an increase in weight from an average of 370 pounds to 800 pounds. (4)

The most startling benefit showed itself in the availability of food, particularly potatoes, which gradually fell in price relative to wages and became the staple of many families.

Population

Fueled by the availability and lower cost of basic food and milk, cleaner water and improved living conditions, there occurred a dramatic increase in population, both in towns and rural villages. According to Toynbee, the population of England was 5.5 million in 1700, showed a growth of 18 percent by 1750, and reached more than 9.0 million in 1800, an increase of more than 60 percent. While many villages virtually disappeared during this period due to the population shift, major cities, turning into centers of manufacturing, showed remarkable growth.

City	1685	1760	1880
Manchester	6,000	30,000	390,000
Birmingham	4,000	28,000	400,000
Liverpool	4,000	40,000	550,000

As part of the Industrial Revolution, the increase in population proved to be a distinct advantage, inasmuch as a pool of ready labor was constantly available. The lot of the laborers, however, did not benefit from the increased competition; wages remained low but the job market continued to expand and proved to be a deterrent to poverty. The growth of the population in England began to level off in the 1800s due primarily to the vast emigration to the colonies, and to North America in particular. Between 1800 and 1880 some eight million English, Irish and Scots left their native lands and settled abroad, with the largest numbers settling on the East Coast of the United States and Canada.

Agriculture

The enclosure laws, while greatly reducing the land available for cultivation under the medieval method of farming, caused the land to be divided into more compact and closely managed farms that yielded much greater output than the old system. Jethro Tull (1674-1741) for example, an educated gentleman farmer, invented a *seed drill,* which overcame the problem of losing hand-sprinkled seed to birds and wind and had the immediate result of sustaining higher rates of seed germination and more yield per acre. He continued to experiment with crop rotation to restore the power of the soil, and devised a program of planting wheat for a year, followed by turnips, then oats or barley, and then clover in the fourth year. In 1770 the yield of wheat had increased to twenty-five bushels per acre compared to the best in France at eighteen per acre.

This mini-revolution in agriculture, based on careful and thoughtful behavior, was a precursor of the engineering inventions that followed, because it generated capital from the sale of the products to Europe and America; the profits therefrom could then be tapped for the employment of thinkers and inventors. Before the mammoth increase in wealth resulting from agricultural productivity, there were few sources of capital available to the scientific community and, as a consequence, little advancement in the art of engineering.

Home Weaving to Factories

Concurrent with the revolution in agriculture was the concentration of the woolen industry into the growing towns on the south coast and center of England. Here factories employing several hundred people emerged in the late 1600s, providing employment for those who previously were the backbone of the residential weaving trade and had moved to the cities in response to the enclosure laws. The art of weaving wool fiber into cloth originated in France and was imported to England as early as 1350, but remained a slow developing industry, concentrated in private dwellings, spreading gradually up the west coast to what is now Yorkshire. All of the looms were powered by the weaver or assistants who perched on a high seat in front of the loom, and with vigorous leg movements caused the machine to operate. The displacement of people to the centers of population provided the manpower to staff the new factories, whose output grew substantially compared to the old system, and generated greater wealth for the owners as well as wages for the workers.

Engineering

The key ingredients supporting the Industrial Revolution were the application of engineering in the creation of all manner of manufacturing tools and the invention of the steam engine. Here for the first time in history, the channeling of an old form of energy, namely *fire*, into an ingenious mechanical device, the *steam engine*, provided man the ability to multiply the force in his bodily frame—and the power of horses and water wheels—many times over. The key to the success of the steam engine lay in the simple but ingenious invention of the *crank,* which allowed a reciprocating motion (of the piston) to be converted into a rotary motion (the flywheel), which could then be used to power all manner of machines.

The steam engine had its beginning in England about 1698 when Thomas Savery, a merchant and inventor, demonstrated that the vacuum, caused when steam in a closed vessel or drum is allowed to condense into water, was sufficient to lift a column of water several feet. Savery developed the principle into a working engine for which he was granted a patent, which by Act of Parliament, extended for thirty-one years. The engines were used for pumping water from coal mines. The problem of water collection at the base of mines was a vexing issue at that time since it severely limited the depth of the mine shaft and compromised the safety of the miners. It was simply not feasible to use manual pumps or pumps powered by horses because of the reliability and continued operation that mine evacuation required. On the other hand, the demand for coal, the major source of industrial fuel at that time, continued to increase, so that the need to find a way to keep the level of water in the mines below the working tunnels became a powerful economic challenge.

The Savery engine answered an immediate need, but its real success was the challenge it presented to other inventors to utilize the principle of pressure differential to force a column of water from a lower to higher level. This principle apparently triggered the inventive genius in Thomas Newcomen, who in 1712 introduced the steam engine to the world.

Thomas Newcomen

Thomas Newcomen (1664-1729), an ironmonger from Devon, was aware of the problem of flooding, which had serious and life-threatening effects on all kinds of mines in Europe, as well as England. In 1703, he started work on the design of a steam-driven pump, which he put into production in 1712. The world's first steam engine, standing more than fifty feet in height and pumping at a rate twelve strokes per minute, developed some five horsepower. But unlike five horses, it could run twenty-four hours a day, every day of the month, without food, but with fair quantities of water and coal.

The Newcomen Engine proved to be reliable and filled a need in human development, such that, for the first time in history, a single man's labor could be multiplied many times over for the benefit of all. More than ninety Engines were manufactured and used in England, Belgium, France, Germany and Scandinavia between 1715 and 1750.

The limiting factor of the Newcomen Engine was that it was operated by the pressure of the atmosphere pressing down on a large piston, on the other side of which was a vacuum created by the condensation of steam in the cylinder. This limitation was solved in 1769 when James Watt (1736-1819) invented an engine based on the pressure of steam from a boiler, forcing a piston to move in a cylinder.

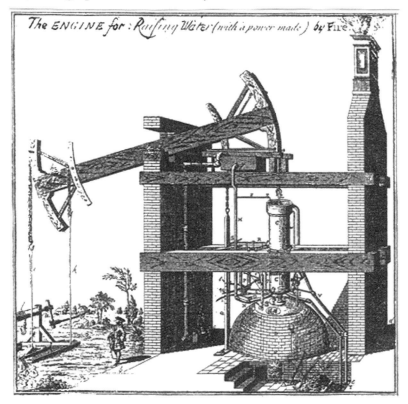

Plate 3 – 1
A Newcomen Engine, 1720, attached to a vertical pump

The vertical cylinder, "C," received steam from the boiler below, which forced out the air. When the cylinder was full of steam, a manual valve shut off the steam and flushed in water, which condensed the steam, creating a vacuum. The pressure of the atmosphere pushed on the piston in the cylinder, causing it to move.

James Watt

In 1765, James Watt, an instrument maker at the University of Glasgow, was given a model of a Newcomen Engine to repair. In the course of his labors and testing, he determined that there had to be a better way of forcing the piston in and out of a cylinder. Rather than using the pressure of the atmosphere pushing against a vacuum created in the cylinder by the condensation of the steam, he concluded that the pressure of the steam from a boiler could be of much more use, particularly if the steam pressure could be raised many times more than the pressure of the atmosphere. His design proved to be successful, and a patent granted by the Parliament in 1769 gave him the right to develop and sell the engine until 1800 without competition. His partnership with Matthew Boulton in 1773 allowed the company to expand and offer the engine for many and diverse applications, particularly because of the supporting inventions in the art of metalworking that occurred in this period.

The steam engine is probably one of the most important inventions in the Western World because it allowed the use of power and energy to be harnessed by small- and medium-sized factories for the first time in history. It also proved to be one of the mini-revolutions that spearheaded the Industrial Revolution. Out of this invention emerged railroads, steamships and factories that transformed the face of England and Europe.

Watt's invention was made possible by the concurrent invention of various machine tools, listed in Table 1.

Table 1
Machine Tools that Supported the Industrial Revolution

1712	Newcomen, in England, builds the first engines
1750	Metal-turning lathes developed in France
1769	Watt patents the Pressure Steam Engine
1775	Boring Mill invented by Wilkinson, in England.
1787	Gears invented in France
1797	Precision Metal Lathe by Maudslay in England
1800	Industrial Lathes in use in France and England
1804	High Pressure Steam Engine by Oliver Evans, Philadelphia
1805	Steam Locomotive invented by Trevithick, in England
1818	Milling Machines invented by Eli Whitney in America
1825	Steam Boilers developed in America and England

Though not in the league of the great engineering inventions, yet vital to the protection of property in an age of thievery and lawlessness, was the invention of the Thief Proof Lock by Joseph Bramah about 1790. The follow-on by his foreman, Henry Maudslay, was the invention of machine tools for the manufacture of the locks and similar small pieces of technical hardware. The team also invented the hydraulic press and the pump for lifting beer from a barrel in the cellar below. (2)

The large beam above Newcomen's Engines, as well as most buildings and ships constructed at that time, were made of wood or masonry. The improvements in the use of coke in blast furnaces finally enabled larger iron beams and sections to be poured in the foundries, and these immediately found application in the construction industry.

Cast and Wrought Iron for Buildings

The use of cast iron for structural purposes began in England in 1770 with the columns in St. Anne's Church, Liverpool, followed in 1775 with the building of bridges in the North of England using cast-iron beams designed and produced by John Wilkinson, an ironmaster from Castlehead. (2. Page 168)

In 1801, after a series of devastating fires in the cotton mills in Manchester, cast-iron beams and columns began to replace the wood construction, and their use in a mill designed by Boulton and Watt is the first recorded application of the material for industrial buildings.

William Fairburn, in his book *Cast and Wrought Iron for Building Purposes*, published in 1854, indicated that the first use of cast-iron beams in buildings dates from 1801 in a cotton mill erected by Phillips and Lee of Manchester using cast-iron beams and columns designed by Boulton and Watt. The beams were 13-1/2 inches in height, 1-1/4 inches thick, with a 3-1/4-inch-wide flange at the bottom. Spaced on nine-foot centers, and with a span of fourteen feet, the beams were calculated to have a load-bearing strength of 8.3 tons. (5)

To determine their actual strength, the beams were subject to gradually increasing load tests until they fractured. Thus the load-bearing capacity and dimensions of these cast-iron beams became a standard, and they were used in all types of construction in England and subsequently in the United States. The whole purpose of experimenting with cast-iron, as opposed to using masonry, was cost. The inability of arches in a masonry building to span any substantial distance limited their use in all but ceremonial and religious structures.

Fire Protection Systems

It soon became obvious to mill owners that fires had to be avoided if at all possible since the loss of the building and contents often resulted in the failure of the enterprise. In most cases, insurance against loss could not be shifted to other parties. Building insurance did not exist. Bonding companies, who offered insurance against loss of contents, through theft or fire, did exist, but their rates were based on the expected frequency of theft or fire. Mill owners found that they could reduce the cost of insuring warehouse contents by consulting with the bonding companies. Heeding their advice with regard to the use of steel doors meant dividing the warehouse into smaller areas separated by thick masonry fireproof walls, and providing large cisterns filled with water on the roof. The cisterns connected to a system of pipes and valves on each floor. Thus emerged the beginnings of a coordinated set of rules for protection against fire in buildings.

The first recorded use of water sprinklers in buildings for the purpose of extinguishing fires was the design of Joseph Jones of Wallshaw, near Oldham, Yorkshire, in 1844. Installed in a cotton mill, the system consisted of a number of hand valves located on the exterior of the mill, each connected to the city water supply, which was maintained at a static pressure of 200 feet of water from a tank on a nearby hill. From the leaving port of each valve, a pipe was run to the rooms requiring protection, terminating in nine-inch-diameter copper globes, secured pressure tight to the supply pipe and perforated with a series of small holes. The globes were hung at the ceilings, every sixty feet in both directions to cover the room. In the event of fire the occupants could flee the space, and the appropriate valve or valves could be opened, which would cause a spray of water forty feet in all directions to cover the fire. For larger conflagrations more valves could be opened. The key to success of the system was the availability of sufficient water at a high enough pressure. (5, Page 120)

In addition to the creation of industry, the Industrial Revolution impacted many individuals who began to apply the lessons of physics to everyday living problems. Typical was the approach to the problem of heating dwellings.

Comfort Heating

The wood fire burning in the center of the living space, providing warmth to those huddled around, while a plume of smoke passed upwards through a hole in the roof above, was a standard of comfort in cold countries for thousands of years before the invention of the fireplace. In the Outer Hebrides of Scotland, the crofters in the 1700s lived in earthen huts fitted with grass roofs twenty-four inches thick, and no flue. The smoke lazily seeped into the grass roofing, giving the dwellings the name of "black cottages," after the color of the ceiling and the curious but pleasant odor which exists to this day in houses that have survived.

In 1240 in England the fire that for years burned in the center of the main hall was moved to an outside wall and fitted with a *metal funnel* several feet above the floor level and connected to an opening through the wall. From this innovation emerged the Norman Fireplace, with the funnel *enclosed in brick* and a vertical stack arranged to convey the smoke upward through the roof. This invention spread through England and the continent and became the standard for almost 300 years until 1600, when a French physician, Louis Savot, displeased with the performance and general smokiness of the fires, invented the *grate*. It consisted of metal rods at right angles, with feet that allowed the fire to be elevated a few inches above the fireplace and allowed combustion air to enter beneath the flames, thereby substantially increasing the temperature and reducing smoke generation.

A century later, in 1713, a French cleric operating in secret under the *nome-de-plume* Nicholas Gauger, using the scientific training learned in university, studied the combustion process. He concluded that the key to controlling the production of smoke and maximizing temperature was the *dampering of the combustion air in and the smoke flowing out*. This meant having dampers or adjustable blades at the inlet to the grate and at the stack so that a balance of the products of combustion could be maintained. In his treatise, *Mechanique du Feu*, Gauger demonstrated the variation of temperature produced by the manipulation of the dampers when the fire was enclosed in a metal sheath and allowed to radiate to the occupied room. (6)

Benjamin Franklin (1706-1790) studied Gauger's work, and in 1740 produced a modified version, named the *Pennsylvania*. It consisted of a rectangular wood-burning unit, encased in a light cast-iron shell, fitted with Gauger's recommended dampers and grate, and provided with a double wall that allowed room air to enter at the floor and rise up through the cavity, becoming heated and thence flowing into the room. Franklin was more than pleased that he had not only solved the problem of smoke blowing back but had reduced the amount of wood burned by a factor of three. He studied the problems associated with fireplaces for many years, toward the end of his life writing his *Observations on Smoky Chimneys,* which described in detail the reasons and gave recommendations to eliminate backflow. His recommendations for multiple flues serving fireplaces on different floors of a building were followed in the design of the Capitol and the other federal buildings.

With the decision to create the new capital city on the banks of the Potowmack River in 1790 came the planning of the first of many Federal buildings and private homes, all of which were heated by means of wood- or coal-burning fireplaces. The original Capitol Building, completed in 1819, contained twenty masonry stacks, each serving back-to-back fireplaces on three floors; so there were at least 120 fireplaces in operation on a cold winter's day in 1825. Many artist's renderings never show a wisp of smoke emanating from the grand structure. Small residential log cabins continued to be heated by a single open-hearth fireplace strategically placed in the center of the dwelling and surrounded by a heavy masonry flue, which when heated in the evening continued to radiate warmth until the wee-hours of the morning. Larger residences were not so fortunate, and like the Capitol were fitted with multiple fireplaces, one at least in all the important rooms, which had to be tended by the staff three or four times a day.

Beginning in the 1750s industrial buildings, mills in the north of England and the Houses of Parliament began to be heated with hot air, allowed to rise up open shafts to the spaces above, with the hot air generated by air ducts adjacent to brick-enclosed fireplaces. The results were a series of fires, many life threatening, including a devastating conflagration at the Parliament Building in London, which lead to Watt's experiments using steam and hot water as a means of conveying heat around buildings.

Initially applied to multi-storied cotton mills, the systems consisted of large iron pipes, six inches in diameter, arranged in banks at the ceilings of the spinning rooms, and connected to steam boilers in the basement. As the steam was generated it would rise by gravity into the piping, and allow the air within the pipes, which is heavier than steam, to gradually sink downward to the boiler header, where it would be manually vented to the atmosphere. The central steam systems proved to be very effective, particularly in the colder climates of north England and in the mill towns of New England. Because of the initial cost on one hand, and the massive appearance on the other, these steam heating systems found no place in the residences of that time. The coal fireplace, refined with dampers, multiple grates and ornate enclosures, dominated the residential heating market in Washington between 1790 and 1860, but it was the invention of the steam radiator that finally brought some measure of comfort to the living rooms and bedrooms. (7)

Heating and Ventilating

James Watt is credited with one of the first attempts to build a home heating system, when in the winter of 1784 he set about making a radiator to heat his study, which was 18 feet long by 14 feet wide with a ceiling height of eight feet six inches. He constructed a box of tin-plated iron, 3'-6" by 2'-6" by one inch in depth, sealed on all sides. It included a manual air vent on the top and a connection on the bottom sufficient to let steam in and allow condensate to drain out at the same time. A hand valve installed in the supply pipe allowed it to be turned on and off. Mounted on edge with the steam coming up from the basement, the radiator got hot, but did not give off the heat that Watt expected. Later scientists showed that the shiny surfaces on both inside and outside the radiator were not good at absorbing and radiating heat from the steam. (8)

By 1799, a Mr. Lee, an engineer from Manchester, showed that the black cast-iron pipes filled with steam did a much better job of giving off heat to a space, and concluded that heat was emitted from a hot body in two ways—firstly by radiation and secondly by conduction. He built his four -inch-diameter pipe radiators into brick enclosures, arranged with an opening at the bottom to let cold air in and an adjustable damper on the top to regulate the flow of hot air drawn up over the hot pipe and discharged into the room. The unit was so successful that he had to turn off the radiators in the vestibule of his house to prevent overheating.

4 . . . SCIENCE IN AMERICA PRIOR TO THE REVOLUTION

Pre-Revolutionary America consisted of the English colonies of New England, principally Massachusetts, New York, and the Middle Atlantic Colonies, including Virginia, together with the colonies of France and Spain. The British monarchy and their appointed representatives governed the English outposts for their benefit and economic gain. There were strict laws regarding competition with the mother country, particularly with regard to the manufacture of cloth and tools, and rules regarding the shipping of Virginia's major product, tobacco, to England. The result was the colonies remained largely agricultural, with little emphasis on higher education. A few educated people wanted to emigrate to the Americas, particularly during the religious upheaval in England that caused the Puritans (Protestants) to leave in droves during the reign of Charles I, to be followed by the Catholics during the Civil War in England from 1649 to 1660. These events led to the population of Virginia and Maryland increasing substantially—Virginia from 15,000 in 1649 to 38,000 in 1670. (9, Page 16)

The Age of Enlightenment, the opening of the minds of people to the possibilities of the Renaissance, was very much driven by the religious beliefs of the time, and to a large degree sought to explain the tangible world and the universe beyond, in concert with those beliefs. A central theme of the Enlightenment was the goal of man, through rigorous study, to unlock the secrets of nature from the smallest plant or life form to the limits of the stars in the heavens. Thus science, the thinking man's art, emerged as a four-pronged field of endeavor, which embraced the study of astronomy, medicine, agriculture and mathematics. Science was not at all the realm of the academic researcher that we think of today. It was the realm of the curious intellectual, usually specializing in one of the four "prongs" of the art, but more than willing to meet and share the struggle for a meaningful explanation of some facet of the universe. Engineering and architecture as we know them today did not exist. The basic theorems of engineering were in their infancy, and the "Natural Philosophers," as they were known, were primarily in England, concentrating on the physical sciences of chemistry, astronomy, physics and mechanics.

The Enlightenment, springing from a core of the love of fellow man, had at its center the belief that science could be used for the betterment of all mankind. The understanding of the flower and the seed could lead to greater agricultural output, which could solve the ever-threatening hunger faced year upon year. Understanding the behavior of the planets and the solar system could lead man to better predict the future and anticipate the impending changes in the seasons. Understanding the human body would enable the doctors to cure the suffering and extend the span of human existence. But it was mathematics that provided the key to the process, in such people as Sir Isaac Newton, who with his simple and enduring laws of nature gave fire to the belief that technical wisdom could lead to the goal that man was seeking—the goal of emerging into an era of abundance and caring, an era of untold power over the frailties of life, a time of finally understanding the message of the Creator. It was in this aura that science began to emerge in America. England's Sir Francis Bacon said it in these words: "Science must be known by its works. It is by the witness of works rather than by logic or even observation that truth is revealed and established. It follows from this that the improvement of man's lot and the improvement of man's mind are one and the same thing."

Science in the America of the 1700s was a gentleman's avocation. The story of Benjamin Franklin is the story of a young man born into humble circumstances, but through his faith in himself and an inner genius was able to rise to the pinnacle of success and be recognized by his peers as a unique leader in the field of science. The son of a candle maker in Boston, born in 1706, he was apprenticed to his elder brother in the printing business. Here he caught the attention of the governor of Pennsylvania as the result of a series of striking and successful anonymous articles published in the local papers and finally attributed to the eighteen-year-old genius. He received help in getting a passage to England, where he studied the latest inventions in printing. Upon his return to Philadelphia he became successful in a printing business of his own, and it was there that he founded the Philosophical Society of America. He also pressed for the foundation of the Academy of Philadelphia, now the University of Pennsylvania. Franklin is best remembered for his experiments attempting to define the nature of electricity, including the kite flying in a thunderstorm and conducting the lightning flash to earth. But above all there is the dedicated thinker, struggling with his peers, to understand nature and bring the best of the understanding to the table of the common man. This man and his career best describe science in America prior to the revolution.

Typical of the time was the work of the English astronomers Charles Mason and Jeremiah Dixon, who were asked to prepare a survey of the boundary between Pennsylvania and Maryland based on astronomical observations. From 1763 to 1768 the two took numerous observations of the latitude and longitude of many locations along the line of the boundary between the two colonies. Their work, while important to the Americans, was published in London in the *Journal of the Royal Philosophical Society* and hailed as an example of the advancement of the science of astronomy.

Another issue of importance to the sailors of all nations was the apparent drift of the compass from the direction of true north that occurred from place to place without any apparent reason. Many theories were advanced but none fit all conditions; so it was decided to prepare a catalog of sightings from many different locations in America and from this data attempt to propose a general theory that would be able to predict the variation from any location. Much work was done and observations recorded, meetings held and information exchanged, and in the end no general theory that explained the compass variation could be advanced. But the participants did prove that coming together and debating the pros and cons of different positions produced a climate of mutual understanding and respect.

When we think of Science in those early times of the colonization of the New World, we must think of a *philosophical* movement, closely allied to the religious teachings of the time, seeking to understand the miracle of life and bring tangible benefits to the population as a whole. We must think of intellectually driven individuals, seeking to recognize the secrets of life in medicine, the window to the universe in astronomy, the behavior of nature in botany and agriculture, and the laws of nature as revealed by mathematics. Later the genius of inventors would bring products to the marketplace, which would give reality to the dreams of the scientists of the 1600s. This reality was the field of engineering.

This flexibility in the use of theoretical knowledge permeated the new nation and allowed the inventive genius of many educated men to solve problems and meet challenges, thereby creating a spirit that became synonymous with Americanism. Within a short space of time all manner of inventions were offered in the marketplace, including a pile driver for use in the construction of bridges, an air pump, farming machinery, and even devices for cleaning wells and sweeping chimneys.

An English immigrant, Christopher Colles, who had trained in mathematics and science, came to America in 1771 and offered his services in "Practical Engineering," and advertised his profession as an "Engineer-Architect," which included the delivery of mills, waterworks and hydraulic engines. He also taught mathematics and philosophy in Philadelphia. In 1772 he was instrumental in the founding of the American Philosophical Society, and went on to build a steam engine, which he demonstrated in 1774, for the purpose of raising water at a distillery. So successful were his projects that he was asked to come to New York and install a water-lifting engine connected to a piping system made of hollowed-out oak logs to provide running water to a new housing development. (10)

Colles's engineering for the distribution of water found a place in the future Capitol. To Christopher Colles, therefore, we must give the title of the "First Practicing Engineer in America."

5 . . . THE REVOLUTIONARY WAR

It must be pure chance that the American Revolution, or the War for Independence as it is also known, occurred at about the same time as the invention of the steam engine in England. It is true that Watt's engines had not yet crossed the Atlantic by the time the war began, so the results of the Industrial Revolution would not be felt in America until the end of hostilities between the warring powers. This means that the war would be fought using the science and techniques in vogue in the 1760s. Engineering at that time had its emphasis on the military; the construction of earthworks, fortifications, roads and means of transportation.

The knowledge for building of fortifications simply did not exist in the colonies at that time, so the leaders of the American army had to rely on the experience gained in their participation in the war against Spain and the forays against the French. Members of George Washington's family had been involved in both events, so it came as no surprise that George would be tapped as one of the military leaders when the war began in 1775.

George Washington

George Washington, the first president of the United States, and considered by many to be the "Father of Our Country," was reared as an English Gentleman in the Northern Neck of Virginia near to the Rappahannock River. George's great grandfather had come to the colony of Virginia quite by chance in 1657 as the mate on the ketch "Sea Horse of London," which was engaged in the transport of manufactured goods to the colonies, returning with loads of tobacco to the port of London. In April of that year the ketch ran aground in a fierce late-winter storm and the mate, John Washington, helped salvage the valuable cargo. As a reward he was allowed by the ship's captain to remain in the colony.

The son of a Catholic clergyman who had been ousted from his church by the Puritans in 1643, John must have gone to sea, as many young men did in that day, to seek a fortune and see the world, but also, in his case, to erase the fact that he would never be able to follow his father in his chosen profession.

John made friends easily, and as a willing and strong farm worker soon impressed his employer, Nathaniel Pope, and Pope's daughter, Anne, so that he received permission to court the daughter. They were married in 1658 and were given 700 acres of farmland and means to construct a house. In the fall of 1659 the couple celebrated the birth of a son, named Lawrence, and subsequently had four more children. As a proper Englishman of stature, Lawrence was sent to England to be educated at the tender age of nine years, returning in 1677 as a man of eighteen with a grounding in the skills needed to manage an estate and take his place in the upper echelons of colonial society.

Lawrence married in 1686, taking over the land inherited from his father, and in the intervening ten years sired three children, John, Augustine and Mildred. Lawrence was never a strong or healthy individual, and finally succumbed at age 38 in 1698.

At the early age of eleven Augustine showed great promise in academics, the skill of writing and the fluent use of the mother tongue, and soon he began to be assigned responsibilities normally reserved for males on the verge of maturity at sixteen or seventeen years of age. He grew to be a tall, muscular man, well over six feet, enabling him to command respect and leadership in the community, and endowed with a knack to barter and trade, began to assemble larger tracts of land in the family name. He married in 1715, and by 1729 had sired three children, Lawrence II, Augustine Jr., and June. In 1730 his wife died, and needing a mother for his children, he courted a financially endowed lady, Mary Ball, who agreed to marriage. In February 1732 she bore him his fourth child, a son named George Washington. (11)

George's stepbrother Lawrence, fourteen years older, was sent to England to be educated, and in 1738 returned to the colony as a polished Englishman. He was soon called to military duty in England's war with Spain, where he exhibited rare leadership and courage, causing him to be celebrated upon his return. Lawrence became George's mentor. The young George spent much time doing Lawrence's bidding, all the while modeling himself after his mentor and learning to behave in the self-assured but well-mannered way of the English upper class. Lawrence, like his father, turned out to be tall and muscular, and it was not long before his younger stepbrother began to sprout up to be taller than all in the family at six feet three inches and a lean 175 pounds.

Lawrence's experiences as a captain in the British Army in the war with Spain were shared with George, who spent many hours listening to his older brother and learning the tactics employed by the British professional soldiers of that time. He also was fascinated with the survey instruments that his father used to plot the boundaries of the family's lands, to the point that Augustine trained his son as a surveyor and allowed him to earn a small income by providing surveys for neighbors. After Augustine's death in 1743, George continued to practice as a surveyor, studying mathematics and writing to the point that he was recognized as a competent professional by his peers.

At age sixteen, in 1748, George was sent by his mother to Belvoir to pay respects to Lord Fairfax, the senior member of the family that his brother Lawrence had married into five years before. During this visit George was invited to accompany George William Fairfax, age twenty three and the son of Colonel Fairfax, on a survey mission to the western part of the colony, over the Blue Ridge Mountains into the Indian country that stretched into the Shenandoah Valley. The party had as its leader James Genn, the official surveyor of Prince William County, who took considerable interest in George Washington's obvious abilities and began to delegate much of the survey work to his student. George displayed an awareness of the great opportunity that his association with Genn offered—the need to be always deferential to the opinions of his superior, but to ask and learn the details of his chosen profession from one of the masters of that profession. Over the six months the survey party spent in the wilderness, Genn provided sufficient training to the young man so that, upon his return to the Northern Neck, George was able to meet with the Commission on Surveys for Virginia at the College of William and Mary, be questioned to prove his credentials, and be commissioned as a surveyor. It is interesting to note that there was no examination by the State, no license issued by a government, but the recognition of a competent professional by the members of that profession.

George began an active career providing surveys for many hundreds of tracts of land in the Shanendoah Valley. He began to purchase land as an investment, some individual housing tracts and other larger pieces of land that would be leased to produce income. In 1750 he bought 456 acres from a James McCracken for a down payment of forty-five pounds and seventy-seven pounds due in a few months. The acreage was then subdivided and leased to tenant farmers.

George Washington's military experience stemmed largely from his service in the British Militia of Virginia during their forays to stem the advancement of the French from Canada down into the Ohio Valley. The French, backed by friendly Indians, were gradually heading south for an ultimate goal of linking with their compatriots in Louisiana. This link-up would provide a barrier to the colonists' ability to continue their march to open up the West. In 1754 the House of Burgesses, the governing council in Virginia, and Governor Dinwiddie agreed that a force should be assembled and moved to the valley to challenge the French. The leader of the expedition, Joshua Fry, was an engineer and retired professor of mathematics from William and Mary College, and George Washington, with the rank of major, was selected to serve as the adjutant for the expedition. Several forts were built and military confrontations with the French occurred from time to time, but it soon became obvious to George that the force was too small for the job of defeating the enemy, so he withdrew to Virginia, resigned his commission and retired to his newly rented home at Mount Vernon. The owner, Colonel Lee, agreed to an annual rent of 15,000 pounds weight of tobacco per year, which at the current rate of twelve shillings and six-pence per 100 pounds, amounted to ninety-three pounds sterling.

George spent his time running the farm and visiting the influential neighbors to gain insight into the government of the region, during which time he met an attractive and wealthy widow, Martha Dandridge Custis, whom he courted from March 1758 until January 1759, when they were married. George had run for a seat in the House of Burgesses during the courtship, and was successful in winning the election in July of 1758. Now, at age 27, a colonel in the militia and a wealthy landowner, he displayed the qualities of a diligent man driven to excellence—faithful, disciplined, quiet in speech and behavior, friendly to all, but sensitive to criticism, which he bottled up inside his rather thin skin. His speeches were not provocative, but based on logic and the obvious desires of a demanding leader. He soon became recognized for his sound judgment and willingness to bring both subordinates and superiors to his way of thinking.

His rise to power stemmed from import duties imposed by the British Parliament in 1767 on various kinds of paper products, glass, paint and tea, which quickly transformed many English colonists into potential revolutionaries, willing to speak up against the government. Virginians, in particular, objected to the tax; soon local meetings blossomed into large gatherings with vocal calls for the abolition of the tax and the freedom of the colonists to support themselves. The House of Burgesses protested to Governor Dinwiddie, who was appointed from England, and he immediately dissolved the local government, which only ignited further anger against the mother country.

Other colonies, particularly Massachusetts, took similar views of the "tea tax," culminating with Sam Adams and a body of men dressed as Indians dumping 342 chests of tea from a ship into Boston Harbor on December 16, 1773. The response from England was immediate, and led to the introduction of additional "Redcoats" being stationed in private dwellings and placing the colonies under martial law.

George Washington and other representatives from Virginia met in Philadelphia early in 1774 to plan a response to the actions of the British Parliament.

In May 1775 a unanimous decision by the Continental Congress affirmed the decision of the colonies to secede from the British Empire and to take up arms against their army in the colonies. When Washington traveled to Philadelphia he inspected several of the local militias and was greeted with much respect and enthusiasm as a colonel who had successful experience against a foreign power. When time came for the Congress to select a leader for the colonial militia, Washington became the national choice over several others from Massachusetts on June 15, 1775, primarily because of his careful and detailed presentation to the members and his ability to rally the army to do his bidding. He thus proved that he was both a military and a political leader, as well as a detailed planner because of his qualification as a surveyor.

The Revolutionary War turned out to be a slow competition between the British redcoats and the American colonials, waged primarily in the good weather months between April and October, with the centers of conflict beginning in Boston and ranging down the east coast of America to South Carolina. Because of the great distances involved, the British, with their superior naval force, were able to transport troops to the battle zones by sea. This meant that the pitched battles of Lexington and Yorktown were slow to build up, with the colonial force moving by foot from Boston, through New Jersey and Maryland, to the battle of Yorktown in Virginia. The task for Washington and his troops gradually grew into the art of encircling the enemy, preventing him from returning to the gunboats, and forcing a prolonged skirmish over a number of weeks. This tactic depleted the enemy's supplies and induced it to surrender on several occasions. It became apparent to the English in London that the rebellion of their American colony, fueled by substantial support of French troops and the French Navy, was turning into a conflict worthy of international attention, not just the repression of a few unruly citizens. Taking a world view of their empire, and the ever growing threat of the French, England decided to relinquish their interests in North America and make peace.

For George Washington and his troops the war had been a cruel and bloody affair, with a persistent lack of supplies, clothing and transportation, and to a large degree micromanaged by the Congress through their control of money. Washington's dedication to his troops and to the principle that he was fighting to free the nation of unjust tyranny, became the pillars of hope to the rank and file and to his officer corps. Washington was not a voluble man, inciting behavior through inspirational speeches and meetings with his subordinates. He kept to himself, particularly in the days when the future looked bleak. He prepared the next action by carefully analyzing the alternatives, all the alternatives, even the ones that would bring fear and uncertainty to a lesser man. Then he would call his staff together and, with comfortable demeanor, issue the next battle plan. He would meet with officers and the troops, in their muddy, cold and rain-soaked garments, and share his optimism and regard for their success. He came to be loved by his men. A tall, powerful leader to be emulated by all for the good of the country.

Conflict between Britain and the revolutionary colonies finally came to a peaceful end in Paris on November 30, 1782, at which time the parties agreed to gradually turn over the sovereignty of all lands to the Continental Congress, and Britain agreed to withdraw its troops and recognize the new boundaries of the thirteen separate entities.

On the eighth anniversary of the battle of Lexington in 1775, the Congress ratified the Treaty of Paris, and on the 19th of April, 1783, met for the first time as a body at peace with England—but very much as a body of antagonists bent on asserting their influence and newly gained power over the peace process. It took some time to bring the parties together in a mood willing to face the costs of the war and to deal with the disbandment of the Continental Army.

For several months after the end of hostilities George Washington toured the colonies, renewing wartime experiences and, as the Commander in Chief, ascertaining that back pay and other promises were kept. Then on December 23, 1783, he met in Philadelphia to deliver his report on the war to Congress, and to offer his resignation as the commander, as well as to present a manifest of his expenses accumulated during eight years of conflict, for which he had not been reimbursed, and to collect his pay of one British pound for his wartime services. Such was the character and moral commitment of this man to see that the nation was the ultimate benefactor of his services. After a tearful series of speeches he took his leave of the representatives, and his wartime military officers who regarded him as something of a brother and a father, so quiet, so committed, so reliable and so powerful.

George had determined to return to Mount Vernon, fold up his uniform and begin the private life of a country gentleman. But "private" it was not to be. The home was constantly visited by all manner of dignitaries, friends, neighbors and politicians, local and European, who came to make or renew the friendship of the world-class figure. The finances of the kitchen were constantly stretched to feed seven to ten overnight guests in addition to the nine members of the family.

As the leading member of the Virginia House of Burgesses he became quickly aware of the need to improve communications and transportation into the western boundaries of the colonies, and with his knowledge of surveying and skills in management, he was persuaded to become involved in a study of the feasibility of using the Potowmack River as a means of transporting barges into the Ohio Valley. Exploration of the two hundred-mile-long river, must have convinced George and his party that the venture was feasible, for in 1784 the House of Burgesses in Virginia authorized the formation of the Potowmack Company, and George was given fifty shares and elected president of the company.

His time as a private country gentleman ended more quickly than he would have wanted, for two years later, in 1787, he headed a delegation to Philadelphia, where the details of the future Constitution of the United States moved in full debate. After nine months of monumental discussion and careful planning by the framers, a document emerged that met the approval of a majority of the colonies, and was accepted and signed on September 17, 1787.

The document now had to be ratified and accepted by all of the new "states," and after much wrangling, the Constitution was accepted by a majority of the voters in each state. Shortly thereafter, during the Fourth of July celebrations in 1788, the demand began that George Washington be the first president. In January 1789, electors from the states met again and agreed on April 10, 1789 to the selection of George Washington as the new president.

Military Engineering in the Revolutionary War

The outbreak of war on April 19, 1775, found the colonies with a cadre of scientists but few persons with any experience in the art of military engineering. The status of medicine was equal to that of the other combatants, but the same could not be said for engineering.

In December 1775 the Congress instructed that a search be conducted to find four experienced military engineers, and during his visit to France in 1776, Benjamin Franklin, with the help of the French Government, obtained the services of four engineers, who came to America and were commissioned into the Continental Army. The four were Duportail, Radiere, Gouvion and Laumoy, with Duportail accepting the command of the newly created Corps of Engineers. After much debate in the Congress, Duportail was given the authority to command and train a nucleus of Americans and foreigners in the art of fortifications and road building. Among the foreigners was Pierre Charles L'Enfant, of whom we will learn more later.

Duportail immediately recognized the lack of schooling in the fields of mathematics and philosophy on the part of most of the American recruits, and recommended to Congress that some form of engineering institute be created to alleviate the problem. Congress did not respond to the commander's requests, and for the rest of the war the four original Frenchmen, supported by nine other foreign engineering officers and one American, a Captain Niven, contributed much to the final victory. Captain Niven, as the first and only American in the original Corps of Engineers, must also be recognized as the first engineer of American origin to be trained in the United States. (10, Page 242)

The war demonstrated the serious lack of engineering talent in the colonies, and led the Congress to finally approve the creation of the combined facility to teach the fundamentals of artillery deployment and fortification construction, both being based on similar mathematics and geometry.

With the signing of the Treaty of Paris in 1783 the Revolutionary War came to an end, and there was an immediate increase in the number of English scientists and men of education who immigrated into the new country. Such men as Samuel Vaughn, Jr., the son of an

English scientist and possessor of experience in metallurgy and machines, were accepted to operate the newly created U.S. Mint.

Patents

Provisions for the protection of inventors were included in the Constitution of the United States in 1787 and combined with copyrights in the clause, "To promote the progress of Science and the Useful Arts by securing for limited Time to Authors and Inventors the exclusive right to their respective Writings and Discoveries." Inventions were protected for fourteen years.

The new United States of America issued its first patents in 1790, modeled after the English law, giving rights to Oliver Evans for his high-pressure steam engine and Eli Whitney for his invention of the machine for milling iron and brass. The patent laws did not prevent the theft of British technology by New England cotton interests, but they did go a long way for the first time in enacting a system of laws that directly affected the products of the inquisitive minds so nurtured by the Renaissance. The ultimate impact of the patent system on manufacturing and invention cannot be overstated. Before the implementation of the rights of inventors to the fruits of their inventions, there was little incentive to place their inventions in the marketplace because they were immediately copied by others for their own use or gain. The result was that inventions were not widely publicized, limiting the infusion of new ideas into the market. Once the U.S. Patent Office began the process of hiring and training professional patent examiners, the documentation offered by a prospective patentee improved to allow a rigorous examination and award supported by very specific drawings and facts. While others became aware of the details of the invention, they were precluded from directly copying those specific details for which the patent had been granted. What emerged as a result of the patent process was a scientific and engineering community bent on improving known patents to new levels, not in violation of the original patent, but offering an innovation patentable in its own right.

Corps of Engineers

At the end of the Revolutionary War, most of the French engineers who had served in the Continental Army returned to France, and this caused the Congress, in 1794, to create a Corps of Artillerists and Engineers, stationed at West Point, New York, with the task of developing engineering courses covering the design of both military and civil works. Transferred to this new corps was a total of 992 rank and file. (12)

The plan did not work, and in 1802 the school was separated from the Artillery, and the Military Academy was created, including a Corps of Engineers, consisting of twelve officers and other ranks. Initially the instructors were mostly French, as were the textbooks, since none in English were available, and the thrust of the academy changed to the training of military engineers. The Frenchman Claudius Crozet was appointed to the academy in 1816 and immediately introduced a rigorous program following the pattern of the *Ecole Militaire*. The following year Superintendent Thayer started the four-year curriculum, complete with examinations, grading and subject matter along the lines of the *Ecole*

Polytechnique. West Point thus became the first school of engineering in the United States, and its program was based on the French model of an immersion in theoretical, mathematical and scientific subjects, employing French-trained instructors and text material used into the 1850s. (13)

To protect the city of Baltimore, America's third largest port in 1800, several French engineers were given the task of constructing a fort to guard and provide defense for the city in the event of war. Fort McHenry, as it was later named, started as an earthworks in 1776, went through several redesigns under the French engineers, and emerged in 1805 very much as it remains today. (14)

The result of the government's decision in 1802 to concentrate on training military engineers meant that there were no facilities in the nation dedicated to the training of engineers for the private sector. There was a need for civil engineers throughout the country. The Congress, by its inaction, apparently had no interest in solving this shortage, with the result being that the need was transferred to the states, who dealt with the issue as best they could. A typical story comes from Virginia, where the services of Frenchman Claudius Crozet proved invaluable.

Crozet served in the French Artillery in the Napoleonic Wars and came to the United States in 1816, becoming an instructor at West Point. He resigned from the academy in 1820 to become the state engineer of Virginia. He served in that post for twenty years, and his sound advice helped to create many of the original turnpikes in the state. Reared in a nation with a strong central government, Crozet found the contracting procedures in Virginia to be somewhat *laissez faire.* The lack of legal authority of the contract documents remained a constant reminder of the spirit of the new nation in which suspicions of central authority were rampant. The behavior of contractors displayed an attitude of self-management without interference from the state. If they felt like making a change in the plans, invariably to their advantage, they would simply go ahead without approval. There was not much Crozet could do about it other than complain to the one body with all the authority; the Legislature. They in turn, mindful of the political power of the wealthy citizens, would often side with the contractor to the detriment of the state. In the long run, therefore, as a direct result of Crozet's talents, the roads in Virginia were much advanced from those of the neighboring states even though they could have been better, or the same for less taxpayer investment.

It was estimated that in 1816 there were no more than thirty trained engineers outside the government in the entire United States. (13)

To ease the severe shortage of technically trained personnel in the nation, Congress in 1824 passed the General Survey Act. This empowered the president to utilize the Corps of Engineers to perform such nonmilitary surveys as studies of roads, canals and other engineering works that he considered to be in the public interest. President Monroe appointed a Board of Engineers under the Army Corps to offer and administer public assistance to the states for surveys and designs of projects, such as the Chesapeake and Ohio Canal project.

In 1831 Congress saw fit to repeal the General Survey Act, which led once again to a shortage of engineers in the private sector, but this in turn caused the creation of new schools of engineering to meet the need.

6 . . . The Beginning of the City of Washington

George Washington retired to his farm at the end of the War for Independence, continued with his surveying practice and, in response to many queries about the problem of transportation to and from the hinterland, began to investigate the feasibility of using the Patowmack River.

The Patowmack Canal

By 1750 settlers had reached the Ohio River, some 300 miles west of the Atlantic Ocean, and it made many business people, including George Washington, aware of the need for communication with these people, and to allow their commerce, both buying and selling, to reach the East Coast. There were no roads, just tracks for horses and people on foot. There were no railroads; they had not yet been invented. The only solution was canals, which had proved very successful in Europe. They had enabled France, in particular, to move produce and people to all corners of the country, given the central government a way of collecting taxes, and in so doing delivered a lift to the economy of the country as a whole.

George Washington (1732-1799) in his early years as a lad of sixteen had helped survey the lands of Lord Fairfax in Virginia, and was aware of the potential of using the Patowmack River as a navigable waterway, provided the waterfalls upriver from George Town could be bypassed. Based on Washington's request, the Virginia legislature in 1784 passed a bill granting a charter to the Patowmack Company for the purpose of constructing a series of canals and locks around the Great Falls and the Little Falls of the Patowmack, two miles upstream from Georgetown and the rapids at Seneca, a mile or so further up river. The engineering concept on which the canal was based assumed that the gently flowing Potowmack would form an ideal waterway to allow the passage of small barges starting at the mountains near Cumberland and terminating at the Port of Georgetown, more than a hundred miles to the east. With the exception of waterfalls near Georgetown, the river presented a smooth body of water, ideal for small sailing boats propelled by the wind, thereby avoiding the cost of towpaths and horses required for typical barges found in Europe.

Washington became president of the new company, and James Rumsey its chief engineer. Born in Maryland in 1743, Rumsey received no formal education. Apprenticed to a cabinetmaker, he learned the art of building and furniture making. He also became proficient as a blacksmith. He became acquainted with George Washington in 1784, showing the General a design for a mechanical boat he had invented that was designed to propel itself through very shallow waters, a condition which prevailed in the Potowmack River during the dry season. Washington must have been impressed with Rumsey's skills because he recommended him to be the chief engineer for the Potowmack Company, a position he held for two years of successful performance. The mechanical boat never materialized, and he resigned from the company in 1786 to continue his engineering research in Shepherdstown, West Virginia.

Excavation of the canal began in August 1785, and two sets of tall lock gates were built in George Town and floated out to the base of the Little Falls. Crews began to hand cut and blast the rock with black powder, and gradually a small basin was excavated on the shore of the river, masonry pillars were built into the face of the excavation, and the lower lock gates were mounted. February 1786 saw the beginning of the work on the Virginia side of the river, with excavation work at the Great Falls.

Dwellings for the workers and their families were situated on the high ground above the river at Great Falls, so by the end of the third year there was a small village to support the company, at Lock Number Two. Washington was active in the venture for the first few years and managed to keep the project financed, with the help of out-of-town bankers. In all, five sets of locks were planned; the main lift at Great Falls and others at Little Falls, Seneca Falls, Shenandoah Falls, and House Falls just upstream from Harper's Ferry. In addition, to allow the barges to pass over the shallow shoals up river, low dams were constructed, and parallel to the dams, channels were cut into the river bank to allow the barges sufficient draft to clear the obstructions.

The water levels of the river varied throughout the year; in the spring the levels were fine, but with the onset of the dry fall season, the river level fell and boats did not have the necessary depth to pass over the shallows. There was also the issue of flooding. No definite hydraulic data about the changes in level and flow in the river were available when the work started. Local inhabitants knew that there were times when the river reached flooding conditions, but they did not or were not asked to share this with Rumsey, or perhaps Rumsey simply did not appreciate the extreme variation in levels that his design would have to cope with. His concept, based on a survey of the river flowing under average conditions, assumed that the problem to be solved was the method of moving loaded barges over the shallow areas in the autumn. Hence the construction of relatively lightweight dams to allow the build-up of water depth for the barges.

The three locks at Little Falls, each with a width of 18 feet, a length of 100 feet and the ability to lift the boats 19 feet above the low tide at George Town, were completed at the end of 1795. The remaining locks, including those at Great Falls, were completed in 1802, and the canal opened for navigation. The total cost of the canal was of the order of $500,000. Operations began in 1803 and it became immediately apparent that the issue of water level of the river had been seriously underestimated. The fluctuation of the water flow between seasons caused the available depth to almost disappear in the dry season and become a raging torrent, breaching the river banks and sweeping boats and large trees downstream, in times of flood. As a result, promised deliveries could not be met and shippers became quickly dismayed that their products were being held up, sometimes for months at a time. There was also the question of damage to the hulls of boats scraped and punctured by the shoal rocks at low water. Rumsey became quickly frustrated with his position; not only was there a flood in 1786, but the finances of the company seldom allowed him to catch up on the wages owed to the workers, with the result that there was much labor unrest and lack of commitment. The quality of work suffered and costs ballooned.

Upon his elevation to the Presidency of the United States in 1789, Washington resigned his interest in the Patowmack Canal Company, which continued to operate for the next twenty years. During this time much attention was given to the changes of the flow of the river, and sufficient data collected to support the decision to abandon the venture. The failure of the canal can be attributed to incomplete engineering assumptions. However, if the designers had waited until sufficient data was available, say twenty years, there would have been no Potowmack Canal Company. In 1821 the affairs of the company were examined by a joint commission of the Virginia and Maryland legislatures, and as a result the charter of the company was revoked and the assets sold to the newly formed Chesapeake and Ohio Canal Company.

The remains of the main channel of the Patowmack Canal can still be seen on the south bank in Great Falls Park, at the point where Old Dominion Drive dead ends at the river. The National Park Service provides a visitor's center at Great Falls Park containing many artifacts and history of the Potowmack Canal.

Pierre L'Enfant

In the spring of 1791 George Washington and Pierre L'Enfant rode on horseback over the territory that had been designated the future capital of the United States by the Continental Congress in Philadelphia. The purpose of the tour allowed the Frenchman to present his initial concepts for the proposed capital of the United States to the new president.

The final location of the federal district had been determined the year before in a meeting between Alexander Hamilton and Thomas Jefferson. Hamilton, representing northern states, desired to have the federal government become responsible for states' debts resulting from the Revolutionary War, while Thomas Jefferson, representing southern interests, desired a location near George Town on the Potowmack.

Jefferson agreed to support Hamilton if he in turn would vote for the Potowmack site. The deal was done; Congress passed the act, but remained in Philadelphia until the city was ready to receive all three branches of government, which in 1800 totaled some 290 persons, from the president to the janitors. (15)

A breakdown of the federal payroll in 1802 included 132 in the executive, 152 staffers in the legislative branch, and seven in the Judiciary. By 1829 the size of government had more than doubled, with 318 in the executive and 300 in the legislature.

George Washington, elected president in 1789, had worked with L'Enfant on the renovation of Federal Hall in New York and felt that the decisive manner in which he conducted himself would be welcomed by an ultra-careful Congress.

Pierre Charles L'Enfant came to America at age twenty-three in 1777 having trained in France as an artist. His father, also Pierre L'Enfant, was the Painter in Ordinary to the King of France, and director of manufacturing of the Gobelin Tapestries situated on Rue Saint Hippolyte in Paris. In this capacity the elder Pierre moved from time to time with the Army into the field of battle in order to record and paint the battle scenes. His paintings are to be seen today on the ground floor of the Palace at Versailles. Young Pierre, at the age of seventeen, enrolled in the *Academie Royale de Peinture et de Sculpture,* where he assimilated the teachings of Andre LeNotre, at that time the most celebrated designer of landscapes in France. It was from LeNotre that young Pierre learned the *art of planning,* which he would bring to America. During his schooling he learned of the start of a war for independence in the British Colonies in America, so he decided to join the French contingency to fight on the side of the Americans and accepted the rank of lieutenant in the infantry. His knowledge of his father's paintings of military fortifications gave him an understanding of the basic earthworks necessary to prepare a defensive position, which was more than most other volunteers possessed. (16, Page 308)

As a result, upon arrival in America, he was transferred to the *Corps de Genie* and assumed the duties of an engineer. He then volunteered for service in the Continental Army as a military engineer, along with a number of his friends, initially paying his own expenses until he received a commission in the Corps of Engineers as a captain. (17)

After the war, with the rank of major, L'Enfant spent a year in France, and then in 1787 returned to New York, where he set up practice as an architect. He prepared the design of a temporary building displaying the Constitution and insignia for the Society of the Cincinnati, of which George Washington was the president. He knew Washington well enough to write to the president in 1789, offering his services for the layout of the new capital city on the Potowmack River. Washington must have been impressed with the Frenchman, not only for the work he had done to convert the New York City Hall into the first meeting hall for the new Congress but for the painting he had done of the general at Valley Forge during the Revolutionary War. Thus, Washington was familiar with the work of the French artist and engineer, and agreed in 1790 to the choice of L'Enfant to prepare a plan for the future city.

The site lay between the Potowmack River and the Eastern Branch (Anacostia River) to the south and east, and a row of undulating hills which rose to the north to a height of 120 feet, near what is Catholic University today. Nearer to the river lay Jenkins Hill, eighty feet above sea level, which commanded a view of the future city and which L'Enfant selected as the site of the Houses of Congress.

Other high points were designated to be the Home of the President, surrounded by the Executive Branch and the Judiciary. L'Enfant included the existing village of Carrollsburg, at the foot of the Anacostia, in his layout, but left the villages of Hamburg and George Town as they were, to be incorporated into the plan later. George Town, established in 1752, was named after George III of England and lay at the tidal head of the Potowmack River, as far inland as ships could go, providing access to the hinterland of the State of Maryland. Belhaven, on the opposite side of the river, provided similar inland access to

Virginia. It was incorporated in 1749 and renamed Alexandria, after the Alexander family who owned much of the land in the vicinity. (18)

The founding of Georgetown has a connection to the practice of engineering in that the presence of the first local piece of engineering work, Magee's Ferry at the foot of Rock Creek, was known to be in service in 1730. In the first quarter of the eighteenth century settlers were moving gradually inland, and by the 1730s the clearing of land and the planting of the staple crop of the region, tobacco, had begun. When harvested, the tobacco was by law required to be brought to a Rolling House for inspection and grading. In 1745 the Maryland Assembly passed "An Act for laying out One Acre of Land, convenient to Rock Creek Landing on the Potowmack River, on the land George Gordon now lives on, and for building a Rolling-House thereon."

George Gordon built the Rolling House in 1747, and it was listed in the "official places" in the state where tobacco could be stored. Soon growers and laborers began to bring their crops over the dusty and muddy tracks from the farming communities, and it was necessary for them to cross the river on Magee's Ferry and be able to find shelter and sustenance for an overnight stay near the landing. The combination of the ferry and the existence of the tobacco commerce were the catalysts to establish the need for a tavern for thirsty farmers. The records of the Prince Georges County Court for 1747, which controlled all of western Maryland, indicate that a "Lysance for keeping a Public House at the mouth of Rock Creek for the Ensuing Year" was granted to Thomas Odell. The following year the land west of Rock Creek came under the jurisdiction of the new Frederick County, which in 1751 granted a license to Joseph Belt "To keep a Public House of Entertainment at the Mouth of the Rock Creek."

It is a curious coincidence that the same year the Maryland Assembly passed an "Act for laying out and erecting a Town on the Potowmack River above the mouth of Rock Creek in Frederick County." The town was laid out on a 60-acre tract of land owned in part by George Gordon and in part by George Beall. On March 19, 1752 the land, now surveyed into building lots, was put up for sale, and the first transactions took place at Joseph Belt's Tavern on March 23, 1752. Georgetown had been founded.

L'Enfant's plan of Washington must have been influenced, to some degree, by the city of Paris, with its wide boulevards, running at angles, and intersecting a rectangular grid of minor streets laid out on a north-south and east-west axis. The plan progressed well until the citizens learned that the streets were to be one hundred ten feet wide, and the avenues one hundred sixty feet, wider than anything in the country, especially Boston, considered by many to be the model for the new city. Further, Washington had negotiated a property purchase whereby existing owners were not compensated for land to be occupied by streets, but did receive some compensation for land to be used for federal buildings. The balance of the land was mapped into plots and the owners could sell these at market prices. As a result of this transaction the federal government acquired some 500 acres for future buildings, and more than 3,500 acres was set aside for roads, without any expenditure to the taxpayer. (15)

On August 19, 1791, L'Enfant wrote to Washington and transmitted the first of his four plans for the city, each being a refinement of the preceding one. This first plan showed the proposed "Permanent Seat of the Government of the United States," drawn to a scale measured in "poles," where one inch equals eighty poles. (A pole is approximately 16 feet.) Street widths, however, were given in feet, very specifically, with the main avenues all with a width of 160 feet, including ten and then thirty feet on each side for sidewalks and rows of trees, and an eighty-foot-wide carriageway in the middle. The plan called for an equestrian statue of George Washington where the Washington Monument stands today, five fountains fed by some of the "23 good springs of excellent water abundantly supplied in the driest seasons of the year." The coordinates of the proposed House of the Congress are given as 38 degrees 53 minutes north latitude and 0 degrees 0 minutes longitude. L'Enfant either did not know or chose to ignore the fact that most of the Western world had agreed that zero degrees longitude passed through the British Observatory in Greenwich, and that worldwide navigation maps used Greenwich as the zero longitude reference.

Running between the Houses of Congress and the Statue of Washington, L'Enfant proposed a 400-foot-wide Grand Avenue, to be flanked on either side by religious and government edifices, and numerous monuments, ponds, gardens and formal walks. (18)

L'Enfant turned out to be a difficult, headstrong, and uncompromising individual, determined to have his way to the point that Washington relieved him, and he retired to Maryland. In 1812 his services were again in demand and he was appointed to the Military Academy at West Point as a professor of the art of engineering by Secretary of War William Eustis on July 7th of that year. L'Enfant declined the appointment and continued to pursue the practice of landscape design until his death in 1825.

Finally in 1909 his body was exhumed from its modest grave in rural Maryland, lay in state in the Rotunda of the Capitol amidst praise and recognition for the work of the artist, and lies today at the top of the hill in Arlington Cemetery.

After L'Enfant's dismissal by the president, his place was taken by his assistant, Andrew Ellicott, a surveyor, who assumed responsibility for the development of the plan and survey of the 100-square-mile District of Columbia, with the help of Benjamin Banneker. On April 15, 1791, the cornerstone of the District of Columbia was laid at Jones Point, southernmost tip of the federal district.

The area selected by George Washington for the future city appeared on the map as a large diamond that included the town of Alexandria at the south end. It then stretched to the northwest along the river, bordered by a forest of oak and other hardwood trees, which in a few places had been cleared to yield open fields for the raising of corn or cattle grazing. Few dwellings were visible from the river. A single unpaved road, run parallel to the river, wound its way through the forest to George Town and thence up into the rolling hills to Frederickstown, as Frederick, Maryland was then known.

Excluding the towns of George Town, Alexandria, Hamburg and Carrollsburg, there was a population density of the order of thirty persons per square mile in 1790, which translated into a rural occupancy of less than one thousand persons for the region. (15)

Once word spread that the site for the future capital had been chosen, an immediate influx of settlers from surrounding counties ensued, moving into the new District of Columbia and to that part designated as the future Capital City. Population began to grow, beginning in the early 1790s, with the building of log cabins in the vicinity of the two streams, Rock Creek and Tiber Creek, as sources of water. The result was the wholesale harvesting of trees for buildings and the attendant formation of paths and byways for foot and horse traffic.

The streets were mud; there were no sewers; water was obtained from a dozen springs and the two creeks and carried in buckets to the dwellings; and horse manure filled the low points where it was washed by rain. Houses were built on the high ground near to the sites of the proposed federal buildings, and the low swamplands along the banks of the river were breeding grounds for flies, mosquitoes and vermin. (19)

Houses and buildings were lit with oil lamps and candles. Heating was by open fire-places. In the cold of winter it was not at all unusual to rise from a warm bed and crack the ice in the wash basin if one chose to wash in cold water. Many homes were constructed of wooden logs, with the result that there was a sudden demand for building lumber. It is hard to imagine that by 1800 there were very few trees of any size standing within several miles of the city—just cleared land, stumps and mud. The original hardwood forest of oak, red oak, hickory, chestnut and birch presented to the early settlers a wall of green supported on robust trunks, many so large it took three grown-ups to touch fingers with their arms around the base. To prepare a site for a small dwelling took many days of chopping, sawing and digging to remove the indigent lumber ,and then weeks of sawing, all by hand, to cut the logs into beams and joists suitable to support the structure.

Compared to New York or Philadelphia, the new Capital City was a construction site. Not that those cities did not have their share of muddy streets; it was the care and attention to lining the main streets with cobble stone, and providing sidewalks free of flood and debris, nudged close to the housefronts, that allowed people to walk in relative comfort. Sundown signaled the time to light the oil lamps, mostly attached to the walls of adjacent homes, providing sufficient illumination so as to make the portable lantern unnecessary. Not so in the growing Capital City, as it was called.

The Congress, sitting in Philadelphia for the first ten years of its existence, had autho-rized President Washington to select the actual site for the new capital. He decided that it should be located on the Potowmack River about where the Eastern Branch (now the Anacostia) joined the main stream. He and the Executive Branch were further charged to erect the first government buildings, which included the President's House, the House of the Congress, the Treasury, War Department and the Navy Yard.

With Thomas Jefferson's advice and assistance, he assembled a plan of the Capital City, based essentially on the proposals of Pierre L'Enfant. Site preparation for the four main buildings began in 1792. This work involved the removal of all remaining trees, rocks and rubble, leveling the land with horse-drawn ploughs and hand rakes, and laying out the boundaries of the proposed buildings with wooden stakes driven into the soil to mark the corners of the foundations.

George Washington, not a confrontational individual, left most of the daily debating and rancor of the Congress to Thomas Jefferson and John Adams. He applied himself to the strengthening of the nation and keeping on even terms with France and England, which moved into the Napoleonic Wars that finally ended in 1815. Washington began to tire of the Congressional battles and longed to retire to Mount Vernon. At the end of his second term, in 1797, his wish came true and he retired from the presidency, welcomed John Adams as the new leader and moved to his home on the banks of the Potowmack. For two years he lived the life of the country gentleman, getting older and less resilient, and finally succumbing to a throat infection on December 14, 1799. He never saw the completed President's House, still under construction at the time of his death.

The city was incorporated in 1802, with Robert Brent the first mayor appointed by President Jefferson. (18)

The Beginning of a City

L'Enfant's plan for the city included the subdivision of the land into building blocks. However, due to imprecise surveys, the plan had to be redrawn by his successor, Ellicott, who is credited with the final layout of the city of Washington. Ellicott's plan, submitted to President Washington in 1792, included the division of the city into 1,136 blocks, with Block Number 1 situated at the intersection of Virginia Avenue and 28th Street N.W., adjacent to Rock Creek. Block No. 1136 fell at 24th and "A" Streets S.E. at the Anacostia River. Each block was then subdivided into building lots, with title awarded to the original land owners prior to 1791.

Throughout this period, the subdivision of the land into lots, each for sale at 25 Pounds Maryland, encouraged much speculation, in particular by the wealthy from Philadelphia, who expected the capital to remain in their city and bought and sold land accordingly. Thus the out-of-towners were ready to buy as soon as Congress authorized President Jefferson to release the land for sale, on the condition that a house would be built on each third lot within seven years. The city commissioners attempted to restrain the speculation, but to no avail, and in May 1800 reported that the city consisted of 109 brick houses and 263 of wood, out of more than 6,000 lots that had been bought by two speculators. By the end of the following year, 230 houses had been added, with another 100 under construction. The price of the lots was listed in "Pounds Maryland" because there was still a tremendous shortage of any other currency that had any long-term value.

Currency

Up to the beginning of the Revolution, the currency used in all of the colonies consisted of standard English paper notes and coins brought into the country and managed by the British-appointed governor of each of the semi-independent jurisdictions. The English money consisted of pounds, shillings and pennies, with twelve copper pennies making a shilling, and twenty silver shillings to a pound. In addition, to speed commerce, several of the colonies began to print their own paper notes, tied to the value of the English pound.

However, the onset of the Revolutionary War caused a change in the policy by the British Government, which led to the banning of importation of their currency into the colony during the war. Some English pounds were available, but they soon became rare items used by the government and essentially unavailable to private individuals

After the war, the chronic shortage of British currency, particularly coins, made the buying and selling of everyday goods by ordinary citizens very difficult. One solution caused Spanish coins to be put into circulation, and this practice was continued for a number of decades after the Revolution. The exchange value of these Spanish coins was tied to a silver Austrian coin named the "thaler." A similar coin of equal value used in Sweden, spelled the same way, was pronounced "daaler." The use of the word "dollar" is an Anglicized pronunciation of "daaler."

Since the Spanish peso coin was similar in size to the silver thaler, the colonists began to use the Spanish coin as the basic unit of the American banking system and called it a "silver dollar." The Spanish coins were used in the new United States until the 1840s, when the Congress finally began to mint U.S. silver dollars and print their own paper currency.

The decade beginning in 1792 saw substantial construction in the city. Not only did the four main federal buildings rise up from barren, muddy fields with the sandstone brought up the Potowmack and down Tiber Creek, but the private sector began to build using brick produced in the new kilns erected on the banks of Tiber Creek, where the Commerce Building stands today.

The New Seat of Government

The Congress moved from Philadelphia to the city in 1802. A few representatives arrived with their wives and children and sought to rent in the vicinity of the public buildings, creating an instant demand for housing. Representatives without wives or families stayed in boarding houses. Curiously, the grown-up sons of the boarding house owners became the first civil servants. At that time the population of the city of Washington was 3,200 while that of the District of Columbia was 14,000. (15)

The view from Jenkins Hill, now Capitol Hill, looked down on a softly undulating open countryside, with the Potowmack River (now the Potomac) on the left, and small dwellings dotted sparsely in all directions and disappearing over the horizon about four miles distant. A mile and a half to the west the outline of the President's House was just visible on a lower hill, with cattle grazing on grassy land on the banks of Tiber Creek. On either bank of the Potowmack, wide swaths of swampy land covered with long reeds gradually merged with gently flowing water of the mile-wide river. In flood seasons the river went to almost two miles wide. Much later the swamps would be filled in and land reclaimed, narrowing the stream to less than half a mile.

Construction of the first four major buildings—the President's House, Treasury, War Department and the Capitol—all began in 1792, with the heavy construction materials moving to the Port of George Town and then on to barges that took them along Tiber Creek to the foot of Jenkins Hill. In 1793 Tiber Creek presented an ideal means of water access to the burgeoning town. It was clear water and tidal, allowing the barges to sail almost a mile east of the point where the creek joined the Potowmack River, terminating at the foot of the building sites for the President's House and the Houses of Congress. However, this access did not last long. The wholesale harvesting of trees, combined with the runoff from higher ground, began a silting process that gradually filled in the creek. The silt reduced the effective barge access such that, by 1804, its length had been reduced from more than a mile to about a quarter of a mile from the main river.

Transportation

The importance of the horse in the development of Washington into an international city cannot be denied. But it was the invention of alternative systems of transportation that finally allowed the population, particularly women and children, to move quickly and conveniently from the more remote farming areas, and about the city itself. The new populated areas had reached the point that walking from end to end took a full day from dawn to dusk. The real challenge to many travelers, however, turned out to be finding a way to cross the mile-wide Potowmack River.

Ferries

In 1797 the only bridge across the Potowmack lay in Harper's Ferry, aptly named because prior to that date there was in fact a ferry. The construction of a bridge the year before turned out to be a great success, and those living farther down the river began to explore the possibility of bridges in their own communities. Commercial traffic, if any, moved *down* rivers and navigable tidal creeks to the established ports, while supplies and manufactured goods did the opposite. What little traffic there was that crossed rivers did so by means of ferries.

At that time there were three kinds of ferries, differentiated by their means of propulsion. All consisted of flat-bottom barges with an accessible platform onto which the people, wagons and farm animals congregated during the crossing. They varied in length between thirty and sixty feet depending on their capacity.

The most elegant, from an engineering point of view, were those that were propelled across the river by the *force of the flowing* stream. This type used a cable, stretched from one bank of the river to the other and securely anchored at both ends. Running on the cable were two large adjustable rollers, attached to the bow and the stern of the hull of the boat, and arranged so that the boat could run along the cable. By drawing one set of rollers inboard and allowing the second set to move outboard, the hull could be cocked at an angle to the flow of the water. The force exerted onto the side of the hull resulted in a component that forced the hull to move parallel to the cable and across the river. To return to the starting point the rollers were reversed.

If there was insufficient flow in the river, the roller system would not work, so a *manual-hauler* system was employed. Here the cable across the river was lowered to a level even with the gunnel of the boat and allowed to run through wooden guides at the bow and stern. Between the guides there was fitted a "gripper," usually a pipe that ran easily over the cable and included a locking plate that could grip the cable to provide traction, or release it and allow the cable to slide. The power was provided by the ferryman, who locked the gripper to the cable and then walked from bow to stern hauling the gripper, thereby pulling the boat. Then, by releasing the gripper and walking it to the bow again, the process was repeated.

Not much used, with the exception of wide bodies of water, were the *barges fitted with sails*, with or without a cable, depending on the speed of the current.

Before 1790 there were three main ferries serving the area, and a fourth smaller one, named Magee's Ferry, established about 1720, that crossed the river at a point just downriver from where Chain Bridge is today. It is shown on a map prepared by Joshua Fry and Peter Jefferson in 1751.

The first, authorized by the Virginia General Assembly in 1738, required that a crossing of the Potowmack be maintained twenty-four hours a day throughout the year. The location is thought to be about where the Arlington Memorial Bridge lies today, and at the plantation of Francis Awbrey on the Virginia side. The rates for crossing the river were seven and a half pence for either a man or a horse. These charges were found to be too expensive for the local population to the point that in 1748 the General Assembly granted a second charter for a ferry run from George Mason's plantation, which ended on Analostan Island (now Theodore Roosevelt island) and terminated on the Maryland shore near Rock Creek. It was known as Mason's Ferry. The price for passage, set by the General Assembly, was four pence for a man or a horse and twenty pence for a chariot and horses, plus four pence each for the passengers. (20, Page 185)

Changes in the bed of the river in the 1840s caused the spit of land that connected Analostan Island to the Virginia bank to be washed away, making the "island" really an island. This event required the construction of a causeway to gain access to the ferry, which by then was called the Georgetown Ferry. After much debate in Congress as to whether they were usurping the sovereign rights of Virginia by granting the citizens of Georgetown their request, the causeway was erected, washed away several times and rebuilt at Georgetown's expense.

From Alexander's Island, the projection into the Potomac where the Reagan National Airport is located today, the Bridgepoint Ferry traversed across the river to the foot of Maryland Avenue. For twenty years before the Long Bridge was built in 1796, the Bridgepoint Ferry, equipped with a sail and oars, shuffled pedestrians from Alexandria to the city several times a day.

From the port of Alexandria, West's Ferry traversed the river to the Maryland side and docked either at Frazier's or Addison's Landing, in the vicinity of Oxen Creek. West's Ferry must have been of the sail and oar type, not only because of the width of the river at that point, but a cable ferry obviously cannot go to two different ports. The cost of a passage for a horse and man was one shilling (twelve pence), high because of the greater distance compared to Mason's. In all, the state of Virginia chartered fourteen ferries across the Potowmack River between 1732 and 1766, with the apparent consent of the state of Maryland, which owned the river. The ferries continued to provide cross-river transportation until the coming of the bridges, beginning with the Long Bridge to Alexandria in 1796, followed by the first Chain Bridge the following year.

The President's House

An Irishman, James Hoban is credited with the design of the President's House. He had trained in Ireland, immigrated to the New World after the Revolution, and practiced architecture in Charleston, South Carolina. A competition prepared by the Congress stipulated an award of 500 pounds Maryland to the winning designer, and with a letter of introduction from George Washington, the committee selected Hoban's sketches and declared him the winner. Hoban traveled to Washington to inspect the site and accept the nomination.

At General Washington's request the President's House, similar in design to Leinster House, the mansion of a Dublin aristocrat, was to be built of stone as opposed to the normal materials of brick and wood befitting the new nation. While there is a distinct similarity to the Dublin mansion, many now feel that Hoban's design had its origin in James Gibbs's *Book of Architecture,* in which drawings for "Design for a Gentlemen's House" show remarkable similarities to the President's House. Gibbs, an architect and a student of Christopher Wren, prepared his book of building details showing various facades, elevations and plans, and it found wide use in England and America by persons offering building designs. (20)

Sandstone for the mansion was mined at the Aquia quarry of the Brent family, just below Mount Vernon on the river, and brought up to the port of George Town. From there it was transported by ferry up Tiber Creek to the foot of the hill just below the mansion. At the time the land for the future city was first explored, Tiber Creek was a broad, clear branch of the Potowmack, fed by a substantial stream, and wide enough to allow ferries to move east, past the mansion and along what is now Constitution Avenue, to a point at the foot of the present 7th Street NW. Tiber Creek was used to transport the building materials for both the President's House, started in 1792, and the House of the Congress, where construction began the year after, and continued to be useful as a marine access to the new town for several more years. However, as the town grew and trees were cut down, the resulting washing of sand and silt into the creek soon precluded its use as a navigable waterway.

Similar to large houses built in England and Europe, the President's House was laid with exterior masonry walls twenty-four inches thick, and interior partitions of twelve-inch brick supporting wood beams and flooring that spanned from exterior wall to interior partition. Four-inch thick polished sandstone sheets covered the exterior of the building, which included marble and limestone pediments over windows and doors.

Central heat had not yet made its way across the Atlantic, so fireplaces were used throughout the mansion, with soft coal as the fuel. Sixteen masonry chimneys, eight each on the front and rear, extended seven feet above adjacent roofs and served thirty-two fireplaces on the first and second floors and the kitchens in the basement. During the day the building received illumination from the natural light of the sun, while at sundown the candles were lit in the more prestigious rooms, and oil lamps provided illumination in hallways and work areas.

Bathing was accomplished by sitting or standing in portable tubs, which were filled and emptied by the staff. All manner of large copper jugs were devised to allow the safe transport of hot water from the kitchen, three floors below, up the servant's staircase to the bathing room. There were no pipes or chrome faucets; these appeared on the scene fifty years later. Wash basins of copper were laid into wooden wash stands, each with a mirror and a drain plug that allowed the basin to drain into a wooden bucket below.

Toilets were elegant, wood-paneled closets, about five feet square, with bench-type wooden seats suitably designed for comfort, each provided with a cutout opening, below which a large china bowl resided. Toilets were serviced and dumped by the staff several times a day. The president's laundry was hung on an outside line to dry, in full view of the passing public, much to the amusement of a visiting Englishman in 1802. (16, Page 40)

To begin with, water was carried by wagon half a mile from nearby Franklin Farm Springs, but in 1833 a system of hollow wooden tree trunks were laid to convey water from the springs to a brick cistern on the property.

The Capitol

L'Enfant's plan called for the Houses of Congress to be placed on the highest point of the future city, an eighty-foot promontory called Jenkins Hill, from which the river, the rest of the future city and the Virginia shores were readily visible. This was in accord with George Washington's concept that in a republic the people's house, not the President's House, should dominate the landscape. The Houses of Congress, soon named the Capitol, were the focal point of the plan, with broad avenues radiating at angles from the center and a system of streets laid out in a rectangular grid following a north-south direction.

To select a designer for the building, a competition was held in 1792, but the submissions were uniformly displeasing to both Washington and Jefferson, to the point that, upon receiving a letter from a Dr. William Thornton of Philadelphia requesting permission to enter a design, the competition was extended. (17)

Substantial immigration from England occurred both before and after the Revolutionary War, and in 1786 William Thornton, a Quaker and a Whig, settled in Philadelphia with the intention of practicing medicine. His training at a British university was typical of the time, providing an undergraduate program of several years studying the first part, which included the basics of grammar, logic, arithmetic, astronomy and mathematics, after which he moved on to the second part to study for the profession of medicine. Since he had no formal training or experience in the design of buildings, he spent several months in the Philadelphia Library researching the subject from the available literature, and in June of 1793 submitted his design for the Houses of Congress, which was enthusiastically received by Washington. In a letter to Daniel Carroll, one of the city commissioners, Jefferson wrote that he found Thornton's offering to be "simple, noble, beautiful and excellently distributed." (17)

Thornton's design was accepted, and in September 1793 the cornerstone of the future Capitol was laid, followed by much ceremony and an outdoor feast at which a 500-pound ox was roasted on a spit.

Because of his lack of building experience, Hoban, the designer of the President's House, was designated to assist Thornton in the supervision of the construction work. However, lack of time prevented Hoban from doing an adequate job, so a French-born architect, Etienne Salspice Hallette, who had changed his name to Stephen Hallet, was assigned to the project, and immediately began to modify Thornton's design. Fortunately Thornton found himself appointed as a commissioner for the city in 1794, from which vantage point he was able to defend his design against the encroachments of several jealous competitors, particularly Hallet. Thornton was rather typical of the University-educated individuals of that time, in that his interests were broad and not constrained by government regulation to the practice of a narrow field of discipline. In his time he was known not only as a man of medicine and the original architect of the Capitol, but found time to devote his talents to town planning, scientific organization, language reform and speech therapy, and is credited as the inventor of various machines, including a steam cannon. (10, Page 369)

Thornton's plan for the Capitol envisaged a three-element structure; two identical north and south rectangular buildings, each 126 feet long and 120 feet wide, separated by a center rotunda of similar dimensions, modeled after the Pantheon in Rome. (17, Page 30)

The Senate meeting room and chambers occupied the north wing, and those for the representatives were in the south. Construction started and it became immediately apparent that there were insufficient funds allocated to the program, and this, together with the shortage of experienced masons, caused the progress to be much slower than had been anticipated. By 1802, when the Congress met in the new city for the first time, the north Senate wing appeared ready for use, but the south wing was far from being finished. It was finally completed in 1807. Between the two wings lay an open piece of land where Thornton's future rotunda was planned. To connect the two wings Thornton designed a wooden corridor, without the rotunda and the dome.

Thornton's reputation, on one hand brilliant and on the other a rather pushy individual who made the best of the failure of others, historically falls somewhere between the two. Winning the original design of the proposed Capitol leads one to think of this man as very inspired artistically; whereas in fact he was a good thinker, quick to reach a conclusion and forcefully able to make his feelings and opinions with others. In the competition for the Capitol design he was able to talk to Jefferson about the shortcomings of the original submittals. In so doing he was able to prepare a design in keeping with the feelings of Thomas Jefferson, who ultimately made the final selection of the designer, and whose own building design skills had much influence on the final outcome.

Toward the completion of construction of the original two wings of the Capitol in 1802, an English engineer named Benjamin Latrobe arrived on the scene, and immediately there began a conflict between the gifted professional, Latrobe, and the brilliant amateur, Thornton. Perhaps the comparison between the two would rate Thornton the "Jack of all trades, and master of none," while scoring Latrobe, "technically correct, even if I go bankrupt in the process." Over the succeeding several years Latrobe invaded much of Thornton's territory with regard to the Capitol, leading to lawsuits for breach of contract and defamation of character. In attempting to find a fair place for Thornton in the history book, it would be prudent to think of him as a lucky individual who arrived at the right place at the right moment, and with a fluent mind, which quickly assessed the situation and filled the void. His influence on the Capitol gradually diminished, and with the destruction of both wings by the British in 1814, the subsequent restoration passed to Benjamin Latrobe.

The death of the revered George Washington in December 1799 was followed by months of mourning, and a bill in the Congress in 1800 to change the name of the capital city to Washington. The city experienced remarkable growth between 1800 and 1812, as did the rest of the nation, helped by the number of indentured laborers coming from England, Ireland and Scotland. These people at the bottom of the economic ladder were willing to work for nominal wages if their masters would pay for the cost of the voyage from England and employ them, in virtual slavery, until their debt was paid. Many of these laborers had acquired skills, such as carpentry, smithing and iron working, and were therefore immediately valuable to the new nation. There were also a number of highly trained and educated individuals who immigrated to the New World, and among this group was the engineer-architect Benjamin Latrobe.

Benjamin Latrobe

In late 1802 Benjamin Latrobe received a letter from President Jefferson to consider the remodeling of the Washington Navy Yard in conformance with an act of Congress earlier that year. The act sought to reduce the size of the military establishment, and the Navy in particular, as a reaction to the decreased military needs of the new nation. (22)

Appointed Surveyor of Public Buildings by Jefferson in 1802 and Engineer of the United States Navy in 1804, Latrobe divided his time between the Capitol and the Navy Yard, having designed a covered dry-dock as his first commission for the U.S. Government in 1802.

Benjamin Latrobe was born in Yorkshire, in the Midlands of England, on May 1, 1764, the son Moravian parents who had fled to England to pursue their religious beliefs. At age three Benjamin started school in Fulneck, Yorkshire, to be followed by thirteen years of education in England and Germany in the arts of science and engineering. Returning to England in 1784, he caught the attention of John Smearton, the leading and most outstanding engineer in England at that time, and studied under Smearton for four years, moving on to the office of Samuel Pepys Cockrell, under whom he studied architecture for four years.

He sailed for America in 1795, living in Norfolk, where he practiced engineering, including a survey of the Dismal Swamps and the feasibility of constructing a canal through them, and the design of fortifications for the port of Norfolk. In 1798 he moved to Philadelphia, having been selected to design the new Bank of Pennsylvania. Between 1798 and 1802 Latrobe not only designed the bank, proposed and designed a water supply system for the city of Philadelphia and supervised its construction, but designed the steam-driven pumping plant to lift the water from the river to a group of cisterns and pipes to serve the city. By the time he received Jefferson's letter and appointment he was regarded as one of

America's leading engineers, particularly in the fields of canal and waterworks construction.

The work at the Navy Yard included the demolition of various minor buildings and the planning of a dry-dock, which would have been the largest in the world had it been constructed. Several submissions of the plan to the Congress all met with rejection, based on the projected cost of the "grand scheme" in a time of conservative "small-central-government" politics. Latrobe's involvement in engineering in the city continued with the planning of a canal, similar to the one included in L'Enfant's design, which would connect the port of George Town to the Navy Yard, thereby saving considerable transportation costs of supplies being shipped from the hinterland.

Typical of engineering services performed by Latrobe was the construction of a steam boiler plant and steam engine, which drove a central line shaft in the main workshops of the Navy Yard. As surveyor of public buildings, Latrobe spent much of his time investigating the latest technology as it applied to the construction and repair of ships. In this connection he proposed that the Navy renovate their existing repair facilities with the construction of the most modern machinery, all driven by a central steam engine. In 1808 the Navy approved Latrobe's plan, and in June of 1810 the boiler components and the steam engine arrived on the site, were installed in the machine shop, and a large leather belt connecting the engine to the overhead line shaft was put in place. The engine, constructed in England by Boulton and Watt, had a twenty-one-inch diameter piston driving the main flywheels and operated on a steam pressure of twelve pounds per square inch.

A number of pieces of machinery, including a stamping mill, a bellows blasted forge and power hammer were all driven by the engine through the main shaft. It was shown that the recovery of scrap iron and its subsequent heating and reworking into useful tools saved the Navy of the order of 6,500 dollars per year.

Benjamin Latrobe was both an engineer and an architect, actively involved in the design of buildings and engineering works of many different types. When he performed designs for an engineering project he would sign the drawing with his name, followed by the word "Engineer." His architectural work was similarly signed "Architect." At this time in America's formation, there were very few architects and almost no people capable of offering engineering services, with the result that Latrobe's skills were in great demand. He had been trained under one of England's premier engineers and was able to convey this credential to many clients in new United States.

Latrobe is best remembered for his diversity. His interior designs for the House of Representatives, prepared between 1805 and 1807, are magnificent. His monumental buildings include the Bank of Philadelphia (1799), the Roman Catholic Cathedral in Baltimore (1805), St. John's Church in Georgetown (1816), the Van Ness Residence and the restoration of the Capitol after the War of 1812 (1814-1817). His designs and drawings for the Washington Canal (1810) and steam engine plants at the Navy Yard (1810) and the woolen mill in Steubenville, Ohio (1814), are typical of the competence of this engineer. (22)

As a man Latrobe grew to think of himself as somewhat above the need to labor and get paid for his services. That he was an honorable man, and a man of his word, there is no question. Many of the commissions he undertook were performed with a desire to deliver superior engineering solutions or sensitive architectural facades, pleasing to his clients, who then took advantage of the man by treating him harshly and neglecting to fulfill their contractual agreements. In 1815, severely in debt, he wrote to his son, "The object is to keep out of debt. You have the advantage of me in this, in that you have not been educated as I was, to believe it beneath a Gentleman to earn an honest livelihood." He felt that his upbringing and education in England and Germany had not prepared him for the frontier life of the new republic, with its uncertainty and lawless behavior. His demeanor was that of an English aristocrat; his speech polished and expressive to the point that many persons with whom he came in contact found him difficult and somewhat objectionable. He experienced much challenge dealing with those whom he considered inferior, such as the construction workers and government servants, with the result that he in turn earned their dislike, which contributed to his failed relationships.

If Latrobe had stayed in England, someone else would be known as the first professional engineer-architect of the new nation, and his finances would have duplicated those of his contemporaries, but his choice of careers in America led him to face financial woes for all his life. He wrote to his sister in 1816 lamenting that , "Though continually engaged in the largest and most expensive public works on this side of the Atlantic, and at the head of my profession, I have failed to accomplish such a competency as would put me at ease for the rest of my life." Such were the feelings of a desperate genius who had failed to attain what was, without a doubt, within his reach. On August 30, 1820, Benjamin Latrobe died of yellow fever caught in the swamps of New Orleans, leaving several design projects unfinished, and a heartbroken but unafraid loving wife.

Washington Canal

The second major engineering project in the new city was the Washington Canal, conceived earlier than the Patowmack canal at Great Falls, but allowed to languish in the new Congress because of the unwillingness of members to vote money for the capital city. The canal as planned followed the bed of Tiber Creek (now Constitution Avenue) which, prior to the beginning of construction of the Capitol in 1793, had been a clear navigable waterway, but by 1802 was mostly silted and filled with debris. It was felt that using the creek bed would reduce the amount of excavation. The building of a canal would provide access to the center of the city and form a direct connection for barges and small sailboats from the ports of George Town and Alexandria. The need for a major access route from the docks at Georgetown into the center of the proposed city was obvious. Practically all the connection with the outside world occurred through the ports of Alexandria or Georgetown. A comparison of the cost and efficiency of hauling masses of cut stone and all the other material necessary for the building of the city, three miles over a muddy road from Georgetown, versus floating it in barges to the bottom of the low hills at the proposed building sites, proved to be no contest. The canal won hands down.

The city commissioners of Washington initially showed interest in the feasibility of the project, but as a result of a cost estimate prepared by Benjamin Latrobe, they decided to abandon the enterprise in favor of Congress providing the funds in 1802 and granting a charter to a privately financed company. The Washington Canal Company, chartered in 1804, engaged Latrobe to prepare a survey and proposed plan of the canal. However, the failure of sufficient financing caused the company to default on its agreement with Congress to have navigation on the canal within five years, so its charter was revoked, and transferred to the Second Washington Canal Company in 1809.

Latrobe became a shareholder in this second company, as well as the chief engineer, employed his son Henry as the accountant, and hired James Cochran of Philadelphia as construction contractor. Cochran had built the successful waterworks project in Philadelphia designed by Latrobe several years before. Finances were again a problem. At a meeting of the stockholders in 1810, Latrobe was asked to cut expenses to a bare minimum, using the least expensive materials, regardless of their long-term reliability. Walls of wood replaced the originally planned stone walls for both canal and locks. The official ground-breaking happened on May 2, 1810, with the chairman of the board of the Washington Canal Company, Elias Caldwell, in attendance, together with the mayor of the city and President James Madison.

Building and construction work in the early 1800s fell under the responsibilities of the designer. He not only prepared the sketches and estimates of cost for the investors, but prepared the working drawings for the artisans and contractors, purchased the supplies and materials for the project, and generally supervised the progress of the work, making changes as necessary to accommodate unforeseen and changed conditions. Latrobe's management style followed the practice he had learned in Germany and England. He employed a "clerk of the works" to keep track of the progress of the entire project, and various superintendents in charge of masonry, carpentry and ironworks, each of whom trained and supervised the apprentices and laborers who performed the manual labor. There was, however, a distinct difference between the apprentices who were learning the art of engineering, and one day would be recognized as professional engineers, and the laborers whose lot in life was manual labor.

Latrobe conveyed his wishes to the superintendents either verbally or by means of hand sketches prepared in the field, and to contractors, such as the manufacturers of steam engines, by preparing detailed drawings more akin to works of art, complete with color, shading and adornments, all signed, "B. H. Latrobe, Engineer." He based the dimensions of the Washington Canal on the waterway he had designed for the Chesapeake and Delaware Canal in 1804, with sloping sides twelve feet apart at the flat bottom, and twenty-one-feet wide at the waterline, giving a depth of water of three feet. The banks on both sides were two feet above the water, twenty-seven feet wide and provided with horse towpaths twelve feet wide on either side of the canal.

As directed by the company, in order to save money, the original lock walls were built of timber, against Latrobe's recommendations; he had proposed stone walls similar to his experience in England. Two main sets of locks were in the original design—the Tiber Locks, about where Seventeenth Street crosses Constitution Avenue today, and the Eastern Branch Locks, close to the Navy Yard. In 1811 the Tiber and Eastern Branch locks walls, built of wood, were in operation, only to face serious rotting from the start; they were replaced with stone-faced elements in 1816. (22)

The Washington Canal was designed to allow barges from George Town and small sailboats from Alexandria to move down the Patowmack River for about half a mile and then enter the canal at Tiber Creek, at a location about three hundred yards on the south side of the present White House. The excavation ran almost due east, along what is now Constitution Avenue, and passed just below the foot of the hill on which the President's House was planned. To minimize the depth of the excavation, sets of lock gates were located just east of the Tiber Creek entrance point, and on the Eastern Branch where the canal reentered the river. The Potowmack River is tidal, rising and falling about three feet on a typical day. To put the tidal change to good use, the lock gates were opened at high tide to allow the canal to fill, and then closed to retain as much water as possible, thereby creating a pond on which the barges could navigate, even though the level of the river had fallen several feet. This concept allowed the excavation costs for the work to be greatly reduced since the barges had a draft of less than two feet, while the main river, which was tidal up to Great Falls, rose and fell three feet under normal conditions.

The Washington Canal initially proved to be a success in that much heavy material for the federal buildings was moved with relative ease. It also provided the main means for bringing food and supplies to the citizens of the district, from Alexandria and George Town.

The canal had been dug by hand, with picks and shovels on the swampy soil just beyond the river's edge. No curbing at the edges was provided, with the result that rain-water washed soil and garbage from the land into the canal. This caused considerable maintenance. To prevent the floor of the canal from silting to the point that it would not fill to a level needed by the barges, crews were constantly working to remove the sand and garbage. On occasions when traffic was low, sometimes for weeks at a time, the lock gates were left closed, with the result that the water dried up and the influx of sewerage, laying in pools of fetid water, became a major health hazard, and a source of stench in the summer.

The canal proved to be a major means of transportation from its inception in 1810 until the 1830s, when the Baltimore and Ohio railroad began to provide a means of bringing freight from the Port of Baltimore directly to the heart of the city. This avoided the sea route to the port of Alexandria, transferring goods to a ferry, then to a barge, which could navigate the canal.

The canal remained operational until the late 1860s and was in use when the new cast-iron dome of the Capitol was under construction during and after the end of the Civil War. As part of a massive program of street and sewer improvement that began in the 1870s, the canal finally became obsolete and was filled in, paved and named "B" Street (later Constitution Avenue). All that remains of this piece of engineering work today is the diagonal Canal Street between South Capitol and 3rd Streets SW, and a gatehouse at Constitution Avenue and 17th Streets NW.

Plate 6 - 1
Pierre L'Enfant 1754 – 1825
Washington Historic Society

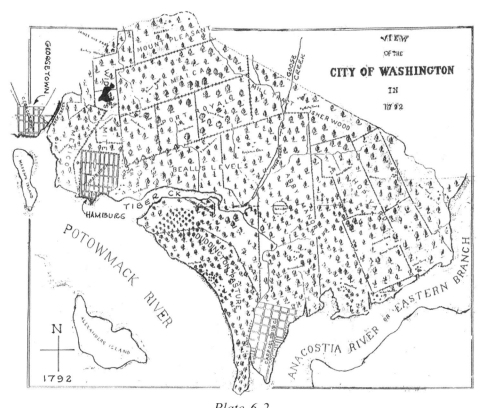

Plate 6-2
View of the land for the future city of Washington showing the towns of
George Town, Hamburg and Carrollsburg as they were in 1792

Plate 6-3
View of the future city of Washington from Georgetown, 1800
The group of houses in the left foreground is George Town.
The bridge over Rock Creek leads to the Village of Hamburg.
Jenkins Hill, the site of the future Capitol, is on the horizon.

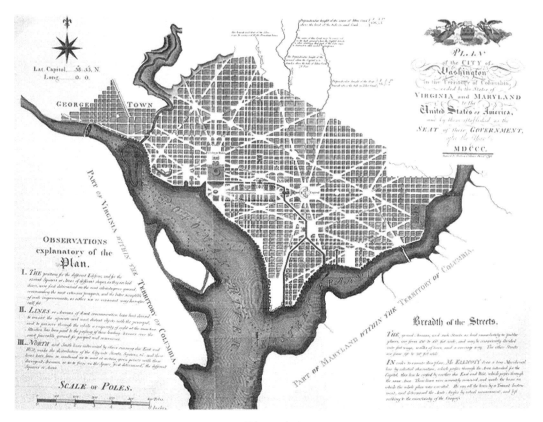

Plate 6-4
L'Enfant's plan for the capital of the United States, 1791
Completed in 1800 by Surveyor Andrew Ellicott, the plan shows the layout of the
future city , drawn to a scale in poles, and includes the Washington Canal passing
the President's House and the Capitol.

Plate 6-5
Pierre L'Enfant's Tomb, Arlington National Cemetery, 1925

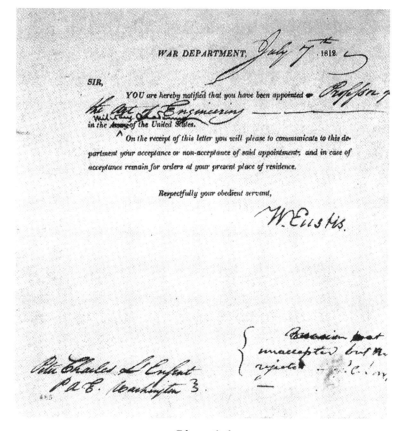

Plate 6-6
Pierre L'Enfant's appointment to West Point Military Academy
as a professor in the Art of Engineering, 1812

Plate 6-7
East Front of the Capitol of the United States
Originally designed by William Thornton and adopted by
General Washington, President of the United States, 1790

Plate 6-8
Washington Navy Yard viewed from the Anacostia River
Latrobe's Drydock sits on the river, with the Capitol behind and
the President's House farther to the left, 1805

Plate 6-9
Manual lock gates, typical of the gates designed by Benjamin Latrobe for the
Washington Canal; similar gates were used on the C & O Canal

7 . . . THE WAR OF 1812

James Madison: The Fourth President; 1809-1817

Born in 1751 in Virginia and educated at Princeton University (then the College of New Jersey), Madison turned out to be a thoughtful, quiet but dedicated individual who felt chosen by nature to help create the American Union. By 1776 the ardent student of government shared in the writing of the Virginia Constitution, and at the age of thirty-six had moved on to the debates in Philadelphia structuring the Constitution of the United States.

In 1807, as President Jefferson's secretary of state, he suggested that the ongoing war between England and France seriously limited the economy of the nation. The capture of American ships by the British reduced the flow of commerce with most foreign nations on one hand, while their activities and those of their Indian allies west of the Alleghenies impeded expansion of American settlements to the west. With his election to the presidency in 1808, he decided to adopt a belligerent policy toward both England and France.

England in 1812, still smarting from the loss of its largest colonies and locked into a contest with Napoleon, found time to harass shipping on the coasts of North America and indulge in the practice of "impressing" captured American seamen, against their will, into the British navy. Coupled with British incursions into the Canadian border, the pirate-like behavior of their navy caused the United States to consider an armed response.

Madison found himself confronted with the prospect of being the first president to declare war on a European nation, which he did in 1812, supporting incursions by American forces into Canada. The town of York (now Toronto) came under assault, was burned and partially destroyed, together with a British squadron on Lake Champlain, giving the Americans the first victories in the war.

In response, in 1814 Britain sent ships and troops up the Potowmack River to the Navy Yard and engaged in a day-long battle with Continental Army in what became known as the Battle of Bladensburg. This event became a turning point in the growth of the city of Washington.

The day after the Battle of Bladensburg the British marched toward the city of Washington and the word was given to the inhabitants to flee, with the result that every available means of transportation was crammed with goods and furniture, with their owners marching behind through the port of George Town and on to the hills towards Frederickstown. By the time the British arrived the town was deserted, with the exception of groups of vandals who broke into homes and businesses and stole whatever was available. The British were well disciplined and had orders to torch the four main federal buildings but to leave private property alone. In fact, they acted as enforcers of civil law, detaining a number of thieves, since the local police had fled along with the bulk of the population. Soldiers removed the miscreants to their boats, anchored at the Navy Yard, where they were kept in custody. When word finally reached the Americans that the British had done their deeds and wished to leave, the inhabitants and local authorities returned to their homes in the city and made peace. The British then sailed away and the town returned to normal, with the exception of the gutted and blackened President's House, the House of Congress, and the burned out Treasury and War Department.

Congress set about at once to restore the damage, beginning with the two Houses of Congress. It was hoped that the walls of the buildings could be salvaged, and inspection by Latrobe indicated that the walls of the Senate were reusable, but those of the House were burned to the point that they were structurally unsound and had to be demolished.

The President's House, though totally burned and destroyed on the inside, proved also to have sound walls, so that renovation of the interior could begin at once. To conceal the black sooty stripes emanating from many of the windows, it was decided to paint the building, since efforts to wash and remove the staining had proved impossible. This over-painting with white pigment caused much mirth among the citizens of Washington, who began to refer to the building as the "White House," a name that has stuck ever since.

The interior had a face-lift with new wood paneling and decorative plaster finishes, but lighting remained the domain of the candle and the oil lamp. There was no interior plumbing other than the carefully designed commodes which were emptied at the dead of each night by the "night carts," removing the day's waste and providing empty containers for tomorrow. Running water would come in 1833 through hollow wooden log piping, replaced in the 1860s with cast-iron piping.

Fireplaces provided heat for each occupied room, burning hard coal in cast-iron grates and emitting the pleasant warmth that was so conducive to the contraction of respiratory disease in winter. The days started early in both winter, when daylight was at a premium, and summer, when the morning hours were given to labor and conversation. The afternoons, being hot and humid, were times for sitting and doing as little as possible. The daily habits in those times were much more dependent on the weather and the availability of adequate light of the sun, and the feelings of comfort more akin to the availability of food than the temperature. Being cold in the winter of 1815 was normal and expected. The degree to which the human body can tolerate changes in temperature in a room that swings from 10 to 90 degrees Fahrenheit between winter and summer are seldom tested in modern society because of the ability of engineering to maintain nearly uniform temperatures indoors, regardless of the outside temperature.

It was decided to place the Treasury to the east of the President's House. A very conservative edifice able to match the grandeur of the neighborhood emerged on Fifteenth Street, while the War Department was moved to the west. The city viewed by a visitor arriving at the docks was one of buildings, many partially finished or abandoned, without windows and surrounded by dusty paths or tracks. There were actually five inhabited neighborhoods in the city in 1815: the President's House, the Houses of Congress, the Navy Yard, and the original villages of Hamburg and George Town, all separated by open land on which cattle grazed and low bush thrived. A congressman writing to his wife described the setting at the Houses of Congress: "Around the Capitol are seven or eight boarding houses, one shoemaker, one tailor, a washing woman, a grocery shop, a stationery shop, a dry-goods store and an oyster house. This makes the whole of the Federal City connected to the Capitol." (17)

During this rebuilding time the Congress met first in Blodgett's Hotel on E Street, which at that time also contained the Post Office and the Patent Office. There was pressure from states that had been denied the location of the capital city to abandon the vulnerable site on the Potomac and relocate inland. President James Madison defended George Washington's original selection, and, after a spirited debate, the motion to relocate was defeated and Congress proceeded with rebuilding. Fearing that disgruntled members would change their minds, a temporary but elegant brick building, known as "The Meeting House," was hurriedly built on the site of the present Supreme Court. Congress met there until 1819, at which time the restoration of the north and south wings of the Capitol were complete. (21)

Charles Bulfinch, an architect from Boston responsible for the rebuilding work after Benjamin Latrobe retired, then proceeded to build the center section between the two wings of the Capitol. This included a rotunda with a low, shining copper dome finished in 1829. Bulfinch, born in Boston in 1763, had an incredible ability to learn diverse branches of the arts and sciences. He graduated from Harvard at age eighteen and spent the next seven years studying in Europe. Returning to Boston in 1787, he began to practice a combination of engineering and architecture—street lighting, storm drainage and road building together with such works as the State House in Boston in 1798.

He began his design of the rotunda in 1818. Neither branch of the Congress, the House of Representatives or the Senate, claimed jurisdiction over the rotunda, with the result that it became the arena to lobby the members, complete with stalls selling all manner of trinkets "from ribbon to pianos." (21)

To improve the flow of material to the city, the Washington Canal was dredged to the south and east around the foot of Jenkins Hill and then south to the eastern branch adjacent to Carrollsburg. Benjamin Latrobe provided the engineering for the Washington Canal Company and employed a cadre of Irish workers to do the digging. The work was finished in 1815; the canal was opened with much fanfare, but Congress at once realized that the canal had effectively cut off the southern part of town. Latrobe prepared designs for the bridges, which were built across the canal at 7th and 12th Streets.

The Navy Yard, burned by the locals to prevent equipment falling into British hands, was skillfully rebuilt under Latrobe's supervision, including a 600-foot-long barracks, a 900-foot-long workshop and miscellaneous dwellings and stables. The biggest attraction of visitors to the yard proved to be an ingenious "dry dock," designed by Commodore Rogers. It consisted of a sloping ramp of sufficient dimensions to carry the largest ship in the Navy, and a system of pulleys and ropes capable of hauling a vessel on rollers up a ramp and into a large hangar-like building. One hundred fifty seamen powered the giant windlass and pulley that hauled the ropes that were attached to the boat.

Not only did the Navy repair ships at the Washington Navy Yard, but it also embarked on a building program; the largest in the nation at that time, which included the frigates *Essex, Potomac, Brandywine* and *Columbia*, each equipped with forty-four guns.

Initially the War of 1812 proved to be an economic disaster for the young United States, with the sacking of the city of Washington. However, after the withdrawal of the British, a later Naval victory in New Orleans led the population to believe that the war had been won and resulted in a surge of economic activity. Madison followed Jefferson's policy of expanding the U.S. Navy. However, while Madison had a firm grasp on the political future of the country, he did not have a plan for meeting the demands for transportation so urgently needed to serve the nation. This need was filled in 1825 with the election of John Quincy Adams to the presidency.

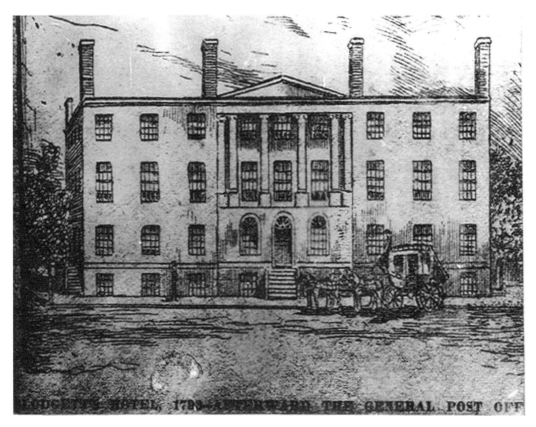

Plate 7 – 1
Blodgett's Hotel, 1793
Washington's first grand hotel, designed by James Hoban, the architect of the White House, it housed many members of Congress until 1810, when it was bought by the government to provide for the General Post Office and Patent Office; it was occupied by the Congress for several years while the Capitol was restored after the great fire of the War of 1812.

Plate 7-2
Capitol of the United States after the War of 1812
Viewed from the west, the Senate wing on the left was restored, the House wing on the right was demolished and rebuilt, the open space between the wings was designed by Dr. Thornton to accommodate a future rotunda, added by Bullfinch in 1820

Plate 7-3
The President's House after the War of 1812
On the 21st August, 1814, the entire interior of the building was destroyed by fire; inspection of the walls determined that they could safely be reused and the house was rebuilt; to cover the burn marks at the exterior windows, the building was painted white, hence the term "White House"

Plate 7-4
Washington Navy Yard, 1815
Benjamin Latrobe's dry dock for the building and repair of Naval ships is on the right of his Navy Yard Boiler Plant.

United States Ship-of-the-Line Columbus at Anchor

Plate 7-5
United States Ship of the Line: "Columbus"
This state-of-the-art Man-o-War, designed and built at the Washington Navy Yard circa 1825, was typical of the three masted battle ships that saw action in the War of 1812 on the Great Lakes and Atlantic Ocean

8 . . . Engineering a City
1814 – 1850

The end of the War of 1812 ushered in a period of substantial expansion in the economy, population, and the application of engineering principles to solve the challenges faced by the city of Washington.

One major concern was the flammability of buildings. The extensive use of wood, particularly for structural purposes, finally reached its zenith in public buildings about 1800. The Capitol, the President's House and three other government facilities had been easily burned to the ground because the floors and floor supports were all constructed of wood. Once the floor timbers were aflame nothing could save the building. The fire departments had to transport water in tanks to the site of the fire since there were no fire hydrants or underground water piping. Water was pumped by hand into hoses, which typically ran out of water after twenty minutes of use. The net result was that small residential fires might be brought under control, but large buildings and warehouses could not be successfully dealt with in the event of fire.

Based on the experience of English builders, the use of wood in monumental and commercial buildings was discontinued and the practice of embedding cast-iron beams in brick or cement became prevalent. The iron beam provided the necessary structural support to span from one wall to the next, while the brick encasement provided the thermal mass to shield the iron in the event of fire. Fireproof brick arches were designed to span between beams and support the floor above, which allowed the use of fire-resistant floor finishes. This is but one of the kind of technical upheavals that cities were facing. Other issues on the leading edge of social behavior included the need to improve travel and communications, to find substitutes for candles and whale oil lamps, to solve the cold and damp in all kinds of buildings. All contributed to the spread of disease and death in winter. There was pressure to find ways of transporting loads of material and agricultural products from the hinterland to the coastal cities.

It was indeed fortunate for the nation that a man with foresight and training came to the presidency in 1825.

John Quincy Adams: The Sixth President; 1825-1829

Born in Massachusetts in 1767, the son of the second president attended Harvard College and at the age of twenty-seven was appointed U.S. Ambassador to the Netherlands. He subsequently served in that capacity in Germany and Russia, where he was exposed to the rapid development of industrial nations of Europe. James Watt's steam engine was emerging as the natural means of powering these new economies, and the ease with which masses of agricultural products moved on the canals of England, France and Germany was carefully noted and studied by the ambassador. He soon became aware that the success of the new United States would, to a large degree, depend on the introduction of roads, bridges, canals and railroads. Also the availability of clean potable water, together with an emphasis on the application of labor-saving inventions, in particular the steam engine, was high on his list of priorities.

One key aspect to the achievement of happiness and the accumulation of wealth was the use of engineering technology. It allowed greater safety, productivity, efficiency, shorter working hours, better communications, lower cost and increased wages for the same market price.

Upon his election to the presidency in 1825, he set about the task of creating a central government with the funding and skills to support an economic development program. In his first annual message to the Congress, delivered on December 6, 1825, he laid out a federal program which included:

1. The construction of national roads to serve the hinterland
2. The provision of technical assistance to build canals
3. A federal program to build bridges at critical locations
4. The expansion of the Navy and Naval shore facilities
5. Creation of a system of standard weights and measures
6. The erection of a national observatory with astronomer
7. Creation of a state university in the nation's capital to provide technical training for engineers and surveyors. (23)

With his proposals and foresight Quincy Adams became the first leader of the nation to recognize the need to bring the power of engineering to help in the expansion and survival of the economy. The population of the United States had grown from four million in 1776 to more than twelve million in 1825. Even with this growth there was a severe shortage of labor and a resulting emphasis on mechanization, ingenuity and invention. The wooden plough used for hundreds of years in Europe was replaced with a new cast-iron unit invented by Jethro Wood in 1819, to be followed by an all-steel plough designed by John Deere in 1831. These inventions occurred as a result of the change in national character from agrarian to industrial.

Quincy Adams's leadership began to influence Congress, which at that time was fiercely committed to states rights, to think in terms of the impact of federally supported programs, which crossed state lines but brought benefits to the states and the country as a whole. In the succeeding years the temperament of the state legislators began to soften and their representatives in the Congress embraced the notion that a balance between states rights and federal needs was possible. This became apparent in the development of policies relating to communication and transportation between adjacent states and between the interior and the Atlantic Ocean. As a result the Congress began to support the construction of bridges spanning the Potomac River, which then divided the District of Columbia into two parts and which took a days travel by boat from the towns on the Virginia side to the port of Washington.

What followed was a series of programs to enable the building of bridges, canals, roads and railways, and the beginning of the utility infrastructure for the new city, including water, sewers, street lighting and gas.

Chain Bridge

A good example of the result of brave engineering planning is the story of Chain Bridge, which began forty years before the assent of Quincy Adams to the presidency. It is a story of what happens to a construction project when unknown or unforeseen conditions strike.

The need for better access to Virginia became an immediate concern to the tobacco farmers on both sides of the Potowmack River when they learned that the Congress in New York had designated George Washington to select a site for the future capital city. It became known that the site lay just east of George Town, where the only passage across the river was Magee's Ferry, dating from 1720. Three other ferries existed, somewhat larger, but were unsatisfactory in that they were slow and unreliable for large loads, and did not meet the needs of a growing economy. So in 1791 a group of investors formed the Georgetown Bridge Company and were granted a charter by the State of Maryland, which owned the river, to build a toll bridge across the Potowmack at a point three miles upstream from George Town. This location offered the narrowest crossing of the river, and presumably, the lowest construction cost. What the investors and the designers did not know of the quiet gorge, with its substantial rocks projecting out of the stream and banks at various points ideal for bridge supports, was the fury and velocity of the river under flood conditions. We now know that the river floods every ten to fifteen years, rising thirty to forty feet above the low-water level. This information could not have been available to the Bridge Company.

Designed by engineer Timothy Palmer as a wood framed structure, it opened in 1797 and lasted till 1804, when it collapsed. Replaced two more times, the last, in 1808, was called the Chain Bridge since it was constructed with a main span of suspended iron chains 136 feet long carried by masonry piers set into the river. The designer, James Finley, hailed from Uniontown, Pennsylvania, where he attended school and then apprenticed to a firm of builders, where he was exposed to the construction industry, in particular bridges and dams. Concerned with the failure of a number of bridges, he devised a suspension system employing heavy wrought chains supported on substantial masonry columns buried in the river bottom or on the banks of the river, if possible. He is credited with the successful application of his concept, ranging from his earliest, spanning seventy feet, to his later designs, where spans of 200 feet were successfully undertaken. The Chain Bridge lasted two years before being swept away in a flooding Potowmack River. (24)

In 1810, with the involvement of the federal government, bonds were issued to finance the erection of a new suspension bridge, and the Georgetown Bridge Company levied a toll for each crossing until 1833, when the structure was sold to the District of Columbia. At that time, in need of serious repair, the federal government took title to the span and rebuilt the structure as a wooden truss, which lasted through the Civil War, in 1865. New versions of the Chain Bridge emerged toward the turn of the century and are dealt with in later chapters.

The Chain Bridge proved to the citizens of Washington and investors that the ease and safety of a bridge crossing was something to be pursued. It was with these thoughts in mind that investors looked across the mile-wide Potowmack River separating the city from the Port of Alexandria, and determined that a bridge was the right solution.

Long Bridge

Washington's plan for the District of Columbia envisaged a diamond-shaped property with each side ten miles in length straddling the Potowmack River, with the majority of the habitable area in the State of Maryland, while Virginia contributed the balance. Prior to 1796 the only way to get from one state to the other was by boat from the Port of George Town to Belhaven, as it was named before being changed to Alexandria, after the Alexander family who had extensive land holdings in the vicinity. With the creation of the new capital city straddling the river, the need for a faster and safer method of crossing the four miles between the two ports became obvious.

The feasibility of a bridge had been confirmed by earlier surveys of the depth of the river. So, in 1794, a consortium of investors obtained permission to erect a bridge one and a quarter miles long across the river at a point just north of where the Washington Airport is today. For this enterprise they engaged Timothy Palmer (1751-1821), later known as the "Father of American Bridge Builders," to construct a crossing consisting of wooden piles driven into the clay bottom of the river and supporting wood frames spanning the twenty-foot distance between piles. The bridge decking consisted of wooden planks about six inches thick. Finished and ready for carts and foot traffic in 1796, the bridge survived until the flood of 1807, after which its condition was deemed unfixable and it was abandoned.

In 1808 Congress granted the Washington Bridge Company the right to build a toll bridge to connect Virginia to the capital city, parallel to Palmer's Bridge. This time much heavier wooden piles were driven into the riverbed over a distance of almost a mile, and included a draw span large enough to permit the passage of ships to the Port of George Town.

Completed in 1809, the bridge connected Virginia to the point where Maryland Avenue ended at the river, and greatly improved the communication for commerce and access to the city, since its width and strength far exceeded Palmer's design. Known as the "Long Bridge," it saw several major renovations and repairs during its twenty-year life. It was partially burned by the British during the War of 1812, rebuilt in 1816, seriously damaged several times by floods in the following few years, and finally rebuilt entirely in 1831 by the government to include a paved road. (24)

Water

For any city to survive it must have a reliable source of water. Typically all of the early settlements on the East Coast of America were sited on rivers capable of providing an abundant supply of fresh water, and the location of the future city of Washington was no exception. The river, with various spellings (when surveyed by Thomas Jefferson's father in 1746 it was the "Patoumak"), extends from Point Lookout on the Chesapeake Bay more than 400 miles to the northwest, with its source in the Allegheny Mountains on the border of West Virginia. The river is tidal and navigable for the first 200 miles from the Chesapeake, where at the Little Falls near Georgetown a series of waterfalls forms the headwater for boat traffic.

In 1608 an expedition by Capt. John Smith to the head of the navigable river reported on the clarity of the main channel and that the surrounding area was fed, "With many sweet rivers and springs, which fall from the bordering hills." Obviously the water was pure and potable at that time, but the first settlements began a process of degradation which worsened as the years went by. Major Pierre L'Enfant noted in his plan for the city that, "Piney Creek (Rock Creek) whose water, if necessary, may supply the city."

In fact, from the first settlements of farms in the late 1600s to the arrival of the Congress in 1802, the residents obtained water from wells and springs, the largest of which, Franklin Square Springs, provided water to the downtown. Later, through piping made of hollow logs, a reasonable supply of water was brought to the President's House and adjacent government buildings. This system of wooden hollow logs was still in use at end of the Civil War. (24)

The Capitol soon experienced the need to find a reliable source of water, and in 1833, it was disconnected from the local wells, and took water from a system of pipes, which originated at a large spring at Smith Farm, some two-and-a-half miles north. The water was piped into two brick reservoirs on either side of the Capitol; one for the Representatives and one for the Senate.

In spite of all the harsh conditions brought on by the climate in both winter and summer, the city began to expand. Population increased from three thousand in 1800 to more than thirteen thousand in 1820. Congress was in session during the winter, and left town each spring, returning in the fall, after the harvest. They therefore did not have to bear the sultry humidity that descended in the summer, which caused the Diplomatic Corps to declare Washington a tropical "hardship" post, qualifying for extra liquor allowances and more frequent home visits.

Congress's role in those early years was primarily to collect sufficient taxes to fund the military establishment and pay the costs of the government. They were not interested in funding any kind of improvement for the Federal City, with the result that there was no money for schools, streets, water supply and drainage.

Beginning in the early '20s, small industry and commercial enterprises began to move into the city, in particular those that supported the needs of government, such as printing, banking, surveying and real property conveyance. The biggest challenge in the city was transportation. The Washington Canal provided a vital service, shipping goods from the

Port of George Town, but did nothing to relieve the needs of settlers a hundred miles to the west. People moved by horse and wagon, and in a very few places, roads could allow the use of horse-drawn buggies, but generally roads were impassable in the rainy season and winter snow.

Europe and England had a good track record of using canals and waterways for the movement of all manner of material, so it was not surprising that people began to look for similar opportunities in America in the 1830s.

Table 2
Growth of Washington

Date	City of Washington	District of Columbia
1800	3,200	14,000
1810	8,200	24,000
1820	13,000	33,000
1830	18,000	39,000
1850	40,000	51,000
1870	109,000	131,000
1900	276,000	276,000
1940	663,000	663,000

The Chesapeake and Ohio Canal

In 1800 the population of the United States west of the Allegheny mountains was less than one million. By 1830 the number had increased to almost 3,500,000. These settlers were predominantly of English heritage, with a minority of Irish, German and Swedish immigrants, all filled with the desire to advance and take part in the dream promised by the Constitution of equality and opportunity for all. The impact of these settlers on the economies of the local states was profound, and their buying power not lost for a moment on the merchants in the eastern seaboard, particularly New York, Pennsylvania and Maryland. Tapping the western markets included, as the major hurdle, the transportation of goods and services across the mountains and into the Ohio Valley.

The Eire Canal, connecting the Hudson River to the Great Lakes, completed in 1825, proved to be a major contributor to the opening up of the Mid-West. Canals in both France and England had demonstrated their usefulness in moving loads much more efficiently than could be accomplished over the roads of that time. By 1818 a major thoroughfare called the Western Road connected the Port of Baltimore to Wheeling, Virginia, and the comparison between the capacities of the Eire Canal and the Western Road became starkly evident.

On the major roads four horses could pull a one-ton load eighteen miles in a day. On a flat water canal, four horses could pull a 100-ton load twenty-four miles a day. Taking into consideration the cost of operation and maintenance, it was estimated that the canal was more than thirty times as cost effective as the road. (25)

The cost to move a one-ton cargo by road from Buffalo to New York was $100. With the opening of the Eire Canal the rate dropped to $12 and the time to complete the trip was reduced from twenty to eight days.

With these statistics in mind, the proponents of a waterway connecting the Potowmack River to the Ohio brought heavy pressure on Congress to authorize the formation of a canal company, which would have a major impact on the wealth and importance of the new city of Washington. Under the authority granted to them by the General Survey Act of 1824, the Corps of Engineers were directed to assist the Canal Company in establishing feasible routes for the proposed excavation.

The Corps surveyed more than 260 miles of potential routes from Washington through the Cumberland Valley and prepared an estimate of construction cost that indicated to build the canal would require the expenditure of $22 million, as compared with the expectations of the investors, which was of the order of $5 million.

Canal supporters, naturally unhappy with the Corps' estimate, organized to discredit it and hired engineer James Geddes to determine a realistic cost for the project. Geddes had worked in New York on the Eire Canal and knew canal building. He came up with a projected cost of $4.5 million to extend the canal to Cumberland.

Work began in 1828, and in 1850 the canal reached Cumberland, at which time the cost had reached $11 million. This cost was the same proportion of the National Gross Domestic Product in 1850, as was the cost of putting a man on the moon to the GDP more than a hundred years later.

The Chesapeake and Ohio Canal Company was an investor-owned venture, with Benjamin Wright as the chief engineer. He was given the task of connecting the Potomac River to the Ohio River, thereby forming a commercial link to the hinterland, which would benefit the competitive position of Washington against its rival Baltimore.

Earlier, in New York, Benjamin Wright was one of three American engineers, along with Canvas White and James Geddes, with minimal surveying and engineering training who were selected to design and lead the construction of the Eire Canal in New York in 1817. There were no trained civil engineers available, or engineers with extensive canal experience, so the State of New York selected these three and allowed them to travel to Europe and observe the techniques of canal building. Upon their return, they were turned loose to build the canal in New York State. It soon became obvious that these three could not supervise and manage the entire length of the work, so they hired untrained men as foremen, gave them on-the-job instruction, met frequently, required reports, and moved slowly, so that by 1819 they were staffed with a crew capable of making decisions and carrying responsibility. This was the classic British method of educating engineers; an apprenticeship with close supervision until ready to assume responsibility.

On July 4, 1828, President John Quincy Adams broke ground in George Town for the new Chesapeake and Ohio Canal, which coincidentally was the same day that the Baltimore and Ohio Railroad broke ground. Work on the canal started in 1830, and in 1833 an extension connecting George Town to the Washington Canal was constructed in order to bypass the continual silting that blocked the entrance at Tiber Creek.

The canal proceeded, first with local labor, which proved unsatisfactory since the workers, mostly from nearby farms, had to leave in the planting and harvesting seasons. Later, with an influx of Irish and German immigrants who proved to be much more reliable, the pace of digging and blasting rock improved remarkably. The canal reached the foot-hills of the Appalachians in 1843, and on October 10, 1850, was connected to Cumberland, Maryland, under the leadership of engineer Charles Fisk. The total length of the excava-tion from the locks in George Town to the terminal in Cumberland approached 185 miles, and had been constructed under some 350 different contracts. (25)

To raise the barges from the high tide level of the Potomac to Cumberland required the building of seventy-five sets of locks, each serviced by a lock-keeper and his family. They lived in a house, provided by the company upon the condition that the keeper would be available twenty-four hours a day to open and close the gates for the barges. The canals were capable of operation day and night, as opposed to the highways, where night traffic was all but impossible due to the dangerous condition of the roadway, inadequate lighting, highwaymen, and the need to rest and change the horses.

The engineering concepts and design of the canal were satisfactory, and considering the success that waterways enjoyed in Europe and England, the investors must have been confident that the C&O would meet their goals and expectations. However, this was not to be. Throughout the twenty-two years it took to do the work, labor was a continual problem, as were the many lawsuits brought by the rival railroad and one of its principal investors, Charles Carroll, who owned land in the direct path of the canal and steadfastly denied the necessary right-of-way. Legal action between the canal company and the rail-road held up excavation in the vicinity of Point-of-Rocks for more than three years until the courts finally verified the canal company's right-of-way and work resumed. Timing could not have been worse. The success of canals in Europe and the Eire Canal in New York all occurred at a time when the only competition was roads. But the invention of the steam locomotive by Trevithick in England in 1805, and its subsequent development over the next fifty years, meant that by the time the C&O Canal reached Cumberland in 1850, it was competing head-to-head with powerful locomotives capable of hauling many times the capacity of the barge system in much shorter times. There was also the problem of flooding. From time to time the Potowmack River would rise to a level where the canal would be inundated; banks were washed away and the canal would empty, stranding barges for days until repairs could be made.

Perhaps the most memorable piece of engineering occurred at the Paw Paw Bends, a series of twists and turns in the river as the Potowmack enters the foothills of the Appala-chian Mountains. The canal had been designed to follow the watercourse of the river, but at Paw Paw this meant cutting a canal six miles long through rock for the majority of the distance, and realize only one mile of western advancement. The alternative was to blast a 3,100-foot-long tunnel through the mountain, construct the canal in the tunnel, and thereby save five miles of rock excavation. Initial geological investigations indicated that the stratified and shelflike nature of the surface rock would persist through the mountain and be fairly easy to blast loose and remove. But this was not to be. The mountain proved to be solid, so the initial estimate of a two-year construction time dragged out to be twelve years and three hundred percent over budget. When completed in 1848 the Paw Paw tunnel was hailed in technical papers and by the European press as a marvel of engineering, and an example of the progress and competence of American ingenuity.

Under the original design, the C & O Canal was to terminate in George Town, with the contents of each barge transferred to larger ocean-going ships in the harbor. However, the masters of George Town imposed substantial costs to each shipment, with the result that the C & O Company began to explore the feasibility of bypassing George Town entirely by extending the canal as an elevated structure above the river. If the barges never entered the waters of the river, then the charges would be eliminated.

Aqueduct Bridge

In addition to the main canal that paralleled the Maryland side of the Potomac River and terminated in Georgetown, there emerged a plan to extend the canal across the river to the Virginia side. The cost of unloading a barge at the Port of Georgetown and transferring the cargo to a sloop that took it to Alexandria, where it would have to be again transferred to an oceangoing vessel, turned out to be expensive as well as time consuming. The operators of the Port at Georgetown turned out to be less than willing to allow cargo to pass through their facility without levying substantial duty charges. If a way could be devised to have the barges from Cumberland unload directly to the ships anchored at Alexandria, the cost savings would be considerable. Thus, as early as 1832 the Corps of Engineers was instructed to survey the main river and determine the feasibility of constructing an aqueduct across the river and a canal on the Virginia side that would terminate at the Port of Alexandria. With such an arrangement the C & O Canal could bypass Georgetown and would present a continuous body of navigable water from the mountains to a tidal shipping point.

The proposed aqueduct would be about twenty feet wide, with a water depth of six feet, contained in a rectangular masonry sheath long enough to span the river—about 1,500 feet—and supported to clear the flood level by thirty feet. The engineers report indicated that the project was viable, and with funding from the Congress, work by the Corps began the following year. The story of the design of the Aqueduct tells of engineering skill that had advanced in two hundred years since its inception in France and England, to what might be termed the "modern age." The quality and skill displayed by the designers and draftsmen supervised by Lieutenant M. C. Ewing of the Fourth Artillery and Captain William Turnbull of the U.S. Topographic Survey is still today quite remarkable. The drawings describing the enterprise are a work of art. Compared to construction drawings for the twenty-first century, which cover in detail *what* has to be done but not *how* it must be executed (the "how" is covered today by reams and volumes of standards, codes, laws and directives), the drawings prepared in 1832 cover in three dimensions each step of not only what was required but how the workers should build the aqueduct.

The plan to support the elevated waterway included the construction of twelve masonry piers, each 65 feet long by 20 feet at the base and 60 feet tall, set into the bed of the river on intervals of 105 feet. To enable the laying of the foundations of the piers and the building of walls below water, a "cofferdam" was erected at the site of each pier. A cofferdam is nothing but a temporary structure, set into a dam or river, with walls that extend down below the water and into the mud at the bottom. Arranged in a circle, in this case about eighty-five feet in diameter, once the walls are all in place, the water contained inside the can be pumped out until the soil and mud at the bottom of the river are exposed and gradually dry out. There is then a circular dam, sitting in the middle of the river, with water around the outside but dry on the inside, so that with ladders extending the full height workmen can begin the task of building the foundation for the pier.

In the case of the Aqueduct, steam-driven pumps, including wood-fired boilers and steam engines, were floated on barges and anchored near the cofferdam to empty the water initially and then remove leakage and rainwater during the six to eight months it took to build each pier. Other barges carried the stone and cement, cranes, ladders, walkways, derricks and lumber, and plied between the shore as needed. At the completion of one pier, the cofferdam was removed and set up at the next work site, until their appeared twelve gray stone towers rising thirty feet above high-tide water level. Each tower had been planned to face upstream with its narrow dimension and clad with hard stone capable of defending against floods and ice flows, floating trees and debris.

The task of building the elevated canal then began, and by 1844 the first barges moved over the Potomac River and headed down the newly built Alexandria Canal. The completion of the aqueduct provided an impetus to the C & O Canal Company to reach its target of connection to the commerce of the Ohio River.

The aqueduct remained operational as a canal until the 1880s, when declining waterborne commerce took its toll and it was shut down, drained, disconnected from the C & O Canal, and paved over to become a major vehicular thoroughfare connecting Georgetown to Virginia. Aqueduct Bridge, as it became known, survived into the 1920s, when it was demolished after the building of the new Key Bridge.

Soon after its completion in 1850, the Chesapeake and Ohio Canal began to prosper. There was a steady increase in the barge traffic. An increasing number of barges parked at various locks and at the Potomac end of the canal was evidence that a fledgling industry of barge building, centered mainly at the head of the canal in Cumberland, was beginning to take hold. The number of operating barges reached more than five hundred in the early 1870s, leading to congestion and substantial waiting time to traverse the locks in George Town, and get down to the level of the river.

To solve this problem, the most outstanding piece of engineering associated with the C & O was designed. It was named the Incline Plane, and allowed a floating barge to gently descend down a slope from the canal to the river forty feet below. The key to the design was a massive flooded steel tank, capable of allowing a barge to enter through doors at the canal level, and then the tank, together with the floating barge, were allowed to run on wheels down the inclined slope to the river. There the massive tank was submerged and the barge floated out, reducing the time to clear the locks by more than sixty percent. The Incline Plane was so successful that it was hailed as an engineering marvel. A model presented at the 1878 Paris Exposition was acclaimed by engineers and scientists as an outstanding piece of engineering art. For twenty years the Incline Plane was a feature of the C & O Canal until it was destroyed in the flood of 1889 and never rebuilt. Barge traffic was on the wane and the canal company must have realized that their venture was coming to a gradual economic end. They elected to go into a receivership to the Baltimore and Ohio Railroad, which operated the canal until 1924, when another devastating flood washed away the walls of the canal in the vicinity of Chain Bridge. This caused the water in the canal to empty, stranding what few barges remained in service. For the owners it must have been the last straw, because they decided to stop operating and close down business for good. It remained dormant until 1938 when, as part of the refinancing of the B & O Railroad, the canal and all the land from Georgetown to the Allegheny Mountains was ceded to the federal government. They in turn placed it under the jurisdiction of the National Park Service, where it remains today.

The experience of the Chesapeake and Ohio Canal demonstrates the necessity that engineering work must *function;* it must work and work efficiently. It must *produce* more than it *consumes,* in economic terms, or it will become obsolete and be replaced. Upon its termination as a functioning piece of engineering in 1924, the canal went dormant, and would have been replaced by a more efficient highway had it not been for the efforts of Supreme Court Justice William. O. Douglas to convert it into a piece of static art (a national park), which produces, not function, but feelings—feelings of delight in the great outdoors, the preserved pristine nature of the countryside as it was in the Maryland countryside almost two hundred years ago. It is indeed good that some engineering marvels of a bygone age can be so transformed and preserved.

The demise of the C & O Canal is also part of the process of society moving from systems that are less efficient, less safe, more expensive to operate and more dependent on humans (and animals) to those which do a better job of meeting the ever higher demands of modern existence. In the case of the C & O Canal, and canals in general throughout the world, the invention of James Watt's steam engine and Trevithick's application of it to the invention of the steam locomotive spelled the end of commercial canals. Railroads began their march on to the center stage of transportation.

Railroads

When the Congress moved from Philadelphia to Washington in 1802, most members traveled by sea from Boston, New York and Philadelphia to the new capital on the banks of the Patowmack River. The passage from New York was four days of pleasant sailing compared to the road journey that took almost twice as long and was much more stressful. Consideration had to be given to the possibilities of being accosted by highwaymen or asked to pay a new toll at every minor settlement along the two hundred-mile journey. Since all of the cities of the new United States were on navigable waters, either rivers or lakes, there was no complaint from the traveling congressmen; they could go from home to the Capital via water in relative comfort and safety.

Meanwhile, in England, the issue of intercity travel was becoming more important. The engineers who had designed the steam engine for stationary power systems had obtained extended patents from the Parliament that protected the reproduction of their inventions in any field of endeavor. James Watt (1736-1819), who had obtained patents on the low-pressure steam engine in 1769, and had the rights extended by an Act of Parliament in 1775 to the year 1800, held a virtual monopoly on the development and use of the steam engine in every application. Watt was opposed to the increase in pressure of the steam in the cylinder for safety reasons. He firmly believed that an engineer's first task was the design of boilers and engines that were safe. He was adamant that pressures in excess of twelve pounds per square inch were life threatening. He maintained this position until his patents expired and he withdrew from the manufacture of engines in 1803.

With the expiration of Watt's patents, engineers were free to begin experimenting with the effects of higher steam pressures, and on both sides of the Atlantic designs emerged that would change the face of industry forever. In America, Oliver Evans of Philadelphia produced a boiler that could sustain a pressure of forty pounds per square inch, more than three times Watt's theoretical goal. Simultaneously, in England, Richard Trevithick (1771-1833) produced a high-pressure boiler, mounted on wheels, which drove a steam engine connected to the front wheels, and the locomotive was born in 1805. The continued development of the locomotive together, with the research in methods of safely hauling a train of engine and passenger cars, and finally produced the wrought iron rail and the twin cylinder engine in the middle 1820s. Here at last in the history of man was a way to convey persons safely and quickly from point to point over land at a speed that far exceeded the fastest stagecoaches. Railroad companies began to proliferate, so it was no surprise when the merchants and land owners of the East began to pick up on the economic possibilities of rail lines connecting the producing and shipping areas of the nation together.

In 1827 the newly formed Baltimore and Ohio Railroad requested and received assistance from the Army Engineers to survey a route through the mountains of Western Maryland for a new rail line out of Baltimore into the Ohio Valley. The Corps did a remarkable job, and on July 4, 1828, ground-breaking for the new railroad was held in Baltimore. Not only had the Corps done the survey but they were directly involved with the laying of the first rail track from Baltimore to Ellicott City, thirteen miles distant. By 1834 the line had reached Harper's Ferry; in 1835 a branch line was laid into Washington; and in 1842 it entered Cumberland, some eight years before the C & O Canal. By 1853 the railroad had connected to Wheeling, West Virginia. There was no contest; the railroad had superseded the canal and become the dominant means of transportation in the United States.

The rail line into Washington terminated at Third Street and Pennsylvania Avenue, a brief walk from the Capitol on Jenkins Hill. Washington "Station" became the starting point for a series of horse-drawn "taxis" that bounced over the rutted and muddy streets, all the way to George Town, three miles distant. To clamber aboard a taxi in the down-town area, one generally waited at one of many small, stone footbridges that spanned across the gutter at the curb in order to cross the refuse and horse dung that had accumulated where the road met the sidewalk.

The arrival of the railroad in the nation's capital should recognize that the key to success was a partnership of the federal military providing surveys and studies, and the private sector taking the financial risk of the actual construction. Considering the acute shortage of trained civil engineers in the private sector, it is fortuitous that the Congress, which had a history of avoiding assistance to the states, was willing to pass an act allowing the only trained group of talent to get directly involved in such a time of need.

In 1831 the Congress repealed the General Survey Act, and the partnership between the military and the private sector came to an end. What should have followed was the beginning of a drain of trained West Point graduates leaving the Army and going into the private sector, but the loyalty of the officer corps and the security offered by a regular source of income induced most to stay for careers in the military.

The termination of the B & O Railroad at the foot of Capitol Hill had an immediate influence on the development of Pennsylvania Avenue. Hotels and boardinghouses sprung up together with the beginnings of the retail trade of Washington. The visitors to the city, who before the emergence of the railroad would have arrived by sea, now appeared in ever increasing numbers at the hotels along the "Avenue," and were more interested in the local scene than the Europeans, whose interests were confined to the government. The communication between Baltimore and New York began to influence the construction industry and the makeup of banks. For the first time in the short history of the nation, the "East Coast" began to emerge as a homogeneous economy, rather than the separate countries of Boston, New York and Philadelphia that heretofore had existed in the minds and practices of businessmen. Through the application of engineering, people were able to enjoy a freedom and ability to travel great distances at affordable prices in safety and relative comfort.

Steam locomotives that powered the railroads generated their steam from the burning of coal, which produced the heat that boiled the water, but in the process produced brilliant light in the combustion chamber. For several years no one paid much attention to this phenomenon, until the 1840s, when the safety and inefficiency of candles came to the attention of inventors. Was there a way to use coal for the production of safer and more brilliant lighting. As it turned out, research had been done on coal gas for a number of years, particularly in Europe.

Gas

In 1845 James K. Polk entered the President's House, and into a town of 45,000 persons who lived along the ridge of the river from George Town to the Navy Yard in brick and wooden houses, enduring the mud in winter and the dust in summer. The main thoroughfare connecting the cluster of houses and shops around the White House to the housing near the Capitol was Pennsylvania Avenue. In 1802 the Congress had appropriated money to provide oil lamps on a few of the main avenues, but the roads were so bad that few ventured out at night, and the city virtually shut down from dusk till dawn. (19)

In 1792 in England, "The Father of Gas Lighting," William Murdoch, demonstrated the production of a flammable gas by heating coal without setting it alight and collecting the gaseous products, which, when lighted, burned brightly and gave off heat. This procedure of distilling coal had been discovered in 1681 by John Becher, but no practical use had been made of the discovery. It was not until 1767 that the Bishop of Llandaff in Wales succeeded in purifying the gas given off in the making of coke for the iron industry. It was that invention that propelled gas into the industrial market as a source of both heat and light.

In Washington in 1847 James Crutchett was granted a contract to provide gas lighting for the Houses of Congress. Crutchett had come to the city from the Midwest, where he had experimented with various types of flammable gasses, such as hydrogen-carbide and "rosin gas." He bought a house on North Capitol Street, where he continued his research. In 1846 he succeeded in lighting the interior and exterior of the house with gas lamps, nine in number, which attracted crowds of onlookers. This spurred a group of activists, who had petitioned Congress for four years in a row to approve a charter for a gas company in Washington, to renew their efforts.

Crutchett, with the help of stories published in the local newspaper, got the attention of the Congress and was granted a patent and a charter for his company to provide gas lighting for the two houses of Congress and the grounds around the Capitol. The plant produced coal gas.

Coal gas is produced when coal is heated in a "retort," a closed vessel of cast iron situated in the combustion chamber of a furnace. With the furnace fired and hot, the coal in the retort is raised to a temperature where it begins to break down into the "vapour of carbon," as methane was called in those days, and other gasses. The breakdown of all the products included methane 25%, carbon monoxide 10%, and hydrogen 55%, with the by-products of tar and coke. The gasses are piped off and stored in large tanks called "gasometers" and then piped to the customers. (8, Page 437)

Crutchett set up his gas plant on the Capitol grounds, ran piping into the building and installed gas lamps in the chambers and a massive lamp on the top of the Capitol dome. The light on the dome could be seen for miles. However, it was unreliable, so the following year Crutchett's contract was canceled. The chief clerk of the House of Representatives, Benjamin French, was responsible for administering Crutchett's contract with the government, so upon its termination French realized that there was a good opportunity for some other entity to continue to provide the gas lighting to the Congress. He associated with a number of Washington's business leaders, and on April 12, 1848, a petition to grant a charter to the Washington Gas Light Company was forwarded to the Congress.

The new company purchased patent rights to Crutchett's plant, renovated the beacon on the top of the dome, and began to operate the plant and furnish gas to the Capitol. The plant was located on the Capitol grounds, where Independence Avenue and Third Street is today. Washington Gas Light Company thus became the first gas utility in the United States to be chartered by the Congress; it is the oldest public utility in the Washington region, and the longest survivor of companies chartered by the Congress. The original investors in the company included John Callan, a druggist; Mayor Bradley; Jacob Bigelow, a lawyer; William Harrover, a hardware merchant; and William English, a Treasury clerk who rose to become a congressman from Indiana.

The first invoice rendered to the Congress on July 29, 1848, in the amount of $2,127.36, included a letter from John Callan, president of the gas company. In it he stated that the bill covered lighting for the two houses of Congress, post offices, passages, offices and stairs within the building, the terraces and walkways on the exterior, and the lantern on the dome. He stated that most lamps burned continuously, day and night.

The invoice also showed that there was on hand, "2011 gallons of whale oil," from which it is concluded that not all of the oil lamps had been taken out of service. The superintendent of the plant was paid $89.50 a month, or about forty cents per hour, versus the laborers who stoked the boilers, who received twenty-five dollars a month, or twelve cents per hour. (19)

The massive gas chandeliers serving the Senate were not satisfactory and were replaced at a cost of one hundred dollars, while the cost of exchanging unstated numbers of lamp glasses was three dollars each. The statement concluded with the assertion that the annual cost of lighting with gas is expected to be less than $6,000, compared to previous expenditures on whale oil, which ran over $10,000.

The structural stability of Crutchett's dome lamps, with their massive wood supports that swayed dangerously in high winds, became the subject of concern for the occupants of the Capitol, who feared that the dome could collapse, so the Congress agreed to the demolition of the lamps and supports for the sum of three hundred dollars. The wood columns were given to the Washington Monument Society, who converted them into a boom crane for the lifting of the stone blocks being used in the building of the monument.

The congressional charter gave the gas company the rights to extend gas service to other parts of the city, so with the future in mind, land was purchased on Louisiana Avenue at Tenth Street for the sum of $3,600. Construction began on a larger plant, including a newly invented gasometer, and office building. The plant was located on the site of the present Justice Department Building. At that time Louisiana Avenue was located where Indiana Avenue is today, and ran from the canal in a northeasterly direction toward Judiciary Square, where it intersected the original Indiana Avenue.

By December 29, 1848 the President's House received illumination from the newly installed piping system, paid for by the government, that connected the plant, up Pennsylvania Avenue, to gas lamps throughout the building. Gas lighting was extended to most adjacent government buildings, but the selling price of the product, at eight dollars per thousand cubic feet, was out of reach for most private citizens. In order to survive, the company instituted a program to sell gas lighting to the major hotels and department stores, including the Willard Hotel on Pennsylvania Avenue.

In 1850 the price of gas was reduced to six dollars and forty cents per thousand cubic feet, and the company purchased the underground gas mains from the government and extended the piping to the more affluent part of town, on Massachusetts at Connecticut Avenue. The demand for gas increased, so in 1851 the company built a new coal gas plant on the Washington Canal at Maryland Avenue and Maine Avenue, a few blocks west of the Capitol. At that time Maine Avenue ran parallel to Maryland Avenue between Third and Sixth Streets, but has since been abolished, and the present street parallel to the Washington Channel renamed Maine Avenue.

Service was extended into George Town in 1852, and in 1854 the George Town Gaslight Company obtained a charter from Congress and laid new underground lines in parallel to those of Washington Gas, but primarily served street lighting customers.

By 1856 Washington Gas was serving 1,700 customers from George Town to the Navy Yard and had more than thirty miles of piping. The gas plant on the grounds of the Capitol had been removed, and connections to the plant at Maryland Avenue served the Capitol.

These arrangements continued until 1860, when a large coal-gas plant, the West Station Plant, was erected at 26th and G Streets NW. Located at the entrance to George Town, the plant included two large gasometers, gas tanks eighty feet in diameter and seventy feet tall, coal loading docks and boiler plant. This was followed in 1888 with the construction of the East Station Plant at 12th and N Streets SE.

In their time these were state-of-the-art facilities and efficient enough to allow the price of gas to be reduced further.

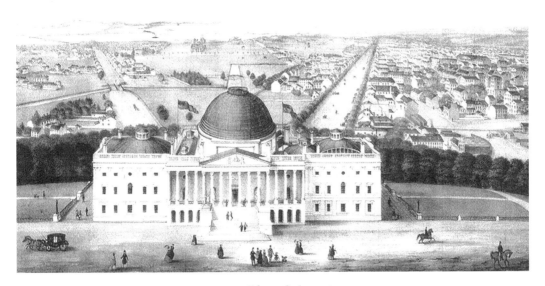

Plate 8-1
View of the city of Washington, 1840
Pennsylvania Avenue to the right and Maryland Avenue to the left
with the Washington Canal crossing Maryland Ave.

Plate 8-2
View of Washington looking west from the Capitol, 1852
The Washington Canal flows past the new Gas Works;
the Smithsonian Castle and "B" Street are to the left

Plate 8-3
The Original Chain Bridge, 1808
This was the fourth bridge spanning the Potomac River;
designed by James Finley

Plate 8-4
Chain Bridge during the Civil War, 1865
Built circa 1840, this wood truss bridge lasted until 1874
and was replaced by a steel truss

Plate 8-5
Stone Footbridge, downtown Washington, 1840
To board horse-drawn taxis many businesses and wealthy property owners
installed small footbridges at the curb of the road to avoid stepping
in the refuse and horse manure that was washed into the gutter
by rain or street-crews in order to keep the streets passable

Plate 8-6
Longbridge across the Potomac, 1865
The Railroad Bridge, erected in 1860, ran parallel to the road bridge built in 1830;
the two bridges connected Maryland Avenue in the city to Virginia

Plate 8-7
C & O Canal near Georgetown, circa 1870
Horse-drawn barges awaiting passage into the locks
above the Port of Georgetown

Plate 8-8
James Crutchett's house on North Capitol Street, 1848
This was the first house lighted with gas in Washington

Plate 8-9
Tower with gas light on the dome of the Capitol, 1848

8-10
Gas plant at Maryland and Old Maine Avenue, 1852
Showing the Capitol to the left and gas storage tank on the right;
the Botanic Gardens now occupy the site

Plate 8 – 11
Aqueduct Bridge, 1850
View of the bridge from Virginia looking toward Georgetown; the barge is anchored, but will move forward and to the right, turning into the Alexandria Canal; a narrow footpath on the left provides access across the river including horse-drawn buggies

Plate 8 - 12
Aqueduct Bridge, circa 1900
The canal to Alexandria has been abandoned and the bridge converted to horse-drawn traffic

Plate 8 - 13
Aqueduct Bridge, circa 1915
View from Virginia with Georgetown University on the left and the "Old Car Barn"
on the right; the original 1830 piers are still in place

Plate 8 – 14
B & O Railroad Train Crossing Maryland Avenue
This passenger train is heading for the Baltimore and Potomac Station
at the corner of "B" Street (Constitution Ave.) and 6th Street N.W.,
where the new National Gallery sits today; the station and branch line
heading north on 6th Street were demolished in the early 1900s

9 . . . A CITY MATURES

Sixty years after the first growth forest began to be cleared, the city of Washington started to take on some of the airs of a capital city. A partially paved Pennsylvania Avenue ran straight between the Capitol and White House. Most residential streets were still mud and dust depending on the season. Maryland Avenue, following L'Enfant's plan, led straight to the Long Bridge and Virginia, and pulled by smoking engines of the B & O Railroad, three passenger cars could be boarded at nine o'clock sharp for the day-long trip to New York.

What Americans in the twenty-first century would consider the most basic and necessary services, such as water, sewer, pest control and street lighting, were still in very poor condition. Water in particular demanded the attention of the Congress. For a town of 40,000 persons, the reliance on wells and springs, which sometimes failed to deliver in the dry season, became an urgent problem to be solved.

Washington had gone through several forms of local government, all very much under the watchful eye of the Congress, which still feared investing in a sound infrastructure because the city might be viewed warily by constituents in the hinterland, who generally lived in much worse conditions. However, Washington was the Capital City, host to foreigners in new embassies, so there gradually emerged a maturing in thinking on the part of both Congress and local politicians to begin building the city services.

Many Europeans seriously questioned the chances, and wisdom, of the new United States in their goal of creating a capital city out of the wilderness. Most foreigners had expected New York or Philadelphia to be chosen as the seat of the federal government. There was, therefore, genuine surprise when the word got back to Europe that a new city was to be created in a wilderness on the banks of a major river half way between the Northern and Southern states.

The boldness of the colonists in challenging the divine right of the English monarchy had produced a reaction among the thinkers of Europe. They were unwilling to openly speak out and embrace the concepts of democracy, until the revolution in France, accompanied by the removal of the French monarch, lighted a small candle of faith in the belief that the individual, perhaps, is supreme in the rule of men. The new Congress, barely fifty years old, was very conservative in its thinking about the advantages of a large central government. The myriad social programs that we are accustomed to today were unknown in 1850. The focus of government emanated from the state legislatures, which raised the bulk of the money to support local needs, sending a small amount to Washington to fund the Congress and the military, in particular the Navy, based on the Anacostia River. As a result little money to invest in improvements to the capital city came from congressmen, mostly from rural and frontier constituencies, who saw no reason to embellish the new city with such luxuries as paved roads, sidewalks, street lighting and recreational facilities.

With private money, a small dock at the foot of Maryland Avenue, sporting a jetty and landing for three ships, allowed direct access to the city and avoided the time-consuming task of getting from Alexandria by coach across Long Bridge. Visitors began to arrive in the new Port of Washington, and the accounts of these wealthy and titled Europeans usually started with the shock and disappointment they felt at seeing a muddy and sparsely built town on the side of a low range of hills, spilling down to a waterfront bereft of all but the most basic public facilities. However, the stories these visitors told usually changed after they had conversed with the leaders of the new city, who convinced their guests of the sincerity of their belief in the new country and their dedication to making the new city expand in numbers and quality of services.

The expansion of George Washington's city from a muddy cow patch in 1800 to a thriving town in 1850 confounded many. Europeans who had never visited the colonies of Africa or America had no idea about the ability of these hardy people to survive and prosper in the harshest of conditions, and would leave the city extolling nothing but admiration for the new Americans and their prospects of success. Inevitably the Congress recognized the need for new government buildings, in particular after the fire that destroyed Blodgett's Hotel, built in 1793 at 8th and E Streets, which housed the post office. Then the fire of 1833 that gutted the Treasury. Congress voted money for a number of buildings, including a new treasury, post office, city hall and patent office.

After a depression in the 1830s, when land values sank and many landowners declared bankruptcy, a spurt in construction took place which included thirty churches, two public schools, a new jail, and public baths on North C Street between 4th and 6th Streets, where the district court sits today. Washington streets in the 1850s were designated as either "north" or "south." North C Street ran from East 15th to West 23rd Streets; the four quadrants that divide the city today were to come in the next century.

Plumbing, with running fresh water discharging into waste water piping, had been invented in England in the late 1700s. However, the absence of piping in the streets of Washington and a reliable source of water precluded the introduction of indoor facilities in the majority of private residences. New public baths, served by a spring and including hot water for bathing, were a huge success. Just around the corner from the baths were Brown's and Gadsby's hotels, both on Pennsylvania Avenue, and two of the city's premier watering spots. Both benefited by the patronage from the baths but began to exert pressure on Congress to solve Washington's water supply problem so that they could install indoor plumbing for their guests, many of whom were congressmen.

Water Supply

The Capitol building was served by two brick reservoirs fed from springs several miles to the north, and it became obvious, after a serious fire in the building, that the water supplies to the city were inadequate. It became necessary to evaluate alternatives and make plans for the future. There were no engineers in private practice at that time who could undertake the study of the water problem, so the Corps of Engineers was tapped to determine the options for serving Washington with an adequate supply of drinking water into the foreseeable future.

The officer chosen for the task was Lieutenant Montgomery C. Meigs, a graduate of West Point, who performed the study at the direction of Congress. Meigs's proposals were such a success with the representatives that he was promoted to the rank of captain.

Montgomery Meigs was born on May 3, 1816, in Augusta, Georgia, and spent his childhood years in Philadelphia. His father, Dr. Charles D. Meigs, a noted and wealthy obstetrician, and his mother, Mary, lived in Philadelphia and were the parents of ten children, with Montgomery the eldest.

A bright and hard-working young man, he proved to be a reliable son, assisting his mother with daily chores and leading his siblings in their schoolwork, while developing qualities of leadership learned from his father. At age seventeen he entered the U.S. Military Academy at West Point, graduating near the top of his class in 1836, with a thorough grounding in the art of civil and military engineering. At that time the emphasis of the academy's program focused on the rounded education of future leaders of men. The syllabus broke the three-year course into "percentages," with each percentage repeated year by year in more detailed and comprehensive instruction. A breakdown of the components were:

> 20 percent: mathematics.
> 20 percent: natural and experimental philosophy
> 20 percent: engineering
> 20 percent: military exercise and strategy
> 10 percent: drawing
> 10 percent: French (12, Page 42)

During his training it became a real joy to Meigs to understand the workings of mechanical things, like a new cement mixer that arrived at the academy and failed to function as advertised. He visited with the workmen and their supervisors to determine the cause of the problem, and received permission to join the construction crew on a temporary assignment, providing it did not interfere with his academic schedule. Upon graduation he was assigned to various military bases as post engineer, responsible for the construction and maintenance of the buildings, fortifications and roads. It was from Rouses Point in northern New York that Meigs received orders to move to Washington in 1852. Throughout his career he was an avid writer and recorder of events, beginning in longhand but soon switching to the newly invented "shorthand." Isaac Pitman had devised a system, which he named "phonography," in which words were broken into phonetic components and assigned a symbol, making it possible to write or record conversations a rate six to seven times that of the most experienced longhand writer. Meigs began to use Pitman's Shorthand for his daily journal. He soon found that the degree of detail and the sheer volume and depth of his understanding of daily meetings with his superiors made him a valuable member of the management team.

Meigs and his wife, Louisa Rogers, whom he had married in 1841, moved in with Louisa's mother and lived in her home on H Street between 9th and 10th Streets. He frequently complained in his journal writings that the salary of a captain in the Army, assisted by an allowance from his father, was insufficient to meet the needs of his family. He compared his income with that of the contractors under his supervision, who were able to add a substantial percentage of the construction costs of the projects to their personal income.

His duties in Washington brought him in contact with wealthy contractors and with congressional representatives, top administration officials and members of the scientific community, and on occasions, invitations to dine at the White House.

His study of the alternatives available for providing a reliable source of potable water to the city of Washington considered taking supplies from the Potomac River near the Port of Georgetown. (The Potowmack changed to Potomac about 1840.) But the lack of sufficient elevation and the probable need to build a substantial steam-driven pumping station led him to look at the river upstream from Great Falls. Here the level of the river reached more than seventy feet above the elevation of the city, which meant that a pipe or aqueduct filled with water could flow by gravity, substantially reducing the pumping costs and improving the reliability of the system.

Meigs's plan called for the construction of an enclosed brick waterproof tunnel, eight feet in diameter, from the Great Falls on the Potomac, twelve miles northwest from the Capitol, terminating at a reservoir near Georgetown, where the mud and light solids could settle out. The Potomac River had been ceded to the State of Maryland in 1792, but the Congress, in an act of 1853, allowed Washington to obtain the necessary water that it needed, and Meigs was authorized to proceed with construction.

With an appropriation of $100,000 made in September 1853, excavation started with a force of three hundred men. The first task, to construct a stone and concrete dam across the width of the river at Great Falls, proceeded without any problem, and connected with an intake on the Maryland side containing the necessary immense cast-iron valves to enable shutdowns to occur and repairs to be made. Three tunnels, nine feet in diameter, were started, connected to the intake building, and the foundation of that part of the aqueduct that ran above ground level was begun. Work continued until 1859, when, for lack of funds, construction stopped. Congress voted additional funding in 1860, but with the onset of the Civil War, Meigs was transferred temporarily to other duty, and did not return until the end of 1861. Upon his return work was resumed, and in 1863 the first water flowed through the aqueduct to the city. Meigs celebrated the final hookup to the Capitol by planting a large pipe in the grounds in front of the building and turning it on to emit a twenty-foot-high fountain gushing upward and flooding the streets below, much to the wonder of the citizens so used to minimal water supplies.

The aqueduct, not unlike their Roman counterparts built two thousand years before, was a masonry structure which allowed water to flow by gravity from the inlet to the discharge point, at controlled velocities, and with a constant slope from start to end. The difference was that Meigs's conduit was based on technology, invented, refined and tested over many years by engineers in France and England, and brought to the United States after the Revolution.

Engineering cannot be successful without its implementation by dedicated mechanics. Meigs was either lucky or able to motivate the personnel working under his direction, because the quality of the stonework and the waterproofing allowed the aqueduct to operate for twenty-seven years before it was taken out of service for the first time. The aqueduct ran partially underground and at times broke the surface to span ravines and streams. The most noteworthy of these is the bridge across the Cabin John Valley, where Meigs designed a granite arch with a span of 297 feet, which was the longest masonry arch in the world at that time. The bridge was paved many years later, and is still a viable means of traveling the road to the village of Cabin John by automobile.

Where the aqueduct crossed Rock Creek, a small river that spills into the Potomac near Georgetown, Meigs designed an arch, 200 feet wide, consisting of two 48-inch-diameter cast-iron pipes. Each was arched to span the creek and provided with sufficient curvature to support the weight and anchor the horizontal thrust into masonry abutments. The design carries the bridge and automobile traffic to this day.

Concurrent with the need to bring a reliable and adequate supply of water to the city was the issue of the growing number of representatives and senators from new states that had joined the union and were crowding the available office space, never mind the jammed seating conditions in the House. Meigs at that time was in the midst of his tunnel from Great Falls to Georgetown, when he was advised that a potentially more volatile issue, the expansion of the Capitol building, had been brewing for a number of years and could fall into the lap of the Corps of Engineers at any moment.

Expansion of the Capitol Building

As early as 1843 there was already concern in the Congress that the Capitol building was too small to accommodate all of the representatives, particularly those from the ever-increasing number of Midwestern states. Then, on May 28, 1850, the Senate announced a competition, open to all, for a design extending the building to the north and south, with new meeting chambers for both the Senate and the House at each end. The prize of $500 would be awarded to the winner, and four entrants were found to be acceptable, so the prize was divided four ways and the material turned over to Architect Robert Mills to prepare the final design. However, President Fillmore objected, alleging that the Senate's competition was illegal since a previous act of Congress had given to the president the authority to select the designer and spend up to $100,000 on the construction work.

After much lobbying by the contestants, the design submitted by Thomas U. Walter was selected by President Millard Fillmore. Several weeks later, without notification to the Congress, the corner stone was laid on July 4, 1851, and the work began, under the control of the Department of the Interior. The original 1825 building measured 352 by 229 feet, and the proposed expansion would increase that to 750 by 350 feet. The design called for extensive use of cast iron, prompted by a disastrous fire that had destroyed the library in the Capitol. Now the ceiling beams and decorative covers over the roof trusses were all cast iron, while a glass ceiling panel covered almost the entire center of the proposed chambers and provided natural illumination to the spaces during daylight hours.

There were many changes and progress was slow, so in March 1853, concurrent with the beginning of the Cabin John Aqueduct, responsibility for the construction was transferred to the Corps of Engineers, under the direction of Captain Montgomery C. Meigs. The original plan submitted by Thomas Walter had the House and Senate chambers on the west side facing the Mall, subject to the hot afternoon sun. The theory behind the west-facing windows propounded that they could always be opened to provide a cool draft and the necessary ventilation to the smoke-filled chambers. However, Meigs did not agree and altered the plan to include a series of offices, small chambers and cloakrooms around the periphery of the chambers so that they had no direct access to the outdoors, and neither did the corridors between the chambers and the outside offices. The origin of Meigs's concept probably lay in requirements by the representatives to have access to the meeting chambers without having to meet the general public at every access point.

The new House Chamber consisted of a room 139 feet long, 90 feet in width, with a glass ceiling suspended 36 feet above the floor. Member's desks occupied the lower level, while a visitor's gallery surrounded the room on three sides. The Senate Chamber, arranged in a similar manner to the House, provided a room 113 feet long and 80 feet wide with a similar ceiling configuration. (35)

In 1853 Charles F. Anderson, the original designer of the heating and ventilating systems for both the new Senate and House chambers, proposed a "down flow" concept in which supply air, providing both fresh air and heat, would be pumped from large air-handling units in the basement up to the attic, and distributed above the glass ceiling. From the ceiling space the air passed through a series of open grilles and was allowed to enter the occupied spaces from above, gradually floating down to floor registers or open grilles, where it would be picked up and returned to the main heating units.

It should be stressed that there were very few buildings in the world, at that time, where the question of airflow was a consideration. Most edifices conceived by the leading designers did not consider the issue of environmental satisfaction, or embrace a concept where *air motion and quality* would determine the acceptance of the space by the users. Sufficient to say that the original design of air distribution for extension of the Capitol in 1855 broke new ground.

Anderson's concept was influenced by the failure of the ventilation system in the House of Commons in England, where the air was introduced from floor grilles low into the chamber and allowed to rise to the ceiling, where it was either exhausted or returned to the central equipment. The alternative was, of course, as Anderson proposed, to supply at the ceiling and allow the air to diffuse into the occupied space and be drawn down over the occupants and finally exhausted at the floor to the outdoors.

Captain Meigs, however, did not agree with Anderson's concept. He preferred the "American" system in vogue at the time, in which the air was discharged at the floor around the occupants feet and allowed to rise to the ceiling, where it was either exhausted from the building or returned to the air-handling units in the basement. Meigs, after much consideration, decided to instruct Anderson to alter his design to conform to the "American concept." There was already evidence at the British House of Commons that the "up flow" system did not perform as advertised. Anderson resisted pressure to change his design and, after a confrontation with Meigs, resigned as designer of the mechanical system.

After a frantic review of potential candidates from New York and Boston, Robert Briggs, a civil and mechanical engineer from Philadelphia, was retained and is recognized as the designer of the revised heating and ventilating systems for the new wings of the Capitol. Meigs then spent several weeks reviewing the credentials of local contractors and concluded that he would have to contract with an out-of-town firm. He finally settled on Nason & Dodge, Contractors of New York, as the mechanical constructors of the heating and ventilating system.

Joseph Nason (1815-1872) left school at the age of seventeen and worked for the Boston Gas Light Company, where he was challenged with the methods of handling gas and the ways of controlling the flame to produce the most light under varying conditions of pressure in the distribution main piping. He moved to England to further his knowledge, where he made the acquaintance of Thomas Russell, whose family was in the business of manufacturing pipe and intended to establish a branch of the company in New York. Nason, aware of the opportunity to run the New York operation for Russell, entered into a partnership with his brother-in-law, James Walworth, and bought the American company founded by Russell. The business consisted of selling pipes of various lengths, all pre-threaded and arranged to fit into elbows, tees and crosses as the plumbing or heating system demanded. This approach of pre-threaded pipe eliminated the need for plumbers in the field to measure and cut screw threads onto each piece of pipe in order to make a connection to another pipe, thereby reducing errors and the cost of assembling piping systems.

Nason moved quickly into the theory and practice of building steam heating plants, including boilers, their piping systems and radiators. He successfully installed a heating system in a cotton mill in Lowell, Massachusetts. This success led to others, and by 1850 Nason was well-known in the business world of Boston and New York for his ability to bring comfort in the winter to hotels, ballrooms and large buildings. His design to heat the Boston Custom House by the use of steam-engine driven fans that forced air over pipe coils and up shafts to the occupied spaces above is believed to be the first use of a forced air system in the United States. (7)

Nason's relationship with the engineer Briggs resulted in the marriage of the theoretical professor and the accomplished mechanical engineer, producing a truly unique team to perform the work on the extension to the Capitol.

Lighting for each chamber during daylight hours would be accomplished by allowing natural light to penetrate through roof-mounted skylights, clear glass panels arranged in a hip pattern and running the length of each space below. Cast-iron framing trusses supported the skylights, providing an attic space some fifteen feet in height. On the bottom of the trusses, milk-glass ceiling panels were mounted—each panel engraved with federal and state symbols—to form a translucent plane, emitting light to the floor below.

Open gas jets, arranged in rectangular rows above the lower glass ceiling, provided illumination at night. On the House side there were 1,500 gas-lighting jets, and on the Senate side 1,200.

Separate forced-air systems furnished ventilation to each chamber. Each unit included a steam-engine-driven centrifugal fan wheel, one sixteen feet in diameter serving the Senate, the other eighteen feet in diameter serving the House. The fans were advertised to deliver 100,000 cubic feet per minute (c.f.m.) of outside air, but later tests showed capacities more of the order of 40,000 c.f.m. Each fan wheel had a cast-iron hub and a series of iron rods that anchored wooden blades to the hub, which in turn was carried on a horizontal iron shaft with bearings. The whole unit was carried on cast-iron stanchions, adjacent to which stood a vertical steam engine with crank that drove the fan wheel at 120 revolutions per minute.

The air discharged through masonry conduits and vertical shafts, and was allowed to enter the chambers through floor-mounted openings at the main level, and through grilles under the seats in the galleries. Mechanical rooms were located in the northwest and southwest corners of each cellar, which ran the length of the additions on the west face of the building. Smaller fans were installed to serve offices and committee rooms of the House and Senate.

Separate coal-fired boiler plants were provided for the House and Senate sides, each plant containing four fire-tube, low-pressure steam boilers in underground boiler rooms on the west side of the Capitol. The design of the boilers was a joint effort between engineer Briggs and Nason & Dodge, who produced a detailed specification and submitted it to Meigs for approval. The specification contained the following:

(1) "These Boilers are to be of a modified locomotive form, with firebox, and fifty-four upper and fifty-eight lower tubes: to be sixteen feet extreme outside length, and six feet one inch extreme outside width."

(2) "They are to be made throughout of the best Baltimore Charcoal Plates, double-riveted in all parts not exposed to fire, and single riveted where exposed, with five-eighth Albany rivets. Stays, stay bolts and other forgings to be of best Ulster iron."

(3) "Tubes are to be of wrought iron, lap welded boiler flues, three and a half inch external diameter."

(4) "Boilers are to be proved before leaving place of construction, by a hydrostatic pressure of one hundred pounds per square inch. And are to be further proved in their places, after delivery, by a steam pressure of one hundred pounds per square inch, and are to be tight under this pressure." (31)

The boilers were constructed in the boiler rooms, not factory fabricated as they would be today. Plates of steel, boiler tubes, castings, and small steel parts arrived on barges on the Washington Canal, having been unloaded in the Port of Georgetown. Shipping documents prepared by Morris Tasker & Co. of Philadelphia on July 3, 1856, confirmed the shipment of 259 boiler tubes consigned to Georgetown on the vessel *John R. Price* for delivery to Nason & Dodge for the U.S. Capitol Extension. The shipping costs were $2.50 per ton. The boiler plates were rolled into semicircular sheets, drilled at the edges with holes every two inches, and then mated with another rolled sheet, fitted together to form a barrel, and then joined with red hot iron rivets, hammered by ironworkers to form a tight joint. The longitudinal seams were then "caulked" pressure tight by carefully chipping the joint line with a caulking tool, which forced the metal to slightly deform and squeeze into the joint, making it tight under a pressure of 100 pounds per square inch. The boiler tubes were inserted into the drum, held in place by "tube sheets," and then the ends were carefully rolled with a hand tool to expand them, pressure tight into the tube sheets. In this manner each boiler was constructed and then erected on a brick base, including a combustion chamber in which the coal was burned, causing the water in the boiler tubes to boil and turn to steam under pressure.

Being locomotive-style boilers, they were mounted on brick bases to provide for an ash pit beneath each fire box, and allow the operator to shovel coal into the fire in sufficient amounts to maintain steam pressure within limits, and to hand rake the ash from the pit and shovel it into a wheelbarrow for dumping outside the boiler room.

The smoke breeching outlets from each boiler were tied together into a common flue pipe, which tapped into the masonry chimney that discharged above the roof. The vertical stacks, conveying the products of combustion, were located in the middle of the large columns located between the original building and the new additions.

The steam from the boilers was fed into heating "elements" mounted in the main discharge corridor from each supply fan. Each element consisted of parallel loops of iron pipe, about two inches in diameter, arranged to form a heating unit with twenty rows, and vertical down-feed pipes about three inches on center.

Each chamber, one for the Senate and one for the House, included a "crawl space," about four feet in height, beneath the main floors, which allowed the air to circulate to all points of the space above and discharge through floor-mounted openings beneath the members desks. Air was also conveyed to the galleries through masonry shafts and discharged into the stepped floor below the seats whence it flowed out through small openings. Exhaust air was allowed to flow through slots at the edges of the glass ceiling and was captured above the ceiling and pumped out through the roof to the atmosphere.

Members of the House of Representatives moved into a finished building on December 16, 1857. The Senate was not completed until two years later, due to the difficulty of delivery of steel up the frozen Potomac River in the winter of 1858, and on January 4, 1859, the Capitol expansion was declared complete.

The "old" part of the Capitol, finished in the 1820s, was originally heated by means of fireplaces, and as part of the 1855 extension, it was decided to introduce central steam heat to various spaces that had suffered under a lack of heat for a quarter of a century. The first step was to install hot air furnaces in the cellar. Each furnace consisted of a small metal chamber with steam piping leading to a "heating element," a pipe coil with multiple rows, arranged to allow air from the cellar to rise by gravity through masonry shafts to each occupied room. It did not prove to be successful, and in 1865 a program to remove the furnaces was initiated. It was completed in 1869, when all spaces in the original 1825 building were heated by steam radiators. (32)

Problems with the Capitol System

There were complaints from the members as soon as the system was put into operation in 1859. Taken together, the complaints included drafts, overheating at times, underheating at others, dust and dirt brought in by the outside air, lack of humidity in the winter, too much heat from the skylights and the 1,200 gas jets above the ceiling, and the general smokiness of the chambers.

The first step taken to meet the many complaints included a prohibition of smoking in the halls that surrounded the two chambers and in the chambers themselves. In its place the use of chewing tobacco was encouraged and special spittoons, with congressional insignia, were ordered placed in strategic locations, within range of each member.

An investigation by Captain Meigs in late 1859 revealed that:

(1.) Basement masonry tunnels, used as air ducts, were found to be clogged with construction debris and fine sand, which was carried in gusts through the floor grilles whenever the fans were started.

(2.) Floor grilles were examined and many were found to be blocked with a 1-1/2-inch-thick layer of dried spittle and tobacco juice. The registers were apparently being used as cuspidors.

(3.)The provision of insufficient outside air contributed to the general "closeness" of the House Chamber. The number of members far exceeded the number in the Senate, and the quantities provided were the same for both.

Hygienists were just beginning to learn that the human body gives off considerable amounts of protein and decaying body oils, especially when bathing is infrequent.

The House and Senate chambers were, in effect, interior spaces with no windows to the outdoors. The standard concept of fresh air entering through open windows did not apply, since on the perimeter of each chamber ran an encircling corridor, and then offices and committee rooms on the exterior of the building. These exterior rooms, fitted with operable windows, had adequate outside air and quickly became the favorite venue of business for the members unless the full House or Senate was in session.

Control of the air temperature posed a real challenge for the building operators. Steam-heated "elements," the forerunner of the heating coil, were manually controlled based primarily on the "feel" of the operator located in the basement some distance from the occupied chambers. Runners, young men working for the representatives, would shuttle to the boiler plant with the information to turn up or lower the heat as temperatures moved from warm to cold in the winter. The same was not true in the spring and fall, when the small quantities of outside air had little or no effect on the space temperatures, particularly during evening debates, when the full force of the 1,500 gas lighting jets above the glass ceilings radiated to the occupants below. The roof was copper, not insulated, which had an adverse effect on both summer and winter meetings.

To provide some measure of air control, manual registers, or air valves, controlled from the floor were fitted into the air outlets below each member's desk. This modification gave some help to the occupants so long as there was excess heated air in the floor below, but gave no relief if the air was too cold.

Concurrent with the comfort problems experienced in the two new chambers, there emerged the issue of the completion of the building, and possible modification of the Bullfinch Dome, which many felt appropriate for the original building but did not lend sufficient grandeur to the expanded structure.

The Dome of the Capitol

To the thousands of visitors who photograph the Capitol of the United States each year and the many stories and news articles that are written about the Congress and the country, no other symbol better reminds the reader that the story is about the city of Washington than a view the Capitol with its imposing and historic dome. The massive, slightly off-white structure dominates the building on which it resides and brings to the viewer a feeling of peace and stability.

From an engineering point of view, the designer of this marvel of early iron construction remains clouded in the somewhat turbulent history of the time and the personalities who played their parts in its creation. The "original " dome, designed and built by the Boston Architect Charles Bulfinch in 1819, included a combination of masonry and wood structural members supporting a copper-clad dome. Somewhat taller in scale than the original designer, William Thornton, would have wanted, its proportions were in keeping with the style and political presentment that the president felt suitable at that time. The elements, however, decided that this dome would not last for eternity, and severe degradation of the wood structural members caused it to be removed in the 1840s. For a while the rotunda of the Capitol survived with a flat roof.

Some ten years, later during the addition of the new north and south wings for the House and Senate, a sketch of a new all-iron dome, by one of the unsuccessful entrants for the building competition, C. B. Cluskey, surfaced, was modified and presented by Architect Thomas Walter to the Congress. Their immediate enthusiasm and approval of the suggestion led to authorization for a detailed design.

What followed was a contest of power and intrigue mainly between the two major players, architect Thomas U. Walter and Montgomery C. Meigs, the military engineer in charge of construction. And then there was the third player, the quiet and competent draftsman-designer August Schoenborn, a German-born draftsman who possessed drawings of similar domes successfully constructed in Europe. It is unclear who can be classified as the "structural designer" for the work that followed. The document that charmed the Congress into giving the go-ahead, presented by Thomas U. Walter in December 1854, showed an exterior elevation of the Capitol capped with a massive dome.

Walter's thinking must have been influenced by the revelation in Clusky's sketches of constructing the upper part of the dome of iron, rather than masonry. The fact that Schoenborn possessed drawings of all-iron domes, brought from Europe, must also have added assurance that an all-masonry structure was not the only solution.

It was Walter's thinking, however, that the lower "drum" portion of the dome, the peristyle, including forty columns surrounding the peristyle, should be constructed of masonry and marble supported on a low attic, with windows, and new masonry walls. Meigs, concerned with the ability of the existing masonry walls to support the new attic and peristyle all constructed of masonry, prepared tests to determine the crushing strength of the old brick. From his tests he concluded that the original masonry walls did not have the structural strength to safely support an all-masonry dome.

He recommended that ways be found to drastically reduce the weight of the dome, which led to its redesign, eliminating the attic, constructing the peristyle of cast iron, and changing the forty marble columns to thirty-six hollow cast-iron sections. At Meigs' suggestion, these hollow columns were carried on cantilevered, wrought-iron brackets bolted to cast-iron box frames set into the existing masonry walls of the rotunda. This design concept produced an appearance such that the base of the peristyle had a visual outside diameter of 126 feet, but was supported on the original ninety-six-foot diameter masonry rotunda. This concept required no additional masonry work other than the restoration of the existing walls after the box frames were set in place. The proposed brick and stone attic was eliminated, and in its place a lightweight sheath of cast-iron paneling extended down to meet the existing roof line. This modification reduced the weight of the dome, and its construction cost, while preserving the basic appearance of the design, and allowing construction to proceed without having to extend new masonry walls from the peristyle, four floors down, and excavate to the foundations of the building.

The structural system that supported the outer covering of the dome consisted of thirty-six curved, trussed ribs of wrought iron, claimed by Schoenborn to be his design. Each rib, 120 feet in length, resting on the original rotunda walls, gently curved to form the outer shape of the dome. Each rib in turn consisted of twenty wrought-iron trusses, bolted end-on-end. Each truss was about six feet tall and had a width of about eight feet at the base, which was then gradually reduced to about four feet at the highest point of the dome, termed the Tholos.

Each truss section was cast in New York by James, Fowler, Kirtland and Co. The hollow, cast-iron columns, produced in Baltimore, Maryland by Pool and Hunt at a cost of 3.4 cents per pound, were delivered to Washington by wagons. The trusses were bolted together, section by section, using three-inch-diameter wrought-iron bolts and nuts.

The exterior skin of the dome consisted of half-inch-thick cast-iron plates that spanned between the ribs and were held in place with cast nuts and bolts. The total weight of the cast-iron and wrought-iron structure carried by the existing 1819 walls of the original dome was 8,909,200 pounds, to which was added the masonry, weighing 5,214,000 pounds. Walter's calculations yielded a load of 13,477 pounds per square foot on the walls at the basement level, which had a bearing capacity estimated to support 755,280 pounds per square foot. The entire weight of the iron dome and the supporting masonry has a weight of 51,292,253 pounds, or 25,600 tons.

There appears to be no clear evidence as to who performed the necessary structural calculations to determine the thickness of the webs and flanges of the iron trusses, thereby determining the supporting capacity of each member, and, when bolted together, the supporting strength of the dome. A review of Walter's training and experience discloses exposure to mathematics and the physical sciences in the early years, and substantial study and experience in the art of architecture and painting, with no evidence that he offered structural engineering design as part of his professional services. Schoenborn was a masterful draftsman and designer of interior details, also an artist with a skilled taste and broad training, but, like Walter, offered no information that he had the technical knowledge to calculate the forces and size the trusses before they were cast in the foundry. Meigs had demonstrated in the design of the aqueduct from Great Falls on the Potomac, part of which included an arch spanning over Cabin John ravine, that he had a working knowledge of structures, in addition to his engineering training at West Point.

There can be little doubt that Meigs felt he did not receive the credit due him for the design work that he and his team of draftsmen performed. On March 5, 1856, Meigs wrote to the then Secretary of War, Jefferson Davis, under whose command the construction of the dome fell, and at the end of the letter included the following:

> *"I may remark, in conclusion, that while the design of the Dome is referred to in the law as Mr. Walter's, the original drawing, and the more detailed drawings since made, have been prepared in this office, in full and free consultation between Mr. Walter and myself, and that I consider that in whatever credit or responsibility there is to be attached to the work hereafter, we have to share."* (16, Page 308)

It therefore seems that the visual design of the dome of the Capitol must be credited to Walter and the structural engineering to size the trusses and calculate the loads to produce a safe and buildable structure must be credited to Meigs, while Schoenborn should be recognized for bringing the possibilities of an all-iron edifice to the attention of Walter and Meigs.

Other engineering components of the dome included a carefully designed rainwater system to catch the runoff from the high dome and convey it, through a series of cast-iron conduits, to eighteen of the thirty-six hollow columns of the peristyle, and thence into a piped drainage system that spilled out on the roof of the building adjacent to the original rotunda. Rainwater penetration proved to be a problem from the very beginning. The many half-inch-thick cast-iron plates that separated the inside of the dome from the elements were not all identical, and there proved to be myriad possibilities of wind-driven rain penetrating to the inside and able to run down the inside face of the dome or drip down on to inner cupola. The cupola, a domed element visible from the floor of the rotunda, comprised the ceiling of the inner dome and supported the painting of the Apotheosis of George Washington by the Italian artist Brumidi. To deal with the leakage, the top of the cupola was faced with a sheet of tin, sealed water tight and shaped to allow water to run down and be collected by a gutter system, which in turn piped the water to the outside of the dome.

Lighting the interior of the dome at night in 1865 included a system of gas piping which ran around the circumference of the inside of peristyle and terminated in rows of gas jets at the level of the frieze some forty feet above the floor of the rotunda. This approach produced a gentle, golden aura in the interior and was a stark contrast to the lighting in daytime, when the windows allowed natural sunlight to penetrate to the floor of the rotunda and, through a series of mirrors at the second visitor's gallery level, to be reflected on to the Apotheosis painting at the apex of the dome.

While the dome of the Capitol appeared to be moving to a successful completion, notwithstanding the tension between the main players, the heating and ventilating systems, installed as part of the addition of new House and Senate chambers, could not be similarly categorized. Problems of odor, dust, and temperatures that were either too hot or too cold continued. And then the tension between the Northern and Southern states reached a point that all other considerations of government ceased, and there was war.

Corps of Engineers

The Civil War had a major impact on the life of the city, with construction of barracks, the modification of Aqueduct Bridge to a roadway, and the construction of no less than sixty-eight forts for the defense against Confederate assaults. The science of fortifications had advanced very little since the creation of the Corps du Genie in France in the early 1700s, when the emphasis on defense became the dominant strategy, and with it the need to protect one's soldiers behind mounded earthworks. An enemy who elected to mount an infantry charge against such defenses exposed his men to withering fire from opponents lodged behind barriers from which they could direct their rifle shots. Artillery pieces, mostly shielded by the earthworks, could fire onto remote enemy positions in support of the infantry.

The forts ringed the District of Columbia at distances approximately 2,000 yards apart, arranged to cover depressions and flatlands across which attacking forces would have to move, with the placement of the earthworks generally at the high points. At the beginning of hostilities fewer than six hundred armed men were available in all of the city; four hundred marines and one hundred sixty at the city arsenal on the spit of land where Delaware Avenue ended. With the battle at Bull Run ending in favor of the Confederacy, the Congress realized that the time had arrived to fear loss of the capital, and orders were issued to prepare the defenses. Of immediate concern was to fortify the hills along the Arlington Ridge, between Fort Corcoran and Fort Albany, approximately between where Rosslyn and Reagan National Airport are today. The forts were interconnected with walking trenches, and by war's end there were eighteen forts on the Virginia side in a long arc beginning at Fort Marcy on the Potomac and terminating at Fort Willard just south of Alexandria. General J. G. Barnard, the chief engineer, planned the defenses, which when completed allowed for 1,120 field gun emplacements, with 800 guns in place and almost twenty miles of interconnecting trenches.

Overnight the sleepy town was transformed into a city at war, with troops and wagons, guns and horsemen, clanking and crunching at all hours of the day or night, creating clouds of dust on every street except Pennsylvania and Maryland Avenues, the only paved streets in the whole of Washington. Barracks and hospitals sprang up everywhere, mostly wooden temporary buildings occupying parks and open spaces, even the front lawn of the Corcoran Mansion.

As luck would have it, the defenses of the city were never tested in a frontal assault, and as the war dragged on it became apparent that the tide was turning in favor of the Union, with the devastating battles gradually moving to the south. With the war's end the dust subsided, barracks were demolished and troops moved out, allowing things to return to a prewar tempo. The Corps of Engineers found they were allotted new responsibilities.

Post Civil War Engineering

In 1874 the Congress disbanded the Territorial Government, and in its place instituted a commission reporting to a joint committee of the Senate and the House, and gave the Corps of Engineers responsibility for public works and for the design and construction of federal buildings. They were quartered at the Macmillan reservation next to the reservoir, and staffed with a compliment of engineers and architects, under the direction of the district engineer, who reported to the Congressional Committee.

The Corps operated the water supply from the Great Falls intake, through the Dalecarlia and Georgetown reservoirs, into the city, and at the turn of the century, constructed a parallel conduit from the intake on the Potomac, to Dalecarlia, in order to boost capacity to meet growing demand.

The first district engineer was Nathaniel Michler, a hero of the war, who took over the responsibility for both federal and city design and maintenance. He is best remembered for his planning and partial implementation of parks and parkways, and his efforts to drain the notorious "flats," the marshy creeks that followed the banks of the Potomac from Georgetown to Alexandria. (29)

Michler was followed over the years by a succession of dedicated and competent engineering leaders, including Orville Babcock, whose efforts in grading and draining the Mall around the Washington Monument and enlarging the sanitary and storm sewer systems was largely accomplished by the funding of a compliant Congress, with the intercessions of his friend, Alexander Shepherd. The reclaiming, drainage and land filling of the banks of the Potomac; the creation of the Tidal Basin, Potomac Park, the Washington Channel, and the land now occupied by the Lincoln Memorial were all products of their engineering, which created the parklike landscape that we associate with Washington today.

The Virginia side of the river was also surveyed and studied to find ways to of improving the flow characteristics of the water as it scoured the banks in both low and high water conditions; moving floating debris downstream and limiting silting of the estuaries. Landfilling on either side of the Boundary Channel narrowed the Potomac's main stream and created park land below the newly graded and developed National Cemetery. Peter Hains, after whom Hains Point is named, surveyed the Virginia riverbanks to Mount Vernon, and laid the plan for the Mount Vernon Parkway and the future freeways connecting the state of Virginia to the Mall, at what is now the Lincoln Memorial.

In 1885, when the Corps of Engineers finished the Washington Monument, the 555-foot-tall obelisk, started in 1848 and dormant for thirty years, produced one of the outstanding and characteristic features of the capital of the United States. The original monument, planned to be located at the intersection of two perpendicular lines from the Capitol and the White House, had to be moved 120 feet south and 370 feet east of the chosen point in order to avoid soft marshy soil that the engineers deemed unsuitable for the massive obelisk. Originally planned with dimensions of 55 feet square at the base, sitting on foundations measuring 81 feet square, the structure had walls 15-feet thick at the base, gradually tapering down to two-feet thick at the 500-foot level.

Before restarting the building work in the 1880s, the Corps did an analysis of the original foundations. They determined that the potential pressure on the structure created by hurricane force winds would be sufficient to stress the soil at the foundations beyond their limits, and cause the monument to topple over. They recommended that the foundations be enlarged by excavating and pouring new masses of concrete below the original foundation slabs. Congress approved, and for almost a year the site looked like an open cut mining operation, with mounds of earth and tons of concrete being carefully poured, in sections, beneath the original foundations. Once the underground work was secure, cranes moved in and began the task of setting hundreds of massive blocks of polished granite and limestone at just the right angle to give the obelisk its characteristic shape.

In designing the interior cast-iron stairway that extended from the entrance at grade to the observation deck at the top, the engineers made allowances for a future electric elevator. This was just as well, because when the monument opened, the options to reach the observation deck at the 500-foot level were to trudge up the 898 steps or to take the new steam-powered elevator that allegedly took five minutes to traverse the climb to the top.

The obelisk, an art form in which the height is ten times the length of a side at the base, had been determined structurally sound many centuries before by the Egyptians, but had never been constructed with the height proposed in Washington, nor with the potential of standing against wind speeds in excess of a hundred miles an hour. The tower contained no interior structural steel to provide stiffening of the shaft; the entire strength comes from the exterior stone wall, laid block upon block, gradually tapering to the apex, thereby exerting mild forces to the center, keeping the shaft stable.

The Corps found itself involved in many other projects, some of a military nature, but most as part of the process of building the national capital. It is curious that at the end of one of the most vicious wars in the history of the new United States, the Congress looked to the military to move in and fill the role of civilian designer and builder of the next era. For a short span of American history the military assumed the task of providing civilian assistance to continue down the road to peace and prosperity of a nation severely torn emotionally.

Montgomery Meigs, widely respected for his work on the Washington Aqueduct, was invited to design various public buildings, most notably the National Museum on the Mall, prepared with architect Albert Cluss, and the Pension Building at Fourth and F Streets, NW. Both were constructed in red brick, a dramatic departure from the white stone used in many of the other federal structures.

The Pension Building, designed in an era before mechanical ventilation and electric lighting, provided a large, open work floor for the clerks who serviced the pensions from the Civil War. It had a high ceiling, some sixty feet, which allowed the warm air, rising in the summer to open clerestory windows at the peak, to create a comfortable breeze at floor level. The high windows provided natural light in the daytime, adequate for the clerks to perform their tasks. While cost effective in its construction, the building was sarcastically referred to as "Meigs's Old Red Barn." However, the circumferential frieze, depicting events in the Civil War, and the grandeur of the main hall, with its engineering purpose, are reminders of a subtle balance between function and form in the design of buildings.

With the end of the Civil War, attention could be directed toward the solution of problems that had plagued the Congress and their Capitol building since the expansion program of the 1850s. It is hard to accept in the twenty-first century that the Congress of the United States had suffered for years with a substandard mechanical ventilation and heating system. Dust was still a problem, as were cold drafts and occasional overheating. Perhaps the members of Congress were resigned to the sad fact that engineering could not solve the obvious deficiencies in the system. It was in this context that Congress again called on the military to revisit the challenge.

Modification of the Chambers in the Capitol Building

Captain Meigs concluded that the issue of reducing dust had to be dealt with concurrent with improving the amount of clean outside air introduced into the main air handling units located in the basement.

The main outside air intakes, designed to bring ventilation air to the air handling units, were originally installed at ground level on the northwest and southwest corners of the basement. Protected by retaining walls, it was hoped that dust, dirt and combustion odors from the boiler plant would be largely excluded. It did not turn out that way.

Meigs' study also concluded that cold down-drafts near the walls of each chamber could be attributed to the copper roofing sheets, which had tight joints when the roof was built, but now had open seams through which cold air could easily flow. As the years went by, the alternate heat and cold promoted expansion and contraction of the sheets, causing them to open at the seams. As a result, the exhaust fan that was supposed to draw the air out of the attic space was in fact pulling air from the outdoors, through the open seams, and then blowing it back outside.

Further studies by the now ex-architect Thomas Walter and two experts from the Smithsonian Institution, Professor Joseph Henry and Dr. Charles Wetherell, concluded that the lack of comfortable feelings were due to insufficient moisture in the air. They examined the chemical composition of the air, the velocities, and the presence of noxious gases, in addition to the "hygrometrics." Dissatisfaction among the members continued.

More investigations were ordered, and leading scientists were brought in to give their opinions and prepare proposals for their suggested solutions. These ranged the full spectrum, from reversing the flow of air by putting supplies at the ceiling and exhaust grilles at the floor (Anderson's original design), to abandoning the building and starting again. A Congressional committee felt that the latter proposal was very attractive, but the estimated cost of $1.1 million was too low.

Consensus indicated that the problem was the roof. With an area of 17,000 square feet, of which more than 4,000 were glass skylights, and the balance copper sheeting with loose joints through which cold air could readily leak and then percolate down in little "water falls" of freezing cold to the occupants below. To solve this issue, the committee ordered a new fireproof ceiling to be suspended below the roof, thereby cutting down on the leaky copper. Once implemented, the cold down-drafts ceased and internal temperatures became less of an issue. The new ceiling, however, did not solve the dust, which blew into the chambers whenever the fans were started.

The Senate decided to install exhaust fans above the glass ceiling to remove the "foul air" that collected there, and this addition proved so successful that the House followed suit. Floor grilles were removed, and new ducts under the floors were connected to registers located in stair risers. This improved conditions somewhat.

In 1876 further minor modifications to the air distribution occurred, and a commission of distinguished experts made further recommendations, leading to the employment of Robert Briggs, an engineer from Boston, to design the agreed-upon changes. These included an underground fresh air duct, eight feet in diameter and excavated to a point 200 feet west of the House Chamber. The duct consisted of a brick corridor connected to the supply fan, and capable of bringing air in from a tower some ten feet above ground, thereby reducing the intake of ground dust and fine particles.

The main air-handling in the basement was modified to include a "dust cleaning and moistening chamber," fitted with heated water sprays to add moisture and remove dust from the incoming air. In the attic, a 140-square-foot relief louver was installed. The original steam coils were removed and replaced with coils of one-inch-diameter pipe, containing 45,000 square feet of heating surface. They were divided horizontally into two separate sections, separately fed so that the top section raised the air temperature very slightly while the lower section did the bulk of the heating. To control temperature, the coils were fitted with manual sheetmetal doors (called "dampers") arranged so that the operator could adjust the temperature of the supply air by choosing more or less of the hot or mild air flows. Thus, the first known application of "face and bypass dampers," a technique subsequently used by many designers, occurred in 1878 on the main air handling unit of the House of Representatives.

Similar improvements were made to the Senate system, including in 1890, a fresh air tower and underground air duct 400 feet to the northwest of the Senate Chamber. (33)

Homer Woodbridge, a professor at the Massachusetts Institute of Technology in Boston, had begun to emerge as a leading thinker and designer of comfort heating and ventilating systems in the early 1870s. He provided consultation and engineering design for a number of universities in the Northeast and was first introduced to the Capitol by the engineer Robert Briggs. It was Briggs who was responsible for numerous alterations to try to solve the dissatisfaction expressed by House and Senate members resulting from the addition of the two new wings in the 1850s. The two engineers collaborated for two years, after which time Woodbridge became the Engineer of Record for the modifications beginning in the late 1880s.

These modifications were made between 1890 and 1894 to improve the air distribution in the Senate, including the complete removal of the floor, provision of new ductwork, serving an overhead supply system as first proposed by Anderson forty years before. Modification to the central air handling units included the addition of new return ductwork with low return grilles, and the introduction of the first automatic temperature control devices invented in the 1880s.

In 1896 Professor Woodbridge prepared a report to the Secretary of the Interior in which he summarized the changes made in the past several years. He stated that each Senator's desk now received 80 cubic feet of air per minute (c.f.m.), and the gallery chairs 32 c.f.m. The new all-steel fan, 10 feet in diameter, replaced the original 14-foot wheel, and was rated to send 35,000 c.f.m. to the ducts when running at 125 revolutions per minute.

These changes were not the end of the expansion to the Capitol that began in the early 1850s and lasted more than forty years, producing a wealth of new information about what mechanical concepts actually work in monumental buildings, and what do not.

During this time the city of Washington underwent major improvements. Meigs's aqueduct bringing water to the city remained a huge success, but there were still no water mains or underground sewers, and most of the streets still ranged between dust bowls in the late summer to muddy challenges in the winter and spring. All that was about to change.

A City Matures: Infrastructure

In 1984 the late Dr. Lewis Thomas, former Chancellor of the Sloan-Kettering Cancer Center in New York, wrote: "There is no question that our health has improved spectacularly in the past century. One thing seems certain: It did not happen because of medicine, or medical science or even the presence of doctors. Much of the credit should go to the Plumbers and Engineers of the Western world. The contamination of drinking water by human feces was at one time the single greatest cause of human disease and death for us; it remains so, along with starvation and malaria, for the Third World. Typhoid fever, cholera and dysentery were the chief threats to survival in the early years of the 19th Century in New York City. When the Plumbers and Sanitary Engineers had done their work in the construction of our cities, these diseases began to vanish."

Statements such as these bring into focus the contribution of engineering to the well-being and longevity of a society that keenly focuses on the appreciation of static art, in the form of paintings, buildings, and landscapes, while taking the dynamic art of engineering for granted. The power of dynamic art, however, arrives with gut-wrenching fear, and then amazing gratitude with the insertion of a stainless steel sleeve, containing illumination, camera, cutter, needle and thread, into the main artery of a leg, up into the heart ,where surgery occurs to repair a malfunctioning heart valve. With recovery comes a diminution in the wonder of the procedure, as the patient, naturally self-concerned, begins to pick up the threads of daily living, and forgets the fear and apprehension that preceded the operation. This says something about the engineering process. Engineering requires an inquisitive mind, concentration, the need to be involved, the deductive reasoning that starts at the beginning of the process and is involved to the end, where finally understanding creates a feeling of satisfaction.

If the doctor was willing and the patient agreeable to study and share the event in great detail, we would probably make an engineering convert.

Sanitary engineering, while less spectacular than heart surgery, has done much to earn the gratitude of people living under the conditions that prevailed before and during the Industrial Revolution. The moats that surrounded castles of the fifth through fifteenth centuries were intended to make it more difficult for assailants to breach the fortification because of the presence of water, adulterated beyond belief, with waste from the castle, and known to cause illness and death to those who came in contact with the noxious fluid. It is not surprising that the perfume industry thrived in these times.

It is reported that the first flushing toilet was installed in one of Queen Elizabeth's castles in England in 1595, but the dear lady refused to use it on the grounds that it, "cascaded fearfully." So much for the dynamics of engineering.

The first patent for the flushing toilet was awarded to Alexander Cumming in England in 1775, but the state of the art of pipe construction had not progressed to the point that leakage and odor could be eliminated, with the result that outdoor plumbing remained the fashion until the 1840s, when mill-manufactured cast-iron pipe became available. (27)

Pennsylvania Avenue had been partially paved in 1832, using the MacAdam hot tar process, but by the 1850s it was rutted and in need of repair. There were no sanitary sewers, and those few establishments that had indoor plumbing discharged to the storm sewers, which sloped down the hills to the Potomac River.

The first dwelling to have indoor plumbing was the Van Ness mansion at the corner of Seventeenth Street and the canal, where the Pan American Union Building sits today.

John Peter Van Ness, the son of a wealthy New York family, had been elected to Congress, and shortly after taking his seat in 1802 , bought the land designated Lot 171 and engaged Benjamin Latrobe to design an appropriate mansion overlooking the canal. The plan called for the building to be 70 feet wide by 42 feet deep, with six bedrooms on the second floor together with dressing rooms and a family dining room. The main floor included a salon, dining room, library, den and butler's pantry, and on the lower level, a kitchen with servants quarter. The original plans make no mention of indoor plumbing, which was probably installed at the time of Mr. Van Ness's death in 1846. The mansion survived until 1894, when it was bought by the Columbia Athletic Club, together with the adjacent six acres, and turned into a site for track and field events. (16, Page 123)

Maryland Avenue, finally graded and partially paved in 1850, had its entrance to the Long Bridge to Alexandria leveled and improved. The avenue became the connecting link road between the bridge and the Baltimore and Ohio Railroad Station on Pennsylvania Avenue, at the foot of the hill below the Capitol. At that time there were only two main roads in the capital—Maryland Avenue leading to Virginia, and Pennsylvania Avenue running between the Capitol and the White House. Other main avenues, such as Massachusetts and New York, had been laid out and carried local traffic, but led into open fields and a few sparsely developed houses, and then into farmland.

Prior to 1870 the city had an elected mayor who was nominally responsible to the people, but the politics of taxation, dominated by Congress, allowed the mayor little room to increase revenue for the purpose of improving the city. The result was that the city services were poor to nonexistent. Trees had been cut down; there were no sidewalks; most roads were unpaved; and there was garbage everywhere. The Potomac River, like most rivers in Europe and England, where the cities had increased in size, was a foul cesspool in the summer, reeking of human and animal waste. (In London the growth of the city caused such increase in dumping waste into the Thames that Parliament, in the summer of 1859, called a recess because of the stench emanating from the river.) Research into the treatment of sewerage was just beginning, and the traditional method of dumping into rivers was being quantitatively evaluated for the first time in history.

In 1871, after considerable pressure, the Congress finally acted. The mayor and council were disbanded and the District of Columbia became a territory. The governing body, appointed by the Congress, included a governor and council, an elected House of Delegates, and a Board of Public Works, with limited contracting authority but empowered to enter into contracts with the approval of the Congressional Oversight Committee. The charge given to the Board of Public Works was to clean up the city and improve the infrastructure, and included as chairman, Alexander Shepherd, an ex-plumbing contractor. (16)

Shepherd, a man of great charm and political skills, had left his trade after the Civil War, when land speculation was extremely profitable, and became a builder and developer. He was associated with men who controlled asphalt for roads and cement for buildings and, in 1871, with minimal congressional oversight, began a program of renovation of the city's public spaces. Contracts were issued; many to friends who were contractors.

Surveyors and engineers were brought in to lay out a system of storm and sanitary sewers; roads were torn up, piping laid, manholes constructed, sidewalks poured, roads graded and paved, and parks laid out and filled with trees and lawns. More than 60,000 trees were planted. The Washington Canal had fallen into disuse, largely because of the runoff from rain, which carried silt and garbage with it. Shepherd's forces filled in the canal, and a major health problem was cured. By 1874 the city had never looked so good and reflected some of the splendor L'Enfant had hoped for. But the cost, $18 million, was more than the Congress had dreamed of, never mind the lack of direct authorization. There was the inevitable investigation, and the territorial form of government was replaced with a commission reporting directly to the Congress.

From an engineering point of view, Shepherd had brought massive improvement to the district. Washington had qualities that could match the best cities in the world. Citizens were thrilled; land values increased.

Some of his methods support his nickname, "Boss " Shepherd. Typical of the unyielding style he used to bring change to the city is the story of the moving of the Baltimore and Ohio Railroad from its location on the Mall in front of the Capitol. The old railway station was an eyesore to some, historic to others. Its location, in the middle of the area designated as L'Enfant's Plaza, despoiled a vista that was to stretch from the foot of the Capitol to the Potomac River. Shepherd and his planners wanted the station moved to the north, into an undeveloped part of town. The railroad would have moved, but was seeking compensation for the cost of the demolition. So, one weekend Shepherd sent in several hundred men who worked around the clock and removed the tracks and wooden platforms, and regraded the station lot. The president of the railroad was so impressed that he offered Shepherd a senior position if he would leave the board and join the Baltimore and Ohio Railroad.

Congressional hearings produced no wrongdoing on Shepherd's part, but the reports in the press, mainly by his enemies, were damaging, so he was relieved of his post and he left with his family for Mexico. He returned in 1887, and was given a hero's welcome, complete with parade and reception for 6,000 people at the Willard Hotel. (28)

President Harrison, in 1889, appointed a blue ribbon committee including three outstanding sanitary engineers, Rudolph Hering, Samuel M. Gray and Frederic P. Stearns, to advise on the options that were available immediately and those that would solve the long-term problem.

The committee's report suggested that the existing "combined sewer" system, in which sanitary waste and storm water could run simultaneously in the same pipe, be retained. But all future sewerage should be separately piped to a point far enough down the river such that tidal action would not return it close to occupied areas. The chosen discharge location into the river was Marbury Point, south of the present Naval Research Laboratory, where the engineers estimated there was sufficient flow and dilution to accommodate a city of 500,000 persons. The population in 1890 was 280,000, so it was agreed to implement the board's recommendations and install the sewer main and outfall at the river.

The story of Boss Shepherd and his dashing ways is to some degree the story of how the city of Washington operates under the closely guarded scrutiny of Congress. Under the law, the District of Columbia is a federal enclave, not part of any of the fifty states, and it's half million citizens do not have the right to elect *Voting* Representatives and Senators to the Congress. They do elect a nonvoting Representative. But the true power in the district is the Congress of the United States, whose interests lie in the fifty states that elect them, with the result that the needs of the district are low on a list of priorities held by each congressman.

To get things done in the district, therefore, requires the support of one or more congressmen, usually from the neighboring states of Maryland and Virginia, in a project that will bring some benefit to one of the states as well as the city of Washington. This pattern was prevalent in the 1890s and continued into the twentieth century, with the influx of major utilities, such as electric, power and transportation.

Plate 9 - 1
Montgomery C. Meigs, ca. 1858
Captain (later General) Montgomery Meigs designed the system that brought fresh
water to Washington from a dam at Great Falls, Md.; he also played a major roll in
the expansion of the Capitol between 1850 and 1870, including the cast-iron dome

Plate 9-2
Cabin John Aqueduct
Designed by Montgomery Meigs to house 84-inch diameter water conduits
conveying water from Great Falls to the city of Washington in 1863,
with a span of 297 feet it was the longest masonry arch in the world at that time

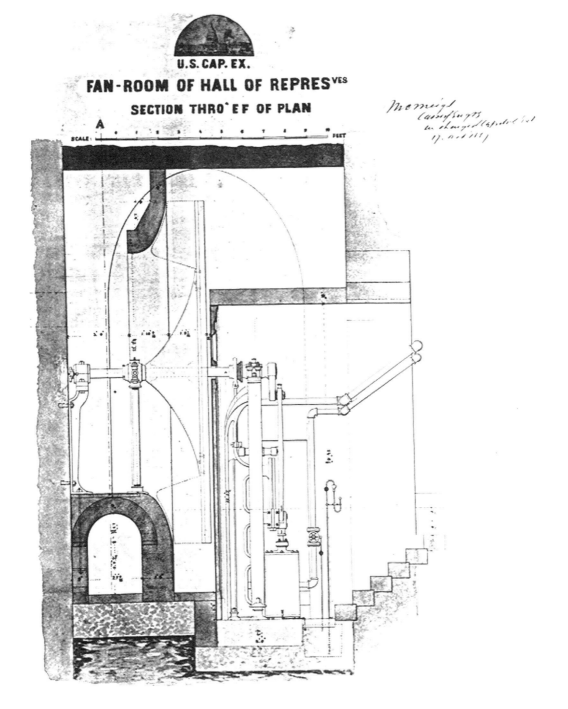

Plate 9-3
Section through a steam engine driven fan 14 feet 6 inch diameter wheel;
installed in the House of Representatives in 1857; rated 35,000 cubic feet of air per
minute at 120 r.p.m.; drawing signed by "M. C. Meigs," Corps of Engrs.

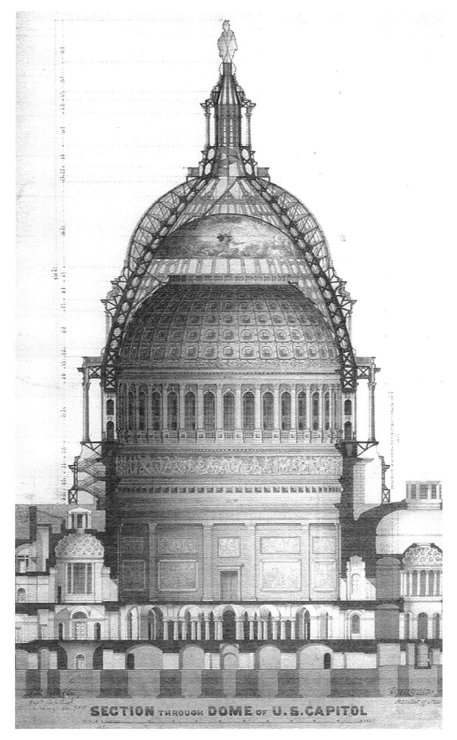

Plate 9-4
Section through the Capitol Dome, ca. 1865
This section shows the wrought-iron framing supporting the dome
and cast-iron tiles that form the outer surface; the whole structure
is supported on the original 1819 walls

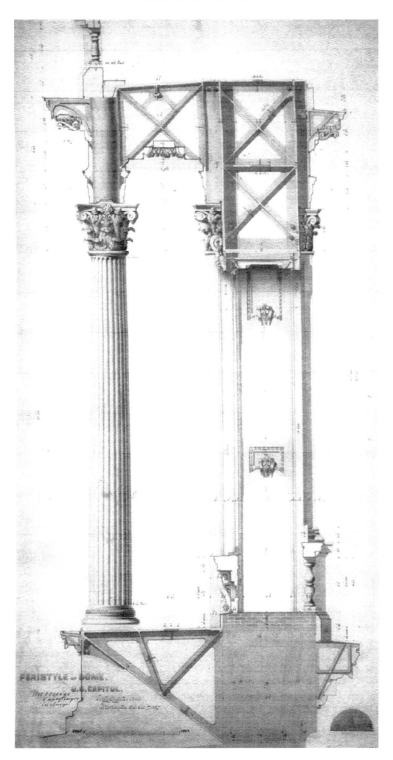

Plate 9-5
Section through the Peristyle of the dome, showing the brackets cantilevered out
from the original masonry walls and supporting the hollow cast-iron columns,
which double as roof drain leaders

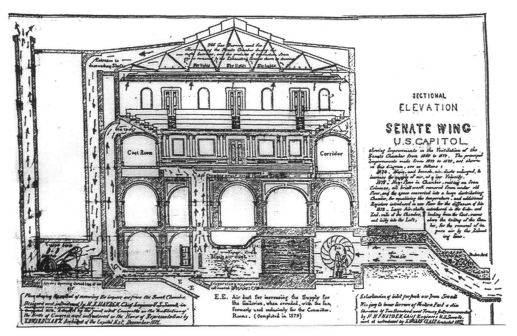

Plate 9-6
Ventilation System of the Senate Wing, 1861
This section through the Senate chamber shows the main supply fan (lower right)
discharging through the heating tubes and up to the Senate floor and balcony
ceiling. Exhaust fan is at the lower left

Plate 9-7
The dome of the Capitol of the United States

Plate 9-8
Alexander Shepherd
Elected to the Board of Public Works in 1871, an ex-plumber and land speculator,
Alexander "Boss" Shepherd is credited with bringing major infrastructure
improvements to the city, including water and gas mains, sewers, roads and
sidewalks, and planting thousands of hardwood trees in new parks

Plate 9-9
Wooden water mains made of bored tree trunks were used extensively beginning in
1800 until 1840, when cast-iron piping became available

Plate 9-10
Pennsylvania Avenue Bridge at Rock Creek, 1860
Two 48-inch-diameter steel pipes supported the bridge and were part of the
system bringing water to the city

10 . . . Public Utilities

Between Crutchett, Meigs, Shepherd, Woodbridge and others, the city of Washington had, by the 1880s, reached a par with the other major centers of population in Europe. The impact of the steam engine and related inventions had all played their parts in helping to move the Western world out of the Medieval Age, through the Age of Revolution, into the age of democracy. It was a time when people reflected on their productivity and success, in their manner of dress, in their style of housing, and in their social behavior. Men were more often than not seen in top hats, black cutaway outer coats and smart black shoes, in the company of elegantly dressed women, comfortably wandering through the new parks or down a clean Pennsylvania Avenue.

Shepherd's underground piping worked wonders on the disposal of sewage and storm water, and his program of bringing potable water to all city residents had a marked effect on individual hygiene. Looking into the future, few people could have imagined that there was a technical revolution of unprecedented magnitude brewing in the minds and laboratories of a few scientists and engineers. This revolution would shortly have a name—electricity.

Riding gently in a horse-drawn buggy in the evening, heading from Georgetown to the White House for a state dinner, the British Ambassador took it for granted that the carbide lamps on either side of the cab were state of the art, and the brushed, polished animal trotting to the beat of hooves, equally so. The invitation had been hand-delivered, several days before; so had the RSVP. Golden oil lamps glowed on street corners, and when the White House came in sight, it was bathed in a more brilliant hue of lamps inside and out. The ambassador kept careful notes, and would transmit them by ship to his government in the morning. They would be received in London two weeks later. What could be quicker? What could do the job better? The answer—electricity.

Electricity

In 1800 Allesandro Volta, a professor of physics at the University of Pavia, demonstrated that a series of dissimilar metals, arranged in sequence but separated from each other by sheets of wool and immersed in salty water, could develop an electrical potential difference between each end. The Voltaic Cell or battery had been invented. The "electrical potential difference" was termed the "voltage." (2)

So persistent was this voltage effect that connecting two pieces of carbon to wires attached to the ends, and then touching and quickly, separating the carbon, could generate a flash of light. The arc lamp was thus invented.

Joule had discovered that by rotating a copper wire coil in-between the north and south poles in the "magnetic field" of a permanent magnet, an electrical current could be generated. This was the invention of the magneto.

From these inventions came the dynamo. Instead of using a permanent magnet to create the "field" in which the coil was rotated, an electromagnet was substituted, and energized by a battery or another magneto. The result was the first machine for the continuous conversion of mechanical energy into electrical energy. This invention occurred almost simultaneously in England by Charles Wheatstone and in Germany by Werner Von Siemens in January 1867. (2)

The almost unbelievable aspect of these discoveries was that for the first time in history it was possible to generate energy in one place and transmit it to another place over wires. For centuries man had relied on waterpower, where the water wheel in one location transmitted the power into a wooden shaft, which turned and gave up its power to a flour grinder ten feet away, but directly connected. There was no alternative. There was no flexibility. Now man had a choice. This is one part of the joy of engineering. It gives any individual choices.

It is also worthwhile to note that the dynamo was a work of art. The combination of fine wiring, precision ground metal, elegantly cast iron, precise assembly and comfortable appearance produced a formidable machine that could create fear in the technically untrained. To the engineer it was like a concerto to a music lover.

With the invention of the dynamo the world had a reliable device for the production of electricity. Foucault, in France in 1844 had invented the carbon arc lamp, but its use was limited by the power sources at that time, but now with the dynamo, the arc lamp came into industrial and commercial use. (2)

The arc lamp is a device that produces an intense beam of white light when an electric current is allowed to jump across the gap between two carbon rods. Initially the rods must touch, and then when drawn gradually apart the current "jumps" the gap and the light occurs. All manner of variations of the carbon arc lamp were produced, some surviving into the movie era of the 1920s. Some creative engineering went into the manufacture of arc lamps, perhaps none better than Mr. Straites patent for a lamp with an electrically powered timer that allowed the carbon rods to be automatically brought closer together or separated in order to control the brightness and eliminate the flickering associated with the carbon arc.

The Architect of the Capitol had experimented with arc lighting, and by 1877 the system had been proven in many street lighting projects and large buildings. It was time to invest in the next generation of engineering improvements. The 46th Congress approved the sum of $2,400 to be spent on arc lights in the rotunda, the dome and a few other parts of the building.

The *Washington Star* reported, "The contrast of the whiteness of the electric light in the Rotunda and Dome, and the yellowness of the thousands of gas burners elsewhere, produced a very fine effect as seen through many windows."

President James Garfield held his inaugural ball in the newly opened Pension Building, now housing the National Building Museum, in March 1881. The building was fitted with the new arc lamps, and there was uniform agreement that no previous event in memory allowed the colorful splendor of the ladies finery to be better seen.

The Heisler Lighting Company, formed in 1882, had among its backers Stilson Hutchins, the owner of the *Washington Post*. The new company had secured the license to Charles Heisler's invention and products. Hutchins set up a generator on the *Post*'s premises to serve both interior and exterior street lighting. The Post Building at 10th and D Streets, NW, became a place to be visited by the local residents and visitors.

October 1879 was another turning point in the march of engineering, for it was on that date that Thomas Alva Edison demonstrated his incandescent lamp, with light emitted by a filament, encased in a vacuum, and fed with a small current of electricity. The importance of this event was not lost on Stilson Hutchins, who persuaded his associates to combine the Heisler Company with a license for the new incandescent lamp, and together they formed the United States Electric Lighting Company in Washington. Initially power was distributed to part of the downtown area using overhead wires on wooden poles, but the District Government soon enacted regulations which stipulated that all utilities would have to run underground.

In 1884 USELCO began to lay the first underground cable in the streets, installed, at no cost to the taxpayer, street lighting along Pennsylvania Avenue, and began to aggressively market electricity to the government.

The company built its first major power plant on the northeast corner of 14th and "B" Streets NW, (now Constitution Avenue). The building lay between 13-1/2 Street and 14th Street on a site where the Department of Labor Building sits today. (To build the Department of Labor Building, 13-1/2 Street and Ohio Avenue disappeared.)

To make electricity on a commercial scale involved the erection of large coal-fired boilers that sent high-pressure steam to horizontal reciprocating steam engines. These in turn were directly connected to dynamos that generated electricity when the dynamo shaft was rotated by the steam engine. To reduce the plume of steam associated with steam locomotives, the exhaust from the engines went to condensers, where it was cooled, turned back into water and could be reused in the boilers. This saved money and made the plant less of an eyesore.

The plant drew cool condenser water from the new Tidal Basin through a brick conduit six feet in diameter constructed from the corner of 14th and "B," passing just south of the Washington Monument, and terminating in a steel intake screen in the wall of the basin. The hot condenser water discharged by the plant was routed in a brick conduit east on "B" Street to the intersection of 7th Street, and turned south to spill into the Washington Channel.

The growth of the electric power market proved to be much slower than the investors in USELCO had anticipated. The government took the position that they would generate their own power when the time was right, and private citizens also did not embrace the new technology as quickly as had been expected. And then, with the arrival of the electric traction motor, the tide turned. The advantage of electric power over a team of horses pulling a streetcar became immediately apparent to the average person and led to the conversion of public transportation in just a few years. In very little time the capacity of USELCO reached its maximum limit, and its managers began to think in terms of additional capacity. This was when a competitor suddenly appeared on the landscape.

Potomac Electric Power Company

Concurrent with the growth of the electric streetcar industry, a group of local investors in 1891 started the Potomac Electric Company to provide electric service for street lighting and residences in the George Town part of the city. So successful was the operation that it attracted the attention of several out-of-town entrepreneurs, one of whom bought the company and renamed it the Potowmack Light and Power Company in 1894. It was sold two years later and incorporated as the Potomac Electric Power Company, a name it has retained for more than a century.

The Potomac Electric Power Company built its first boiler plant in Georgetown in a renovated building at 33rd and Water Streets (K Street) NW, and sent high-pressure steam to a generating plant up the hill at the canal. The plant was equipped with horizontal reciprocating steam engines driving the generators. Initially Pepco served the Northwest portion of the city as well as bringing power to additional streetcar tracks. Fierce competition between USELCO and Pepco over rights to expand into new sectors of the city, and to serve the various streetcar companies, led to the merging of the two in 1899. Pepco has been the source of electric power to the city ever since.

Electricity began to make great strides in the 1900s with the invention of all manner of labor-saving devices aimed at the homemaker, including washing machines, ceiling fans, electric kettles, toasters and electric stoves. Usage showed yearly increases marching upward such that it became possible to predict that the total generating capacity of Pepco, 18,000 kilowatts, would be exceeded by 1910. The company began to seek out a site for a new, larger plant adjacent to a source of water for cooling, and finally selected a location on the Anacostia River at Benning Road, near to the abandoned Benning Race Track.

The Benning Road plant became operational at the end of 1906 and incorporated the latest vertical steam-turbine-driven electric generators. The steam turbine, largely perfected in Sweden, was proving to be more efficient and reliable than the traditional horizontal reciprocating engine, invented by James Watt more than a century earlier. The new plant initially produced 10,000 kilowatts from two turbine-generators, and by 1912 could meet the demand of the entire city with the addition of three 9,000-kilowatt turbine-generators. The original plants in Georgetown and at 14th and B Streets were gradually phased out.

The White House

The White House received electricity in 1889 after Congress appropriated money to install a generating plant and wiring throughout the Executive mansion. A boiler plant and generators, manufactured by the Edison General Electric Company, in the basement of the mansion provided illumination for the residents, including a skeptical President Benjamin Harrison. He was known to distrust the system to the point that the plant operator was required to turn the lights on at sunset, and then off again the following morning.

This arrangement of the key government buildings having their own means of making electricity was the direct result of Congress not having the will to compromise its independence. Electric power was not yet viewed as a "public utility" with controlled rates, and there was still a feeling that submitting to the services of a monopoly could lead to uncontrolled cost increases.

The reliability and obvious advantages of electricity finally led the passage of an act regulating the prices that power producers could levy on their customers. With the result that most federal buildings, including the White House, switched over to the Potomac Electric Power Company.

The Telephone

In October 1877, George C. Maynard laid the first telephone line and connected an instrument at each end, such that the chief signal officer in Washington could talk to his aides at Fort Whipple (now Ft. Myer), in Virginia.

Mr. Maynard, an electrician and telegraphist, had learned his trade working on Alexander Graham Bell's products, and was interested in fostering the business of telephones in Washington. By July 1878 Maynard had installed 120 "electric speaking telephones," in many businesses, such as the Washington Gas Light Company, Willard Hotel, and several government departments, including the White House, Department of State and the Capitol. To provide interconnection between his customers, Maynard set up the first "exchange," a 24-wire peg switch, at 1423 G Street, NW, with Burnet Nevius as the attendant. Two years later Maynard moved to 1420 New York Avenue and contracted with the National Telephone Exchange to operate it, and in December 1879 Maynard sold out to the Exchange and became the general manager of the new venture. In 1881 the company changed its name to the National Capital Telephone Company, incorporated in West Virginia.

By 1883 the company had some nine hundred telephones connected to its switchboard, but the opportunity to sell out to the new Chesapeake and Potomac Telephone Company proved too tempting, so NCTC was bought by C & P in June of that year.

The growth of subscribers was brisk; everyone wanted to be "in communication," as the buzz went, so by 1897 there were 2,000 customers, and this number increased to 10,000 by 1904. As the years went by the numbers increased, and so did the "central offices," where rows of happy ladies with pleasant, helpful voices sat and plugged lines from one connector to another. By 1908 C & P staff "manned" eight central offices. These finally began to give way to the rotary dial telephone, which was introduced to the central city in May 1930, and by 1950 had taken over all the dial service with the exception of long distance assistance.

The previous year a nationwide telephone numbering system had been agreed to, and this was the "2-5" method, in which each dialer had to begin by dialing the first two letters of the exchange being called, and then five assigned numbers. The downtown was mostly the federal exchange, with "FE" the letters. There was Jackson, Main, Dupont and many others, all of which gave the old-time Washington a good idea of the part of town to which they were calling.

With life not getting any easier, the C & P in 1959 provided customers the ability to dial any part of the nation, with the new "DDD," or Direct Distant Dialing network. DDD also allowed automatic billing of long-distance as well as local calls. (36)

Gas

In 1856 the Washington Gas Light Company, from its main plant on Maryland Avenue, and the secondary plant on Louisiana Avenue (Indiana Avenue today), was serving most of the city with coal gas, distributed by underground piping to street lamps and many homes for illumination. Also there was pressure from the Congress to consider a plan for removing both plants to another location in order to allow the further development of the L'Enfant plan on the Mall.

Both plants were on the Washington Canal, which in the 1860s was becoming less and less able to bring the coal barges from the Port of Georgetown and deliver coal to the plants. There was talk of moving the rail lines from the Mall to a new station farther to the east, which would further imperil the required coal shipments to the plants. So, in 1860 a new West Station Plant was built at 26th and G Streets NW, on the site where the famous Watergate Office and Apartment is today. The plant included a coal yard on the Potomac and two massive gasometers, each consisting of a circular steel tank, 100 feet in diameter, open on the top, into which a similar tank, open on the bottom, neatly fit. The lower tank was filled with water, which caused the upper tank to float, provided it was filled with gas. The more gas in the upper tank, the higher it floated. As the gas was sent out to customers via the pipelines, the upper tank gradually sank down, but in so doing it kept a constant pressure in the gas mains, and a constant pressure on the many gas lights and customer use points.

Then, in 1888, the East Station Plant was built at 12th and N Streets SE, just to the east of the Navy Yard on the Anacostia River. Four large gasometers, similar to the West Station, were installed, and the underground lines from the Mall were extended to the new plant. The capacity of the Gas Company was more than doubled, and it was in a position to serve the now-completed Capitol with all the gas it needed.

However, the renovations in the Senate and House chambers, under the supervision of Professor Woodbridge from MIT, were just being completed and included the removal of the 1,200 gas lighting jets from the Senate and 1,500 from the House. Electric lighting was being substituted, with the result that the demand for gas by the Capitol was suddenly reduced. This allowed the demolition of the two old plants at Maryland Avenue and Louisiana Avenue.

It is curious that just when the market for gas lamps was beginning to wane, the market for a new appliance, the gas cooking stove, began to arrive. In 1856, Mr. Willard, proprietor of the National Hotel, became one of the first of many to install gas cooking, and his establishment became sought after for its tender broiled steaks without the smoky taste of wood. (19)

The Gay Nineties lived up to its name in the city of Washington. There was all manner of entertainment in the salons and bars to fit the most conservative or hedonistic tastes; moving pictures were shown in the Willard Hotel and the horseless carriage paraded down the electrically lit Pennsylvania Avenue to Sousa's *Washington Post March.*

Street Lighting

For almost thirty years after the Great Fire of London in 1666, the use of outdoor open flames was banned, since the inhabitants were still in shock after the destruction of a major portion of their city by fire. Prior to the conflagration there had been some attempts at lighting the main streets of the center of the city with open oil lamps and enclosed candles, but it was not until 1694 that the first weatherproof glass-enclosed lamps found their way into the city, to the disgust of homeowners who were taxed to pay for their upkeep.

Prior to that simple invention, the streets of the world were dark, foreboding places infested with rogues and thieves, to the point that people of modest means did not venture out after sunset, and the wealthy employed guards carrying burning torches if they were obliged to be out in the dark. The feelings of safety on one hand, and the number of persons using the streets after dark on the other, persuaded the city to allow the installation of 5,000 oil lamps in 1736, and by 1740 the number had grown to more than 15,000 in the city of London.

With the arrival of Congress in Washington in 1802 came a few representatives who had experienced the advantages of street lighting in New York and Philadelphia, and the need for similar convenience was voiced in the Congress, but at the expense of the municipal government. However, the need to have some form of lighting at the bridge over Tiber Creek at the foot of the Capitol, and other hazardous places where congressmen returning to their lodgings after a night of revelry could find themselves in water or mud, was addressed and funded in 1803. Private individuals had installed and maintained a few oil lamps at various places along Pennsylvania Avenue by 1804, and the city installed similar fixtures at all street intersections between the Capitol and the President's House. However, they were inoperative because there was no budget to pay for the oil and the lamplighter, whose job it was to light the lamps at sundown and extinguish them at dawn. The funding was resolved, and for fifty years the lamplighters were a fixture in the city, gathering praise for their skill in polishing the glass to remove all traces of soot, and trimming the wicks to their most efficient length to maximize light emission and minimize "smoking." The fuel was whale oil, in some cases blended with other oils to help prevent the gradual fermentation and reduce the distinctly fishy odor that was a hallmark of that time.

An industry sprang up with the realization that there was a need for many hundreds of cast-iron lamp standards, which were cast in the city by local foundries, and exhibited the unique art of the producer. Street names, unmarked and unknown to most, were cast onto signs and attached to the lamp-standards, so for the first time a street address could be referenced rather than the then-current method of describing a residence as "the fourth house beyond the second road after Tiber Creek near the Avenue."

After James Crutchett's experiments with gas and the interest of the Congress in granting a charter to the Washington Gas Light Company in 1848, the streets of the city gradually began to be lighted with gas, rather than oil. The reason was economics. It was cheaper to pay the higher price for gas and to reduce the labor of maintaining the street lamps, since the gas lamps required no daily cleaning, filling with oil and wick adjustment. It was also easier and quicker to light the gas lamps, so that a single man could now do what it had taken seven or eight men before.

The gas company began the gradual extension of underground gas mains, starting at the West Station plant on the edge of Georgetown and the East Station on the banks of the Anacostia River. Lines were generally laid in the thirty-foot right-of-way in the avenues, so that by 1865, Pennsylvania, Massachusetts, Maryland, Vermont and Delaware avenues, a total of thirty-nine miles, were served by gas mains. With the change in the form of government in the District of Columbia in 1870, the new Board of Public Works, headed by Boss Shepherd, embarked on a major program of the upgrading of the city's public utilities, and included the installation of sixty-nine miles of new gas mains. The result was that most of the housing existing in the city at that time was served by the Washington Gas Company, and this included more than 100 miles of street lamps. (19)

In the late 1860s, with the invention of the arc lamp, the Architect of the Capitol began to experiment with the replacement of gas lighting by the new electricity. The arc lamp, with its bright white emission, was very much stronger than the gas jet, and ideally suited to the illumination of streets and large outdoor areas. Were it not for the fact that the arc lamp required much more maintenance than the gas jet, its use would have spread and gas would have seen a faster replacement than it did. A few locations in the city did switch to arc lamps, such areas as the parks on the east and west fronts of the Capitol, and the park in front of the White House were ablaze with light and centers of outdoor activity in the summers. The life of the arc lamp was abruptly ended with the invention of the incandescent lamp by Edison in 1879. The monumental cast-iron standards, once modified from oil to gas, were modified again to include electric wiring running in the gas pipe up the shaft, terminating in a socket in which one of the new electric lamps was screwed.

In the early twentieth century, as overhead electric power lines began to parallel all streets, new street lamp fixtures were developed, attached to the power poles twenty-five feet above the road, equipped with reflectors, and now served to illuminate both the sidewalk and the road. The control of the street lighting was now made automatic, with the introduction of timers and light-sensitive switches, so that the lighting could be turned on at just the right time, regardless of the time of the year, and turned off selectively, as the need for security and safety changed, thereby reducing energy consumption and cost to the taxpayer.

The amount of light given out by a light source is measured in "lumens," and the efficiency of the source is measured in lumens per watt. The more efficient the lamp, the more lumens it will emit for each watt of electric power it consumes. At the time Edison invented his light, it produced about ten lumens per watt, compared to a modern lamp at sixteen lumens per watt. Throughout the period from 1920 to 1960 the standard incandescent lamp was widely used in street-lighting applications, until the engineers at the major manufacturing companies began to develop more efficient light sources. This revolutionized the industry, so that today we are able to make lamps that will emit sixty lumens per watt, or almost four times the standard incandescent lamp. This means we can light our homes and workplaces with the same amount of light at one quarter of the cost and one quarter of the consumption of fuel.

From dull dark places of refuge, our cities have become shining jewels of brilliance, far beyond the imagination of those who conceived them in times of the candle and the oil lamp.

Public Transportation

In his delivery to the Columbia Historical Society in November 1946, Mr. E. D. Merrill, president of the Capital Transit Company of Washington, observed that, "History is dull unless there is coupled with the recital of the facts, some hint of the reasons for changing fashions, and some account of the personalities and the human efforts which played important roles in the changes."

"If we can derive from history a suggestion as to the course of human events the study becomes of real value."

The changing patterns of public transportation in Washington were dominated by the changes in technology, the marriage of science and engineering , which made the horse and buggy obsolete and provided the city with a series of improvements in methods of moving masses of people.

The series of improvements began in 1800 with the establishment of a horse-drawn buggy service that originated in George Town at the intersection of Bridge and High Streets and wended its path down "M" Street and Pennsylvania Avenue, terminating at the foot of Jenkins Hill, adjacent to the Capitol. The service ran twice daily mainly for the benefit of government personnel and congressmen going to and from the office. Since most people lived either in George Town, then the center of commerce of the city, or near to the Capitol at that time, the were no commuters and certainly no "rush hour" navigating the unpaved dusty streets.

However, as the years went by the center of business began to move from George Town to "F" Street, which ran between the Capitol and the President's House, a distance of about two miles. With the relocation of the center of business came the need for more public transport. This need was filled by the introduction of twelve-seater omnibuses drawn by four-horse teams. By 1830 a number of competing companies had emerged, providing service not only to George Town, but to the Navy Yard, the docks on Water Street (now Maine Avenue), and up 7th and 11th Streets to the north. Then, in the late 1850s, a consolidation of companies occurred, largely due to the monopolies issued by the district government in an attempt to improve service by limiting competition to two businesses, the Citizen's Line and the Union Line. Both companies had their stables in George Town, in the same building, on the site of the former Capital Transit Terminal building, which still exists on "M" Street at the foot of Key Bridge.

Based on the success of the railroads, which ran on iron tracks embedded in the earth and provided a much smoother, safer and faster means of movement of heavier vehicles, the transit companies in the 1860s began to experiment with tracked vehicles in the cities. They assured the local government that the change would do nothing but improve the adjacent roadbed for private horse buggies. Most roads in Washington, other than Pennsylvania Avenue and a few others, were still unpaved. The introduction of a pair of iron rails in the center of a wide avenue and mounted on deeply excavated foundations caused the streets to be torn up, the rails with their supports laid in concrete, and the roads on either side of the track to be regraded and drained. In 1862 permission to install a rail system was granted, and construction began. By the end of that year the Washington and Georgetown Railroad Company had a line operating between the Capitol and the Treasury, near to the White House, and two years later had extended the rails to 3222 M Street, the location of the original stables. Because of the carefully calculated grades and the reduction in friction of wheels on the metal tracks, the new rail cars were able to carry sixteen passengers at more than twice the speed of the omnibuses, while the number of horses required by each vehicle was reduced from four to two. This improvement in efficiency allowed the fare from the Navy Yard to Georgetown to be reduced from twelve to five cents.

The obvious advantage of a street car on rails had its impact on all aspects of the extension of the city to outlying suburbs, which before were accessed over a very poor road system that limited the value of developing the areas for housing. But with the chartering of the Metropolitan Railway Company in 1864, and the subsequent laying of rails up to the north, areas such as Mount Pleasant were now accessible, and housing began to be built in these newer sections. Horse-drawn street cars were in vogue in Washington until 1886, at which time the president of the Washington Railroad Company, Henry Hurt, stated that the limit of capacity of the horse-drawn street cars had been reached and consideration must be given to alternatives. The limiting factor that caused this decision was the weather. Washington was in the grips of a mini-ice age, as was the rest of the country, and the problems of clearing snow and ice from the tracks, coupled with the diminished power of their prime mover, the horse, in day after day of freezing temperatures required the doubling up of the horsepower, with attendant increased cost.

The temporary solution turned out to be the cable car. Several other cities had been developing a system consisting of a steel cable loop laid in a trench underground between the steel rails. Driven at a speed of six miles per hour by a steam engine-powered revolving drum, around which the cable was looped several times and then allowed to move in the rail trench to the opposite end of the line usually no more than a mile, cable cars were fitted with a mechanism that allowed the operator to clamp onto one or the other of the two cables in the trench when he decided to set the car in motion, and to disengage when a passenger stop appeared. The first cable car ran up 7th Street on April 9, 1890, driven from a powerhouse situated at the foot of 7th and the waterfront. This was followed by the

Washington and Georgetown Company's largest powerhouse at 14th and E Streets, where the District Building sits today, and which powered cables in three directions, up 14th Street, East on Pennsylvania Avenue and West to Georgetown. The cable car system in Washington served as an effective interval between the demise of the horse-drawn vehicle and the arrival of the electric driven cars. It probably would have had a longer useful life had it not been for a disastrous fire in the main powerhouse at 14th and E on the night of September 29, 1897, which completely destroyed the plant. This disaster caused the company to buy horses on a crash basis. Services were restored on October 1st, albeit at a slower pace, using the four-legged sources of power.

From the United States Electric Company's plant at 14th and "B" Street (Constitution Avenue), operational since 1884, electric power could be sent under ground to the central section of the city. However, it was the invention of the electric traction motor that came to the rescue of city transportation.

The development of streetcars, driven by an electric motor from an overhead power line, had reached the point that some cities were ready for their installation. Washington was not. The hitch came from Congress, which decreed that overhead electric lines were prohibited in all parts of the city south of Florida Avenue. Since most electric streetcars then under development were powered by a roller connector that ran on an overhead electric line, the available cars could not be deployed in Washington. Westinghouse Electric engineers and the makers of the cars came to the rescue. They designed a car that could receive its power from an electric copper band, called a "buss," set on insulators in a concrete envelope beneath the street level, and accessible through a slot about an inch in width that opened to the street level above. Each streetcar was equipped with one or more insulated copper sheets, called "ploughs," that extended down through the slot, made contact with the buss, and allowed electric power to flow up to the traction motor.

Streets and rail track could remain undisturbed, with the temporary horse-drawn traffic accommodated during the day, while crews laid the new electric buss at night.

In the time beginning in 1888 and extending to 1905, no less than five transit companies, all using electric streetcars powered by overhead electric lines, were chartered to operate in the northern sections of the city and into adjacent Maryland. At terminals along Connecticut Avenue, 16th Street and Georgia Avenue passengers transferred to the City Company that used the underground electric buss. Gradually over the years the companies began to merge and renovate their tracks to allow the use of the underground buss system. In 1925, with the formation of the Capital Transit, the existing companies were all merged into a capital-wide system that relied almost exclusively on electric street cars using the underground buss and plough system.

Plate 10-1
Annapolis Stage Coach, circa 1802
For a fare of three dollars one could ride from George Town to Annapolis;
the trip took fifteen hours

Plate 10-2
Washington & Georgetown R.R., circa 1865
With the laying of steel rails in the avenues, the number of horses required
reduced from four to two, and the fare from the Navy Yard to Georgetown
decreased to five cents

Plate 10-3
View of Washington at 13th & "B" Streets, circa 1895
The USELCO electric generating plant is at the lower left, between 13-1/2 Street and
14th Street (not visible). The new post office building on 12th Street is in the center

Plate 10-4
Washington: 13th and "B" Streets, circa 1906
The Pepco Power Plant is on the lower left, and Ohio Avenue runs at a diagonal;
The new Museum on "B" Street sits across from the Central Market

Plate 10-5
Pennsylvania Avenue looking to the Capitol, 1865
Tracks for the horse-drawn cars lie in an unpaved road at the corner of
15th Street at the Treasury Building

Plate 10-6
Pennsylvania Ave. at 15th Street, 1885
The streets have been paved and illuminated with gas lamps;
horse-drawn taxis run on metal rails

Plate 10-7
Pennsylvania Avenue at 15ᵗʰ Street, 1896
View from the Treasury Building showing the new cable cars and electric street
lights; post office and Southern Railroad building on the right

Plate 10-8
Pennsylvania Avenue at 15ᵗʰ Street, 1925
The cable cars have been replaced by electric cars served from an electrified rail
buried between the tracks

Plate 10-9
Washington Gas Light Company: East Station, 1888
Situated at 12th and N Street, S.E., near the Navy Yard, three large gasometers, the circular tanks with floating top covers that stored the gas produced in the plant and maintained a positive pressure on the entire distribution system; the plant was demolished when natural gas came to the Washington region

Plate 10-10
The First Electric Motor in the United States Capitol
This is an 1886 D.C. motor made by the Holzer-Cabot Company; the first electric lighting in the Capitol served the Senate Chamber in 1885, and this motor was probably installed about 1892; in 1921 the motor powered a small lathe in a machine shop in Room HT18 in the basement of the Capitol, running on 120 volts D.C.

Plate 10-11
Benning Generating Station
The Potomac Electric Power Company, incorporated in 1896, built the first major
generating plant at Benning Road on the Anacostia River in 1906; the plant
generated 37,000 kilowatts of power at 25 cycles per second, and was the
company's main plant serving metropolitan Washington until WW II in 1940

Plate 10-12
Reciprocating Steam Engine Driven Electric Generator, circa 1900
This 200-kilowatt generator is typical of the units installed in power plants in the
early years of commercial electric utilities; the reciprocating steam engine to the left
drove the piston at a rate of two strokes per second, causing the generator on the
right to rotate at about 100 revolutions per minute, producing the electric current

Plate 10-13
Vertical Steam-Turbine Generator, circa 1910
This unit is similar to the 5,000 kilowatt turbine generators initially installed in the
Benning Plant of the Potomac Electric Power Company;
they produced 25 cycle, 2,200 volt power

11 . . . National Events and their Influence on Washington

Insofar as its impact on the United States in general and the city of Washington in particular is concerned, the lasting effects of the Industrial Revolution were major players in moving the city into a state of political and economic strength. It was these lasting effects that changed the nation from an agricultural economy and minor player on the world scene to the world's leading industrial economy by the end of the nineteenth century. The forces that melded together to yield this remarkable result were a combination of events, which impacted several administrations and the political thinking in Congress.

These forces or events include:

Immigration: An abundant inflow of new citizens

Mechanization: The creation of many labor saving devices

Resources: Supply of land and minerals for industry

Freedom: The ability to manage freely to create wealth

The Flood of Immigrants

Political upheavals in Europe in the second half of the nineteenth century, in particular Germany and the surrounding countries, coupled by reduction in the industrial output of slowing economies and the famine in Ireland, where the potato crop, so vital to feeding the island, had suffered serious declines for several years, influenced many to consider leaving their native land for the foreign shores of the new United States.

The need for workers matched the expansion of the nation westward, where the railroads were excavating huge amounts of earth and stone and laying steel track in an effort to connect the Atlantic with the Pacific shores. The demand for iron and steel had its effect on the mining and steel-producing cities of the East, where Pittsburgh, Cleveland, Canton and Baltimore all showed remarkable growth and the ability to assimilate foreign workers. Government agents in the sparsely settled Midwestern states joined with shipping and railroad company executives in running advertisements for immigrants in the local newspapers throughout Germany, Scandinavia and Ireland.

The year 1830 saw 23,000 new immigrants arrive at the ports on the East Coast. By 1840 the number had risen to 84,000, and to 297,000 by 1850. Between 1850 and 1860 some three million souls passed through the immigration hubs of New York, Boston and Philadelphia. In the aftermath of the 1848 Revolution in Europe, more than one million

Germans entered the country and settled in a triangle of the Midwest enclosed by the cities of Cleveland, Chicago and St. Louis. Mostly these were farming families. Poor and desperate, but determined and committed, they brought diverse skills to propel the land from open plane into ploughed fields with the help of the new equipment and invention.

Factory and construction workers and single men tended to gravitate to the cities, with Washington getting its share of masons, carpenters and blacksmiths, together with a greater supply of unskilled labor. Table 3 is from U.S. Censuses.

Table 3
Population of the District Columbia 1840-1920

1840	43,712
1850	51,687
1860	75,080
1870	131,700
1880	177,624
1890	230,392
1900	278,718
1910	331,069
1920	437,571

From the data it will be seen that the population of Washington, D.C. increased tenfold in the eighty years enclosing the Industrial Revolution.

Among the immigrants from Germany and Scandinavia were many experienced farmers and a sprinkling of bankers and businessmen. These individuals became the leaders of their clans and the founders of all manner of trading companies. Their background and ethics differed markedly from the leaders of the early settlers, who were primarily of the English gentlemanly class. The new leaders showed skills in areas such as negotiation, compromise, friendly trading, and helping each other in a competitive world.

The city of Washington got its share of both unskilled and skilled leaders who entered the housing construction market, with the result that the city's growth to the north accelerated. The suburbs of Mount Pleasant, Schuetzen Park, Petworth and Brookland were all the results of immigrants seeking a better living standard and applying their skills to the art of home building. In these neighborhoods the European style of city housing is still obvious today.

Mechanization

The population growth of Washington paralleled that of the United States, which grew from 17 million in 1840 to 105 million in 1920. Farming output showed substantial gains, with the ports of Georgetown and Alexandria handling the exports of the region, mainly tobacco, flour, wheat and cut stone, while bringing in the products of the industrial north, including machinery, leather goods and clothing.

The main "business" of the city was then, and still is, government. To support this challenge the number of persons required grew exponentially. For example, in 1850 the Patent Office for the first time granted one thousand patents in a single year; by 1860 the number was six thousand. If one considers that the majority of these grants were for labor-saving devices and machinery of various types, it becomes immediately apparent that a massive move to mechanization was in progress. Isaac Singer improved the sewing machine, invented in Massachusetts in 1846 by Elias Howe, for industrial use.

By the application of the steam engine driving lines of newly invented sewing machines, the time to manufacture a man's shirt was reduced from fourteen hours to a little over an hour, with an attendant reduction in cost to the buyer.

Cyrus McCormick, a Virginia blacksmith, obtained a patent in 1834 for a horse-drawn grain-reaping machine, with the capacity for one man to harvest as much grain as seven men wielding the traditional harvest knives. He moved his factory to Chicago in 1840, and four years later produced five hundred reapers per year; by 1856 the number had grown to four thousand. Driven by such changes in mechanization and supported by vast improvements in transportation, the farmers of the Midwest saw grain crops move up from 100 million bushels in 1850 to 200 million in 1870.

While a vital element of the Economic Revolution, the growth in agricultural production alone did not occupy center stage; it fell to the "mechanization trio," transportation, manufacturing and mining, with interlocking functional interests, to propel the country to prosperity and power. Later, in 1902, the U.S. Industrial Commission referred to the emerging technologies as, "probably the most rapid change in the methods of industry observable at any time in history."

Mass production, as we know it today, had not yet emerged, but the process of *worker specialization,* with teams of semi-skilled people, each assigned a particular task, in a sequence that allowed the sum of many small tasks to culminate in reaching the manufacturing goal, began to replace the skilled mechanic, who previously made the parts and assembled the finished device. The output of the agricultural nation provided the greatest segment of wealth up till the late 1870s, but the trend reversed after the census of 1900, when industrial production was more than double the value of farming. Again, from the Patent Office the data showed that prior to 1865 the total number of patents issued since its inception in the early 1800s amounted to 65,000, and from 1865 to 1900 the number was close to 638,000.

The rapid growth in output from mechanized factories in the East and farms in the Midwest created a demand for improved transportation. Attempts were made to meet this demand by much road construction and a few canals. The problem was that there were no satisfactory road vehicles; everything was horse-drawn and slow, as well as uneconomical. Canals were fine for moving large quantities of a single commodity, say grain, from Chicago to New York, but there was no way to use them to distribute the product once it reached its destination.

The outcome was that the bulk of the nation's products began to move on a network of railroads that connected the ports, cities and towns, and even small industrial and agricultural centers. Railroads were actively sought after by the officials of cities and states, who gave generous grants of land and rights-of-way in order to bring the rail lines close to the grain loading points and into the factory yards.

The expansion of the rail line system from 30,000 miles in 1860 moved to 90,000 by 1880, and to 190,000 in 1900, more than the total length of track in all of Europe.

A key addition to the safety of American train travel occurred in 1872 with the invention of the automatic air brake by George Westinghouse. The system employed a steam-driven vacuum pump on the engine up front, connected to all of the cars behind through a flexible hose, with suitable connectors at each car. The pump exhausted the air from the hose, which at each car connected to a cylinder and piston. Vacuum in the cylinder pulled the piston inward, which released the brakes, allowing the car freedom to move. When the engine driver wished to stop the train he opened a valve, allowing air to enter the tube, which released the vacuum, causing the brakes to be immediately applied. Failure of a linkage between any two cars in the train would immediately apply the brakes, saving many lives on runaway cars. Systems such as these were typical of the engineering inventions designed to do a job better or in a safer manner. (38, Page 129)

Resources

With safer more reliable transportation, the development of the vast fields of iron ore near Lake Superior and coal in West Virginia and Ohio began to pick up momentum with remarkable increases in the output of iron and steel. Between 1860 and 1890 the production of coal went from 13 million tons to 140 million tons, while the production of cast-iron increased from 820,000 to 9 million tons. In 1860 the United States ranked fourth in the world in manufacturing output. By 1894 she had moved up to number one.

The impact of many labor-saving devices propelled farming from a "homestead" supporting a family into a production business supporting a workforce using mechanical devices to enhance production, giving meaning to the *agricultural revolution* in America. Between the years 1850 and 1880 the area under cultivation increased by 270,000 square miles, or the area of the British Isles and Sweden combined. In the following twenty years the farmed area reached 412,000 square miles, or more than the area of the British Isles, all of Scandinavia, Holland and Belgium together. (38, Page 141)

Because of the shortage of labor, invention tended to concentrate on the necessary tasks, requiring an excessive amount of time relative to the economic values of those tasks. Prior to the invention of the "Twiner," harvested wheat had to be hand-bound with string or twine into manageable bails, but with J. F. Appleby's mechanical device, perfected in 1879, the volume of wheat that could be economically harvested increased eightfold. The homesteader, with one helper, could do what had previously needed the services of six. The production of corn and wheat increased by 100 percent between 1860 and 1880, making America the greatest exporter of these products in the world. In the following decade the production of wheat and corn almost doubled again, reaching 400 million bushels of wheat and 1.4 billion of corn. An economist, Edward Atkinson, in 1889 wrote, "There has never been in the history of civilization a period, or a place, or a section of the earth in which science and invention have worked such progress or have created such opportunity for material welfare as in these United States in the period which has elapsed since the end of the civil war." Such was the Economic Revolution.

All of these increases in wealth and population had an obvious impact on the federal government in Washington and on the city in general. Housing boomed. Washington never has been an industrial city, but enterprises that supported government, from builders to banks, from brick makers to breweries, flourished. The city moved relentlessly, block by block, to the west and north. Multi-story brick buildings began to dominate the downtown, with the previously open spaces between the Capitol and the White House being filled in with what amounted to low-cost commercial structures, all wall-bearing, with minimal professional engineering input. The volcano of ideas, devices, invention, finance and industry that swept the nation during these years, producing pockets of enormous power and wealth, had its impact on the profession of engineering in a manner that no one predicted, least of all the practitioners of the art.

The Engineering Profession Begins to Change
The story of Benjamin Latrobe's involvement in the Washington Canal Company in 1809 is typical of the way engineers at that time took the lead in a business venture, because the other investors had no power to exert their influence on the technical direction of the project. The success of the enterprise resided totally on the expertise of the technical advisor, and his judgment was accepted as the key to financial reward. To retain the respect of their clients, engineers had to exhibit honesty, identity, leadership, knowledge and good judgment in their dealings with others. From a professional perspective, the key items were identity and leadership. They had to feel a sense of self-respect brought on by a commitment to moral, ethical, mature and honest behavior: the identity; and be compelled to take responsibility to see the project through to the end: the leadership.

Up until that time there was really no difference between the scientist and the engineer, or the different branches of engineering. The same individuals who had learned their mathematics, and the limited published information about steam and hydraulics, moved into the challenges offered by the production of steel, and the manufacture of rails and locomotives, and the hulls of ships equipped with massive steam engines, driven by coal-fired boilers, and the many small manufacturing concerns that were the backbone of the economy. The advancement of the technology occurred by "judgmental trial," the product of the astute innovator, willing to advance the art by careful steps in order to avoid the pitfall of "trial and error." Even so there was an ample supply of errors, particularly in the field of high-pressure boilers, which continued a pattern of explosive failure and the claiming of lives. Throughout this period engineers performed by building on their latest and best creations and by carefully recording their observations for future reference. Relatively small firms were the norm. The practice of the profession almost always included the manufacture, or the offer to design, a unique product; a machine or armament or some project paid for by the client and produced by the engineer and his staff of blacksmiths, machine-shop artisans and draftsmen. There was no "mass production," no assembly line. Responsibility for the design and manufacturing rested with the engineer, and he exhibited his professionalism by bringing his training and ingenuity to the success of each product or service. The mass of recorded observations, carefully bound and filed, began to be shared among like practitioners, out of which grew the philosophical societies in the early 1800s and the technical societies, such as the American Society of Mechanical Engineers, in the latter part of the nineteenth century. There was little competition between engineers. The existence of a sufficient number of projects and the fact that there were not many engineers in practice when compared to other callings allowed the profession to be rather "gentlemanly." There was, of course, no registration or licensing by the state. This would follow later.

The fields of physics and chemistry were in their infancy, but to the degree that information was available, it became a part of the knowledge expected of the mechanical designers, as opposed to civil engineers, the other major division of technology. Men like Maudsley in England and Whitney in America had a command of most of the technical knowledge that had been developed since the Renaissance, and were therefore recognized by their peers to be at the peak of their professions. Men like these were both scientists and engineers, and at that time there was no need to differentiate between them.

The information available was of a practical nature. There was no molecular theory; no basis for predicting the onset of corrosion caused by galvanic action—these concepts would be developed in later years. What these men knew were the limits to which steel could be loaded without failure, based on actual field tests. Beams were loaded with tons of stone blocks, and carefully observed as they gradually bowed and finally broke. The breaking point was studiously observed and recorded, and disseminated to others, such that the body of information became available to all engineers. The people performing this research were individuals, either sole practitioners or the owners of small engineering companies. (5)

What followed next was the emphasis on basic research conducted by the institutions of higher learning, and this rapidly led to the separation of the engineer from the pure scientist. The period in question ranges from the 1820s to the 1870s, by which time scientific knowledge had grown to the point that engineers could no longer actively participate in the fruits of science without an "interpreter," a scientist with interest in the engineering process. The arrival of electric power in 1867 not only created another field of scientific research, but divided the mechanical profession into two parts, with the new specialty of electrical engineering. Civil engineering, the original part of the technical professions, remained largely untouched by the developments in electricity, but it, too, began to be impacted by the scientific research into materials and the development of vastly superior equipment, such as excavators, which resulted from the research.

The formation of West Point and, later, a number of schools such as Rennselear, Stevens Institute and Massachusetts Institute of Technology, became the institutions for scientific research and the source of graduates who entered the field of engineering.

One thing that all these institutions had in common was that the entrant scientist or engineer began with the fundamentals of mathematics, physics and mechanics, and other similar subjects in the first and second years of study, then selected courses in the third and fourth years, leading to a degree in one of the three branches of engineering. The decision was then to stay in academia or move into the other fields. The choice generally was to pursue either scientific research in an academic setting on one hand, or the practice of engineering on the other. Oversimplified, this led to a continuum in which the scientist discovered the principle or phenomenon of an event, with no particular end result or product in mind, followed by the engineer, who, once he understood the scientific theory, visualized applications for the science and developed products and solutions for society's needs.

There is still a debate as to whether technology is science or engineering or both; or which of the two is the most "important." The media generally likes to refer to technology being invented and manufactured by scientists but installed and operated by engineers. In fact, technology is a continuum that begins with basic research, the domain of the scientist, followed by applied research, performed by teams of scientists and engineers, followed by design, manufacture, application engineering, installation, operation and service, all performed by engineers, or technicians under their charge.

In the early years there was a defined amount of scientific and engineering information to be learned and a limited field over which to practice. As the nineteenth century moved along, more and more scientific research led to an ever-expanding body of knowledge. Inventors, usually engineers, took this knowledge and devised an increasing number of more complicated products and systems.

The railroads had a remarkable effect on the economy of the country, with the ability to bring vast quantities of raw material to the steel smelters of Pittsburgh and Baltimore, move farm products in bulk to where they were needed, and allow manufacturing to be concentrated in centers like New England, New York and the South.

One of the results of this ability to move masses of material with relatively low cost was that projects got larger. Depots and terminals, buildings and construction projects became governed by the economics of the enterprise, with the influx of capitalists and investors as the prime movers and decision-makers. There followed an inevitable shift of engineering from the decision-making role to a support role. The larger and more complex the project, the larger were the engineering teams brought to solve a greater, more undefined set of problems. The expansion of various fields of knowledge led to specialization in those fields, which meant that the coordination and management of many specialties became a specialty in itself.

Members of the "shop-oriented" technical societies were happy to see their ranks swelled by the influx of new graduates and, with larger budgets, were able to embark on the development of much needed "standards," covering most of the myriad materials used in manufacturing. Technical associations brought order and safety to an engineered-society without the intervention of the states or the federal government. The members of these associations were the leaders of the manufacturing and building communities, working in concert with consultants to establish limits, characteristics and minimum performance levels to thousands of manufactured products.

For example, they determined the dimensions and characteristics of pipes, screws and other products that must "fit" with another. A pipe made in Ohio must mate precisely with an "elbow" or "tee" made in Maryland. There had to be agreement on the various sizes of pipes to be manufactured, and the pressure limits of each size. The higher the working pressure of a pipe, the thicker must be the walls of the pipe, and the greater the attendant cost. Over the decades hundreds of man-years of technical experience brought societies, like the American Society of Mechanical Engineers, to fill a very important place in the evolution of America into the Engineering Age.

Another dimension was added to this massive upheaval in the form of the cost of scientific research, which became prohibitive to the individual scientist. Innovators working in an academic or industrial setting were able to devote themselves to their research without bearing the financial cost.

On the engineering side, an individual professional could no longer handle the ever-increasing size, complexity and cost of projects. The result was that both professions, science and engineering, found themselves becoming a part of large institutions, universities or corporations with an economic motive.

The numbers bare some analysis.

In 1840 almost all engineers were individual professionals.

In 1890 some sixty percent were self-employed; the balance were in industry or academia.

In 1925 twenty-five percent of engineers operated as independent consultants, in the same way that a physician dealt with and prescribed solutions for his patients. The remaining seventy-five percent worked for government, academia or public corporations.

By 1965 some five percent of engineers were self employed, while ninety-five percent were employed by institutions or commercial organizations. (13)

In the United States in 1900 there were about 40,000 graduates of engineering schools.

By 1950 this number had increased to 500,000.

In 1997 there were more than two million.

The proportion of engineers employed compared to total persons employed in the country went from 13 per 10,000 in 1900 to 128 per 10,000 in 1960, almost a tenfold increase. (13)

Engineers began to practice in teams. The more experienced individuals became the team leaders, supervising the newcomers and checking to verify the accuracy of the work of less-experienced people.

The Evolution of Engineering

The growth in the industrial, agricultural and business sectors created a requirement for technically trained people at all levels of manufacturing, from hands-on mechanics to administrators. Up till that time there were two main channels an individual could follow in the quest to become an "engineer." They were the English or "shop" track (the old way) and the academic track (the new way).

The shop track was an outgrowth of the guild craftsman approach, prevalent in England since the 1500s, and carried through the centuries. In this system the entrant, at the age of fifteen, was apprenticed to a practicing engineer, who usually owned a small manufacturing plant and "made" things for a living. (There were few theoretical engineers.) The entrant learned the trade by beginning at the bottom, and over the next ten years trained in the details of the business to become a mechanic, recognized by the industry and his peers as someone proficient in the "making" of things. For those mechanics who demonstrated the mental capacity to learn to read and write and master arithmetic, the way was open to becoming an "engineer," which took another ten years, so that by the age of thirty-five, a competent engineer emerged.

This engineer became a member of the "shop elite," who began to share their experiences with other similarly trained individuals in meetings and forums, out of which emerged the American Society of Mechanical Engineers (ASME) in 1880. The "shop culture" became more scientific and dedicated to the advancement of society, just as their forebears had striven in the beginning of the Age of Enlightenment two hundred years before. It is important to differentiate between the "shops" and "factories." The shops were in business to manufacture one or two of a kind at any given time, equipped with lathes, boring machines, planers, milling machines and steam hammers, and usually worked on special orders, often breaking new frontiers of engineering. These shops were equipped with all the books on science, technology and institutional reports, and included draftsmen skilled in the production of the highest quality drawings.

Factories, as they began to emerge, were initially geared to produce a single or specialized product, usually designed by a shop engineer, and staffed by many workers with no engineering training.

The second track to becoming an engineer occurred largely by the demand for semi-technically trained individuals to satisfy the demand caused by the expansion of industry at the height of the Industrial Revolution, between 1840 to 1910. Mass production had not yet been invented, but manufacturing shops headed by an experienced engineer were slowly outnumbered by manufacturing plants headed up by an investor, a nontechnical manager who foresaw the profit in the "making" and selling of manufactured products. There was an escalating demand for young, technically trained men, responded to by the academic institutions, which created courses in theoretical science and technology. The academic track could graduate an engineer by age twenty-two, then expose him to a specialized industry for six to ten years, and then move him into an administrative or technical marketing position by age thirty-two. (39)

In the years from 1870 to 1910 the shop elite tended to look down on academia, who in turn made every effort to break into the technical societies and be recognized. The graduates of the academic schools, however, made little attempt to join the technical societies and associate with the elite. Thus, in the fifty years preceding the end of the nineteenth century, there began the split between the "professional" shop engineers and the graduates of the engineering schools. A survey of the engineering graduates for the year 1904 of

Cornell's Sibley College of Engineering revealed that ten years after leaving the school, of 1285 graduates:

> 298 were classified as mechanical engineers
> 170 were classified as electrical engineers
> 107 were sales engineers
> 140 were draftsmen or designers
> 43 were consulting engineers
> 527 were teaching, in business, practicing law or in administrative positions. (39)

In other words, forty percent of the graduating class remained in a field that could be considered to be engineering, while the balance moved into fields that supported an economy that was becoming more and more based on manufacturing. Of the 468 mechanical and electrical engineers, most worked for large industrial companies, where the degree of authority and "professional" responsibility they wielded over their day-to-day decisions is not known.

The competition between the shop elite and the college-educated engineers became so acute that in 1892 various representatives of shop-trained engineers came to Washington to lobby the Congress and the White House to create a cabinet-level Department of Mechanics and Engineering. It would have authority to control all of the engineering work produced by all arms of the federal government. The action was partly in response to the increased competition caused by large industrial businesses, which employed a few engineers and a majority of technicians, and which sought to offer "engineering services" to the government. The "industrials" were far better positioned to offer services on a more competitive basis, since in most cases they were using engineering services as a marketing tool to sell manufactured products to the government. Typically, an industrial concern would generate less than five percent of its income from engineering services, compared to the private practitioners, where the number was one hundred percent. The efforts of the shop-trained engineers did not have the hoped for effect on Congress, but did lead to the beginning of a movement to protect the practice of engineering from unwarranted and unfair competition.

There was also the fact that many of the engineers employed by government were college-educated, without any practical field experience, yet in positions of authority over engineering work. The shop people lobbied hard for the government to employ people who had served an appropriate apprenticeship, but this too died on the vine.

It was at this time in the growth of America that engineering began to evolve into a *technical overlay* of a vast industrial economy. Almost every new industrial plant produced a product that one way or another depended on the application of engineering principles, and it made no difference that the workers in the plant had little or no technical background, as long as they could keep the facility running according to the maintenance books.

Engineering began to be infused into the nation's economy as a series of "steps." At the bottom of the ladder were the most experienced practitioners of the art, bringing their skills to the design of manufacturing machinery, steam turbines, power transformers and the like, and the thousands of smaller inventions such as how to build a tin can that does not leak, or an electrical switch that can be turned on and off safely for forty years without failure.

The next "step" up included the many graduates of engineering colleges and their technically trained coworkers who took the concepts of the "first step" and applied them to the manufacturing process. The designers of the first step had their designs reduced to drawings and plans by draftsmen and technicians of the "second" step, who in turn instructed mechanics and other technicians, of the "third" step, how to make or apply the product.

It was this third step, millions of technically savvy individuals that inhabited manufacturing plants and service industries, that brought a mechanized world to the doorsteps of consumers. These men and women were generally not graduates of engineering schools but were students of training programs instituted by the product manufacturer to impart a rigorous and necessarily focused overview of the technical aspects of the product in question. The computer technician, the copier repair tech and the auto mechanic are all members of this important third step.

At the beginning of the twentieth century, however, the availability of skilled "second" or "third" steppers was essentially zero. The nation was on the verge of widespread mechanization. Skilled "first steppers" existed but were in extremely short supply, and industry had yet to grasp the massive demand for manufactured products that was about to break into the marketplace and the demand for technical services that would accompany the flood.

Thus in many parts of the economy, engineering services were being performed by all manner of persons, some highly trained in the old shop method, some academically trained, and some persons with no engineering training at all. One exception to the trend lay in the practice of civil engineering, which remained very much under the control of the engineering practitioners. Probably because of the nature of civil works that tend to be one-of-a-kind, and not easily reduced to an industrial plant, there remained a clear distinction between the engineer who designed and supervised the work, and the contractors and builders who performed the construction.

12 . . . ENGINEERING IN WASHINGTON 1870-1925

Consulting Engineers

The picture at the turn of the twentieth century for engineers had changed remarkably from that envisaged by Crozet or Watt two hundred years before. The majority of engineers were salaried employees of government or industry, with strong economic and technical drives and little legal responsibility for the outcome of the projects with which they were involved.

The exception to the rule were the consultants. These were individuals who, for a fee, would take on the client's problem and deliver a solution. There were very few consultants in the scientific field because there was no market for their services. On the engineering side there was a market, particularly in the construction industry, where the product was a one-of-a-kind dam, building or power plant, and an owner willing to "rent" the services of a professional for the duration of the project. So the field of consulting engineering began to fill in the role of the professional of an earlier time.

Many of these consultants had spent years in the employ of an industrial organization, mastered a field of engineering related to that industry, and gained a reputation that allowed them to go out on their own and offer services on a contract basis. The process was to a large degree similar to the "old method" of becoming an engineer in the British system. The key to developing a consulting practice was to have a reputation for delivering engineering advice that could be relied upon as a result of delivering successful services to previous clients.

In the late 1800s, with the exception of the federal government, the demand for mechanical or electrical consultation on individual projects was limited. This was not true in the field of civil engineering, however. The growth of the city, while not requiring the input of a structural engineer for the design of buildings, did need experienced individuals to design the infrastructure. This included roads, bridges, sewers, water, surveying and site preparation, all of which fell to individual practitioners with proven expertise.

For the city of Washington the system worked well through the entire nineteenth century. Early buildings and homes were erected by builders who had learned their trade in the Northeast or one of the European countries and later by local craftsmen who had picked up their skills as apprentices to proven organizations. Civil engineering skills were passed from man to man over years of training—the giver, the owner of the engineering practice; the recipient, a young man demonstrating the desire to enter the profession.

Thus, at the beginning of the twentieth century Washington had its first homegrown consulting engineers.

Weller

The first known consulting engineer in Washington was Francis Weller, a civil and hydraulic practitioner in 1902, with offices at 408 C Street SW. Little is known of Mr. Weller other than that his name keeps showing up in the permits and land records of the District of Columbia, and his practice included the expansion of the storm control system started in the previous century by the Corps of Engineers. In 1902 Weller was listed in the new telephone directory as an engineer offering services in the structural and civil fields of engineering. (40)

Weller practiced on his own for a number of years from his office in Southwest Washington, then in 1910 moved uptown to the Hibbs Building. In 1916 he associated with George Weschler, an associate professor of mechanical engineering at Catholic University, who lived at 1243 Monroe Street NE. At that time Marion X. Wilberding, about whom more will be said later, was an instructor of mechanical engineering at Catholic University.

In 1925 Weller moved to the Mills Building on Pennsylvania Avenue, at 17th Street. By 1924 Weller's partnership with Weschler had dissolved, and a new one, Francis Weller Inc., had been formed with Weller as president, Wilberding as vice-president, and Leo Cleary, a graduate of Catholic University in electrical engineering.

Cleary had moved from Connecticut to Washington with his parents in 1912, attended Catholic University, and then worked as a draftsman for the Bureau of Yards and Docks at the Navy Yard until 1924, when he joined Francis Weller. Leo Cleary left Weller in 1928 and joined with Bill Karsunky in a consulting engineering partnership. (41)

In 1934 the record shows that Weller was no longer with the company, and M. X. Wilberding was president, B. P. Hessler and C. E. Edwards were vice-presidents, and L. M. Keck was secretary. Their offices were in the Mills Building.

Wilberding

Marion X. Wilberding, a student at Catholic University, graduated in 1914 and joined the staff as an instructor. He met both Weller and Weschler during this time. He must have started a consulting practice some years later, because in 1924 he had an office at 2833 29th Street NW. In 1925 he joined Weller in a corporation as vice president.

In 1931 Marion X. Wilberding changed the name of the company from Weller to M. X. Wilberding, Consulting Engineer, and moved to 1822 I Street NW, where he practiced for thirty years, establishing the reputation as the leading consulting engineer in Washington.

Many well-known engineers in later years started their careers with Wilberding or Weller. Perhaps the best known is Joseph Hanlein, a graduate of Catholic and Michigan State universities, who joined Weller in 1931 and continued with Wilberding until the 1950s. Joe Hanlein had the reputation as an engineer's engineer because of his thorough familiarity with the theory behind the practice and his willingness to spend hours discussing a project with his competitors in order to produce a satisfactory solution. It was Joe Hanlein who introduced radiant heating to Washington in the late '30s and radiant cooling after the war in 1946. One of his high profile projects was the design of the radiant floor system for the Washington National Cathedral. There is a story of a German engineer who was familiar with the heating, or lack thereof, in European cathedrals, and visited Washington's cathedral with Hanlein one midwinter. He was quite perplexed by the obvious comfort inside the Nave, compared to the refrigerator-like conditions he was used to in his native country. Yet there was no obvious source of heat; even the radiant floor at a 75-degree temperature was not the apparent source. The German went home suitably impressed.

Marcel Hoppe was another associate of Wilberding's. Born in Paris, he came to the United Stated in 1916 and worked in New York. He came to Washington in the '30s, worked with Wilberding and then started his own consulting firm in 1940. (41)

In 1897 Proctor Dougherty, a graduate of MIT, came to Washington and worked as an electrical engineer for more than thirty years with the Treasury Department, which provided design services for all government buildings. He left Treasury in 1928 and started a practice that offered electrical engineering services. He partnered with Wilberding over the following ten years, during which time Thomas Urdahl, a mechanical engineer, became his first employee. (41)

Urdahl specialized in air conditioning, which was becoming more common in the late 1930s, and was the engineer of record on numerous Federal and District of Columbia office buildings. During World War II, he, like most other consultants, worked for the government since there was no other work in the town.

Weschler

George Alphonsus Weschler was born in Oxon Hill, Maryland, in 1881, the grandson of German immigrants who came to the United States in 1809, settled in Eire, Pennsylvania, and moved to Washington in 1864. He attended Purdue University, where he graduated with a B.S. in mechanical engineering in 1910, and an M.S. three years later. He joined Catholic University as an associate professor in 1916, becoming a full professor and head of the Department of Mechanical Engineering for twenty-five years. Wilberding was a student of Weschler's.

In 1924 Weschler started a consulting firm, and in 1927 had offices in the Transportation Building, under the name George A. Weschler Consulting Engineer. 1934 recognized him as one of Washington's leading engineers, with offices at 732 17th Street, just up the street from Weller.

During this period Leo Cleary joined as an electrical engineer, and W. Karsunky left Catholic University, where he taught for ten years, and joined as a mechanical engineer. In 1928 Cleary and Karsunky left and started their own firm.

In 1930 Ted Gooch came to work for Weschler as a mechanical engineer. Five years later, in 1935, he joined Karsunky in a partnership, which continued through the war, and in 1945 Frank Weller joined them, and the firm of Karsunky, Weller and Gooch was formed.

Weschler practiced in both mechanical and electrical fields, and was a consultant to the Architect of the Capitol for a number of major projects. These included the Longworth House Office Building in 1930, the expansion of the Capitol Power Plant in 1949 and the conversion of the buildings on Capitol Hill from twenty-five-cycle to sixty-cycle electric power in 1951. George Weschler died in 1954.

Registration of Engineers

By the turn of the century in 1900 the struggle between the "academics" and "shop elite" had reached the point that most manufacturing was managed by people who had minimal academic training as engineers. The "shop" school of training, in which one was apprenticed under the supervision of men with proven manufacturing expertise, was prevalent in most industries in the United States. These men, on the cutting edge of industries like steel, electric power and transportation, had a strong incentive to do what was prudent and "right," as well as economically sound, so there developed a club of leaders who met to examine what was in their best interests from a technical point of view. There were no professional societies to meet their needs, and in any event, these men were not academically trained or welcomed by those who were. These "shop professionals" decided to create institutions that met their needs.

The American Society of Mechanical Engineers (ASME) was founded in 1880, followed by the Electrical Engineers (ASEE) in 1884. Both of these organizations appeared in response to the need for order and standards in a developing industrial society fraught with all manner of "one-of-a-kind" manufactured products and claims that could not be easily substantiated. The consuming public was clearly at risk, as were the reputations of the responsible members of the manufacturing industry. Both societies set about developing and codifying standards for consumer products such as iron pipe, boilers and pressure vessels, electrical switches and sockets, and industrial power products used by the major manufacturers.

The approach they used was one of establishing "consensus," an agreement between the competing interests to obtain a balance that was best for the public. Primarily they prepared testing procedures and standards, and encouraged interested parties to join a society, subscribe to its principles, implement the testing procedures in their factories, and be willing to have the tests witnessed by independent inspectors. Those products that passed inspection were given a seal, and the buying public was encouraged to insist on products with the seal. The balance of opinions of parties, including buyers, users, manufacturers, sellers, independent consulting engineers and academics, were brought to the committee process in which the standards were written. It is interesting to reflect that the process did not involve the government at either the state or federal level, and there was no attempt by either to usurp the process. In fact, as the years went by federal, state and local governments were happy to incorporate the standards into their codes and laws. Such was the status of the shop-trained engineers in 1910.

The academics, graduates of the academies and private universities, were generally salaried employees in governments, teachers in schools of higher learning, or they worked for the shop engineers in industry. What they learned in their schools of instruction varied from institution to institution. Further, there were no standards required of people who offered services to the public, with the result that many persons with minimal or no academic training and competence performed heating calculations, boundary surveys, road construction, and building "design."

Things got so bad in the western United States that homeowners, lawyers and notaries prepared land surveys for the public records. In 1903, the State of Wyoming engaged Clarence T. Johnston, a 31-year-old engineering graduate, as state engineer. He immediately recognized the problem of incompetent people preparing and certifying land records. Wyoming required that property transfers and access to state-controlled water sources be accompanied by a certified boundary survey depicting the watercourse, streams, reservoirs, and the area of the land to be irrigated. Johnston could foresee the future chaos and legal wrangling that would result from confusing, inaccurate and modified land records. He approached the State Legislature, presented the dilemma and was asked to prepare a bill that would remedy the matter. After much debate and opposition on the part of those who benefited from the existing system, the Legislature passed a law that stipulated the minimum qualifications and training that must be possessed by persons certifying to the accuracy of land surveys in the state.

However the State of Wyoming went further. They claimed a power under the Constitution that left to the states those things not specifically surrendered to the federal government, and sought to exercise that power by the regulation of engineering and surveying. That standards were required in Wyoming at that time is hard to reject; the question of why the State chose to regulate the engineering profession, when the manufacturing industry and engineers practicing in the eastern states were doing the job themselves, is still open to question. In any event, Wyoming, in 1907, became the first state of the Union to require the registration of engineers by an examination administered by the government. Johnston became the secretary of the Wyoming Board of Engineering Examiners.

The following year Louisiana followed suit, and in 1915 Illinois enacted a similar law but included structural engineers as well. Many states followed, and in 1920 the District of Columbia, New York and Virginia passed similar legislation regulating the practice of surveying and mechanical, structural, civil and electrical engineering.

For engineers in the District of Columbia, the Board of Registration included several practitioners already involved in the public domain, and they issued licenses to themselves and others who qualified under the "grandfather" clause of the legislation.

The First Registered Engineers in Washington D.C.
1921 - 1922

Name	License Number	Discipline
Daniel Walser	1	Civil/Structural
Unknown	2	
M. X. Wilberding	3	Civil/Mechanical
Martin Bennett	4	Chemical
Lee J. Purnell	5	Electrical
Henry Snelling	6	Mechanical
Walter Simpson	7	Civil/Mechanical
Gordon Young	8	Civil/Structural
T. J. Hayes	9	Civil/Structural
Robert Davis	10	Civil/Structural
James Daly	11	Civil/Structural
E. Brook Fetty	14	Electrical
John Loehler	15	Civil/Structural
James Gongwer	17	Civil/Structural

Engineers in Government

The years toward the end of the nineteenth century left uncertainty in some of the citizens of Washington about the site chosen to be the seat of government for the nation. A few Washingtonians harbored a fear that Congress would not dedicate itself to the eastern seaboard in the long run because the center of the nation seemed to be gradually shifting toward the west. There were suggestions that St. Louis, Missouri, would be a more accessible capital because of its central location and its accessibility on the Mississippi River, then the main north-south commercial highway. To be permanently anchored as the capital the city needed the federal government to send the right signals to a waiting investment community that felt committed to the original choice. This signal came with the decision by the leaders of both Houses to improve the federal infrastructure under the Corps of Engineers, and to assign the design and construction of several new buildings to the Treasury Department in 1869.

This authority included the design and maintenance of all federal buildings, except those buildings occupied by the Congress, which remained under a superintendent of buildings who reported to the Congress.

The Treasury Department began a search for designers experienced in the art of buildings, and over time assembled a team of engineers and architects that became the design and construction supervision arm of the federal government for fifty years, until the creation of the Public Building Administration in 1925. Their offices on the top floor of the Treasury Building on 15th Street, next to the White House, quickly included such innovations as electric lighting and a telephone for each department, together with sheetmetal ductwork through which heated air was pumped in the winter and untreated outside air in the summer. Treasury, because of its high standards of professionalism and opportunity to work on state-of-the-art projects, soon attracted some of the leading students of mechanical and electrical schools, and offered them experiences far better than those of the private sector. With a near audible sigh of relief, the city welcomed the decision to replace the old War Department building on the west side of the White House with a great new edifice to house the departments of State, War and Navy.

The Old Executive Office Building

The State, War and Navy Building, later known as the Old Executive Office Building, enclosed 640,000 square feet, with 450,000 of occupiable space, thereby becoming the largest office building in the city.

Congress authorized the design to begin in 1871, with the building to be erected in four phases to permit the site to be gradually developed without the necessity of finding temporary quarters for the occupants of the two existing buildings. The south wing, housing the Department of State, was completed in 1875, followed by the east wing, assigned to the Navy in 1879, which allowed the original Navy and War Buildings to be removed, making the site ready to receive the rest of the new building. In sequence, the north wing followed in 1882, with the completion of the whole in 1888.

Because of its construction sequence, it was really four separate buildings put together to appear as one entity. Each wing had its own heating, lighting and plumbing systems.

The original heating apparatus included a pair of coal-fired boilers in each wing, providing low-pressure steam to "heating elements," the forerunner of heating coils, consisting of many rows of iron pipe. The heating elements were located in brick tunnels in the basement and arranged to allow warmed air to rise by gravity up masonry shafts that ran parallel on either side of each window from the first to the fifth floors. Cast-iron grilles in the stools of each window permitted the warm air to enter the occupied space. Similar systems had been used in the Agriculture Administration Building on the Mall, and were a great improvement over the coal fireplace used in the Capitol and the original War and Navy buildings. However, they were not ideal, since they provided more heat at the first floor and gradually less on the subsequent floors above. Their real engineering advancement lay in the ability to provide heat to 580 separate rooms without the need for a staff to stoke the fires multiple times each day, and the admission of relatively clean air to each space, which reduced the necessity to have windows cracked open in the dead of winter. Substantially reducing the number of open fires also greatly minimized the hazard of fire.

The warm air system survived until 1910, when the advances in cast-iron radiators, developed in the 1870-1890 era, were introduced into the building. The warm air system was abandoned, and in its place cast-iron steam radiators, with manual hand valves, were installed in each room under the window, fed by iron pipe risers supplied from a central boiler plant in the basement. Other than removing the boilers in the 1930s and serving the building's heating need from the underground central steam distribution system, the radiators continued to be used successfully until the 1990s.

Wall-mounted or suspended gas lamps in the offices and corridors provided lighting for the original building. With the advent of electric lighting in the late 1800s, the building witnessed the removal of the gas system and the introduction of electric lighting in 1903.

The 1950s saw the building partially air conditioned with the installation of self-contained units in each exterior window, and these units, with periodic replacement, still serve the structure.

The story of the old Executive Office Building is rather typical of the work performed by the engineers at Treasury for the fifty-odd years that they had the responsibility for the design and construction of federal buildings in Washington.

Typical projects designed or supervised by Treasury engineers included:
- The Department of Agriculture Administration Building, designed in 1904 by engineer Franklin Gardner; this building still exists today as the center wing of the Agriculture Building on the north side of Independence Avenue SW.
- The Treasury Building addition by Edward Talcott, the Treasury's chief mechanical engineer.
- Natural History Museum at 12th and Constitution Avenue, designed by engineer Homer Woodbridge 1907.
- The Bureau of Engraving and Printing on 14th Street SW was designed by Marks and Woodwell, Consulting Engineers of New York in 1910.
- The City Main Post Office at North Capitol and Massachusetts Avenue NW designed by Treasury in 1911.
- The Interior Building, now the headquarters of the General Services Administration, at 18th and F Streets NW in 1915.
- The Arlington Building, now the Veterans Administration Building, at Vermont Avenue and H Street NW in 1919.

Typically all these buildings were arranged either as a series of parallel wings extending perpendicularly from a connecting "head-house" or in the form of a hollow donut. The purpose of the configuration was to provide a line of offices on the exterior of each wing, or on the inside and outside of the donut, opening on to a central corridor. With corridor doors and windows on the exterior all open in the summer, a measure of relief by cross-ventilation occurred. A solid door for each office leading to the corridor provided security at night, while a louvered door could be closed during the day to allow air to circulate from office to corridor and provide a measure of privacy.

From coal-fired boilers in the basement of each building, steam at about ten-pounds-per-square-inch pressure circulated up vertical risers to cast-iron radiators under each window, which were fitted with hand valves for "on-off" control by the occupant. Buildings generally were zoned by exposure to north, south, east and west on exterior or interior walls of the donut by the provision of main steam valves in the basement, controlled by master zone thermostats on one of upper floors for each zone.

Many first-class professionals were developed under the apprenticeship employment system in vogue at Treasury. It followed the "old British" way by bringing in promising young people, exposing them to the latest engineering practices and instilling in them a moral and ethical sense of behavior, which is the mark of a "professional." Henry Adams fitted this description to a tee.

Henry Adams (1858-1929)

Chief mechanical engineer in the Office of the Supervising Architect in the Department of the Treasury for twelve years, he left in 1898 to open a private consulting engineering practice in Baltimore, which continued under his name for more than a century. He was president of the American Society of Heating and Ventilating Engineers in 1899.

American Society of Heating and Ventilating Engineers

The society, known as A.S.H.V.E., had been formed five years before in New York as a result of a paper on heating presented by an Englishman named David Nesbit. The paper was so challenging in its conclusions that some of the attendees determined to follow up with other meetings. Invitations were sent to leading engineers throughout the country to join a society dedicated to the knowledge of heating and ventilating, and on September 10, 1894, seventy-five responded and met at the Broadway Hotel in New York. They became the charter members of the new society that included Henry Adams of the Treasury and Homer Addams of Washington, D.C., about whom nothing else is known.

The new society proposed the first ventilation standard in 1896, which recommended minimum amounts of outside air to be brought into buildings. Children should be provided with thirty and adults thirty-three cubic feet of air per minute.

The interest that Treasury employees and the department as a whole showed in A.S.H.V.E speaks well of the professional approach engendered in the government at that time. The art of building design from an environmental point of view was in its infancy. Engineers like Adams had begun to suspect that the interior air quality of buildings, particularly large edifices with relatively tight windows, could be one of the reasons people in the late 1800s were particularly susceptible to influenza. Thus Treasury engineers encouraged the inclusion of the latest innovations in their buildings, particularly the management of heating by the use of the newly invented automatic control systems. These systems, developed by such firms as Johnson Controls, used compressed air in small tubes to convey a signal from a space thermostat to a device, such as a steam valve, in a remote part of the building. Up till that time all of the devices, such as boilers, radiators, water heaters and pumps, had to be started, stopped or adjusted by the hands of a building mechanic who spent his day patrolling the mechanical systems, reading thermometers and pressure gauges, and carefully recording the numbers in a building log. With the invention of automatic controls, the building mechanic's surveillance tasks were reduced from eight hours per shift to about one hour. The use of the new technology released him to be more productive.

To preserve the separation of powers between the Executive Branch and the Legislature, Congress decreed that buildings occupied by staff and other personnel of the two branches be housed in separate buildings. The management, design, maintenance and operation of these buildings should be separate and fall under the jurisdiction of one of the separate branches. Thus the Congressional office buildings used by members of the two houses of Congress and the Capitol Building were not under Treasury jurisdiction.

Congressional Buildings

In his annual report to Congress at the end of 1899, Glenn Brown, the Architect of the Capitol, made reference to an explosion that had rocked the Capitol on November 6, 1898. Considerable damage was done, mainly in the basement. The cause of the explosion was never satisfactorily determined, but it was felt that a leaking gas main was the culprit, so an order was issued to limit the use of gas as much as possible. It was a convenient time since the use of the new lighting medium, electricity, had been tested for a number of years and found to be far superior to the many gas outlets that required daily lighting and service and posed a severe explosion hazard if not properly maintained. The order stipulating that gas should be used in situations that were unavoidable went out, and the program to convert to electric lighting was accelerated.

Homer Woodbridge, a professor from the Massachusetts Institute of Technology in Boston, carefully renovated the mechanical systems of the House of Representatives and the Senate to the satisfaction of the members at the end of the 1800s. One of the keys to Woodbridge's success should be given to the emergence of an automatic controls industry that had begun to develop systems to replace humans for the continuous surveillance of heating apparatuses.

Two boiler plants on the west side of the Capitol, one each for the House and Senate, produced steam and, when unavoidable in the daytime hours, emitted smoke out of one or more of the four main stacks on either side of the Capitol dome. At issue was the kind of coal being burned in the boilers. Since there were two separate boiler plants operated by separate staffs, one for the House and one for the Senate, there were two separate coal contracts for the delivery of coal from different states, as a result of the chairmanship of the committees responsible for placing coal orders. The Senate was furnished with hard coal from Pennsylvania, which burned hotter with minimum smoke and ash, whereas the House used the soft coal from a neighboring state, which gave off quantities of black smoke when the boilers were stoked. The procedure on the House side was to stoke the fires at night, when the smoke was less visible, but the cold winters of the 1870s required the more frequent shoveling of coal into the fireboxes, some in the day time, which led to a negotiation between the House and Senate. To their credit, the legislators agreed that the appearance of the building was of greater import than the need to have separate coal suppliers, so the House switched to Pennsylvania hard coal, but all agreed that this in no way reduced the separation and independence of the two bodies.

Of greater concern to the leaders of both parties were the conditions under which the newer members of both Houses had to compete for office space. The Capitol building originally provided necessary work space for the representatives, but as numbers increased and the size of the staffs needed in a faster-moving world more than doubled, it became obvious to the leadership that additional office space must be added in the form of two new office buildings, one for the House members and one for the Senate. Both Houses passed plans for new buildings, and land—fully built up with residential housing adjacent to the Capitol—was condemned and purchased. Consistent with the separatist construction of the Constitution, wherein the two Houses should be apart and independent, the site for the new Senate office building was placed to the north of the Capitol on Constitution Avenue and First Street NW. The building for members of the House of Representatives was situated more than a quarter of a mile distant to the south on Independence Avenue.

Canon House Office Building

The interest of Congress for additional space came to a head in 1900 with the authorization of a study to determine the extent and probable cost of the proposed new buildings. In 1904 Professor Homer Woodbridge of MIT was again selected to do the mechanical design for a new building, along with architects Carrere and Hastings of New York. The mechanical design included a hot-water heating system with radiators under each window, manually controlled, and the provision of electric lighting and electric-driven ventilation fans throughout. The design was considered to be state-of-the-art.

The design called for a rectangular plan with a hollow center courtyard to allow for the cross-ventilation in the summer, typical of other monumental buildings in the city. Completed in 1907 and providing 397 new offices, it soon became occupied to the point that a fifth floor was added in 1913 to allow for the addition of fifty-one new offices.

Russell Senate Office Building

By 1904 the Senate found itself in the same situation the House had been a few years before, with members renting office space in nearby buildings and taking over committee rooms in an effort to get the people's business done. So in that year a design contract to the same professionals who were working on the new House building was let, and in 1907 Homer Woodbridge had produced a mirror image of the mechanical and electrical system that he had designed for the Canon Building three years before.

The building was designed for operation in the summer, with natural cross-corridor ventilation and open windows on the exterior faces. For operation in the winter, under the window hot-water cast-iron radiation was installed and provided with decorative enclosures and manual control valves. A central ventilation system provided tempered and filtered air from grilles mounted above each corridor door from ductwork suspended above the corridor ceiling

Located on Square 696 of the District of Columbia, the building was bound by B Street to the west (now Independence Avenue), Delaware Avenue, and First and C Streets NE. The building design included a load-bearing masonry wall system with steel beams resting on the walls and supporting poured concrete floors. Structural engineers F. L. Averill and Kort Berle of Washington provided the design. Other consultants included Owen Brainard of New York, Homer Woodbridge Mechanical of Boston, Arthur Ernst, Lighting of New York, and the architect John M. Carrere of New York.

In addition to the state-of-the-art hot-water radiators in each room, electrical conduit laid in the floors provided a system of outlets to serve the desk fans for the comfort of each occupant, and power for the buzzers, clocks and call-bells to alert members to the impending debates and votes to be cast in the Senate Chamber some distance away. At the entrance to each office a wall-mounted telephone with hand crank and polished wooden case, located adjacent to the corridor door, connected the office to a central switchboard. A hand lavatory, with a mirror and hot, cold and iced water faucets, furnished a measure of luxury not seen on the "Hill" before. Central air handling units in the attic furnished tempered air to the corridor ducts in the winter, while windows and the "cross-corridor" doors gave some measure of comfort in summer.

This method of ventilation (air conditioning had not yet been invented) was standard for institutional buildings and dictated, to a large degree, the architectural design of the floor plan. There was simply no way in a climate like Washington's to create interior space separated from the exterior of the structure by partitions and walls, and have the spaces comfortable in the summer. The 1855 design of the Capitol extension, with the Senate and House chambers both surrounded by corridors and offices, was justified on the assumption that Congress would not be in session in the summer, and their separation from exterior walls would be a benefit in the winter. With the advent of air conditioning, the designers were, for the first time, given the flexibility of creating a more efficient use of space, and providing "adjacencies" to minimize travel time and improve communication. The improvement in the quality of the air allowed the size of work spaces to be reduced, and people could work in closer proximity to one another with greater comfort.

Consistent with the thinking of that time, it was decided that a new power plant, providing both heat and electricity for the sole benefit of the Congress, be constructed close to the proposed new buildings.

The Capitol Power Plant, which came on line at the same time as the "New Senate Office Building," delivered electricity to a series of Westinghouse motor-generator sets situated in the basement of the Capitol Building. Each set was driven by a motor that received 125 volts 25-cycle alternating current from the Capitol Power Plant, and was direct connected to a dynamo producing 125 volts direct current for lighting and other purposes in the Capitol Building and the new buildings.

Capitol Power Plant 1906

Concurrent with the provision of additional office space loomed the issue of furnishing the necessary central steam and electric power. The United States Electric Company, USELCO, had built a generating plant at 13th and B Streets NW in 1890 and had marketed the government with minimal success. The White House had constructed its own electric generating plant in 1889. The concept of a "public utility" providing a commodity that was needed by all had not yet emerged in the marketplace. So for several years after the initial steam-engine-driven direct current generators were installed in the Capitol there was movement to provide a larger system for all the houses of the Congress. There was apparently no firm opinion on the extent that electricity in the future would influence people's lives. The discussions amongst some of the representatives were based to some extent on their rural backgrounds, where candles and oil were still the rule. At that time there was in operation a small steam-engine-driven direct current generator in the basement of the Capitol, which provided lighting in the chambers and most of the committee rooms, but the rest of the building still employed gas as a source for lighting. So it was a good sign when, in 1900, Congress decided to build its own generating plant for the production of electricity and heat to serve not only the Capitol, but the proposed new House and Senate office buildings then on the drawing board. The idea of a central heating plant serving a group of buildings had never been done before and was the brainchild of Homer Woodbridge, who presented his study and findings to the Congressional committees, and in 1905 a design authorization for the novel venture emerged.

Owen Brainard, a civil/structural engineer and partner in the firm of Carrere and Hastings, Architects of New York, designed the building and foundations to support the steam turbines and other industrial equipment, while Woodbridge prepared the plans and layouts for the underground steam and electrical distribution on the grounds of the Capitol, as well as the mechanical and electrical work in the power plant.

Together with the Architect of the Capitol, Woodbridge put together a procurement package outlining the requirements of the system, and spent considerable time interviewing prospective designers to determine their qualifications. Many proposals were received and rejected. Woodbridge had to defend the concept before an unconvinced House committee. Finally, the firm of J. G. White, Engineers and Constructors of London, England, were selected to prepare bid packages for the steam heating and electric generating plant and underground distribution piping to analyze the bids and supervise the construction. The selection of J. G. White to be the consulting engineers for the project was not received happily by the engineering fraternity in New York, who felt that the design should be awarded to an American company, and used their considerable weight with their elected representatives to lobby for a reversal of the award. However, J. G. White was up to the task of responding to the pressure and presented letters of support from Babcock & Wilcox, Westinghouse Electric, General Electric, Allis-Chalmers and several other major American manufacturers, all of whom indicated that they would be happy to bid on the project if J. G. White were the designer. White proposed a design fee of three percent of the construction cost, which was negotiated down to two-and-a-half by the superintendent of capitol buildings, Elliott Woods. (42)

The finished plant came on line in 1910 at New Jersey Avenue and E Street SW. It included coal-fired boilers producing steam at sufficiently high pressure to drive four steam turbines, manufactured by C. A. Parsons of England, each directly connected to a 1,000-kilowatt, 25-cycle, 6,500-volt alternating current generator, built by Westinghouse.

Underground cables carried the electricity to the west side of the Capitol building, where the voltage was reduced to 125 volts, through a bank of transformers and fed into the "Dynamo Room" in the basement.

The Dynamo Room housed five motor-generator sets, called dynamos, manufactured by Westinghouse-Church-Kerr of New York. Each dynamo consisted of an electric drive motor connected to a direct current generator. The motors took the 125-volt, 25-cycle current from the transformers and drove the generators to produce 400 kilowatts of electricity at 125 volt D.C, which was used for the lighting in the building. Because of the "flicker" that 25-cycle alternating current causes in an incandescent lamp, the use of D.C. was preferred. (43)

Both the Capitol Power Plant and the Dynamo Room went on line on July 18, 1910, and the Dynamo Room provided direct current to the Capitol until it was shut down on January 11, 1963, by the chief operator, Mr. L. Laser, who first started working at the Capitol on January 6, 1921, and spent his entire career operating the plant.

The entire Capitol complex converted to 60-cycle alternating current power in 1962, as part of the electrical renovations started in 1951 and designed by Mr. George Weschler, consulting engineer. Since the Capitol and other congressional buildings were all converted to operate on 60-cycle (hertz) power, there was nothing that could use the 125-volt direct current produced by the Dynamo Room, so all the motor generators were demolished and removed from the building. The new 60-cycle system included four transformer vaults, each containing three 750 kVA (kilovolt-ampere) 13,200-volt primary transformers that stepped the voltage down to 480 volts for distribution inside the buildings.

At the time of the conversion from direct current to alternating current in 1962, Congress agreed that the Capitol Electric Generating Plant had served its purpose and could be taken out of service. As a result the Potomac Electric Power Company agreed to provide electric power to all buildings as a public utility.

The 1906 turbine-generators in the Capitol Power Plant were shut down and ultimately demolished.

High-pressure boilers in the Capitol Power Plant delivered steam at 250 pounds per square inch into the underground piping, which conveyed it to the Capitol and to the two new office buildings. Steam-pressure-reducing stations at the entrance point to each building dropped the 250-pound pressure to 100 pounds per square inch for distribution to mechanical rooms, where it was further reduced to a using pressure of 15 p.s.i.

The individual boiler plants for the House and the Senate, put on line in 1857 as part of the Capitol expansion, were demolished, including the four masonry stacks on the west front of the Capitol.

The *Evening Star*, on Tuesday, July 25, 1905, wrote, "The unsightly chimneys on the roof of the Capitol are to be removed. This will be done in pursuance to a general plan of improvement, renovation, and repair of the big white building prepared by Superintendent Elliott Woods for the reception of the Fifty-ninth Congress."

Longworth House Office Building 1930

The addition of the Cannon Building in 1904 solved the issue of the need for additional office space for members of the House of Representatives until the end of the First World War in 1919. At that point it became clear to the leadership that another addition to Capitol Hill was inevitable. In 1925 the Congress approved the condemnation of additional private housing west of New Jersey Avenue at Independence Avenue, and voted to approve the construction of a second House office building similar in design to the Canon

Building across the street. A consortium of local architects put together a partnership to seek the project, with George Weschler as the mechanical and electrical engineer. Weschler was well-known as the chair of engineering at Catholic University and had established a consulting engineering firm in the District a few years earlier. He had a solid reputation as an engineer on the leading edge of design in the building industry.

Allied Architects and Weschler were selected to do the project, which was bid on October 23, 1930 and awarded to Consolidated Engineering Company of Baltimore for an amount of $5,270,000.

It was fortunate that the need for new federal buildings and the provision of much needed space for the Congress occurred at a time when the theory of air conditioning was in the process of development. Studies showed that humans feel comfortable at different temperatures and degrees of humidity depending on the activity. And there was little question that spending the day working in an office where the indoor temperature could rise well above 95 degrees Fahrenheit was not conducive to long-term concentration and high productivity.

Willis Carrier had spent much of his professional career developing the science of "psychometrics," which could be used to calculate the relationships between the temperature of air and the amount of moisture that can be carried in air at different degrees of relative humidity. With this tool he began to devise various types of "air-handling" equipment with which he could heat air and add moisture, thereby increasing its humidity. Similarly he experimented with apparatuses that could cool moist air, causing it to "condense," just like mist forming on a cool day.

By actually experimenting with groups of test subjects under various conditions of temperature and humidity, a pattern emerged, showing that the majority of normally dressed humans felt most comfortable in a range of temperatures from about 68 to 78 degrees Fahrenheit when the humidity measured about fifty percent. With this data confirmed Carrier began to manufacture equipment about the time that the Congress became aware of the advantage of indoor climate control.

Plate 12 – 1
Cannon House Office Building
Constructed between 1904 and 1907, it had an area of 671,000 square feet; built before the invention of air-conditioning, its layout conformed to the plan with a center corridor and offices on either side to allow cross-ventilation in the summer; a fifth floor was added in 1913 and air-conditioning in 1937

Plate 12 – 2
Capitol Power Plant, 1910
The power plant came on line in 1907 and included steam turbine-driven, 25-hertz electric generators that provided the alternating current to the Dynamo Room in the basement of the Capitol, where it changed to direct current to serve the building; the plate shows an interior view of the engine room with the turbo-generators and condensers on the rear wall

Plate 12 - 3
Dynamo Room in the U.S. Capitol
View of the five motor-generator sets that each generated 3,200 amps at 125 volts
direct current and supplied all lighting and power to the Capitol Building from July
18, 1910 until the conversion to 60-hertz alternating current on January 11, 1963

Plate 12 - 4
Old Executive Office Building
Constructed between 1871 and 1888, it was the largest office building in the city
with an area of 640,000 square feet

Plate 12 - 5
Structural Frame of the Justice Department Building, 1930
Typical of the Federal buildings designed by the Public Buildings Administration in the Federal Triangle, the Justice Building shows the innovative use of reinforced concrete on the lower floors and structural steel on the upper floors

Plate 12 - 6
Preparation of the Site for New Federal Buildings, 1928
Housing and commercial enterprises between Pennsylvania Ave. and Constitution Ave. have been condemned and the site cleared ready to receive new underground water and sewer; the old post office to the rear remains today as a symbol of 19th century Washington; photographed from the roof of the Central Market on 9th Street

Plate 12 - 7
Washington Monument, 1928
Started in 1848, it was completed in 1885

13 . . . Civil Engineering
1900 – 1940

With the building of Washington's infrastructure, discussed in Chapter 10, and the arrival of major new buildings and utility systems to serve the Congress, included in Chapter 12, we now should look at a parallel field of engineering events that occurred in the city in the first half of the twentieth century, designed by civil engineers.

Civil engineering, the outgrowth of military engineering of the 1700s, initially dealt with those aspects of construction that were non-warlike. It had nothing to do with moats around castles or fortifications, but was needed to support the peaceable elements vital for the conduct of peace after the end of conflict. Perhaps a simpler way to express the differences between the two kinds of engineering is to look at the needs of any society surviving a military conflict and entering a time of peace. The war is over and now we need to build those things that support and enhance the life style for which the war was all about in the first place.

Civil engineering, therefore, brings an art to the table of human concern and provides answers to vexing problems that are in need of a solution. The quality of the water we drink, the disposal of the waste we generate, and the need to cross a river or tunnel through a mountain are all issues that challenge the civil engineer. The city of Washington, on the banks of a mile-wide river, initially regarded the challenge of river crossing as a minor event, dealt with by the building of ferries and other means of sailing. But as the city developed and the need to have fluent transportation across the river and other ravines became obvious, the skill of the civil engineer was called on to provide a solution.

Initially the art of civil engineering included the management of water systems—canals, aqueducts and flood control—but with the invention of cast iron and, later, steel, the direction of the profession changed dramatically. Civil engineering began to explore the feasibility of using the new materials to create metal frames and beams that could span between supporting foundations, over far greater distances than was possible using the traditional materials of stone and wood. The invention of the rivet, a metal pin that when heated red hot could be hammered into different shapes, allowed metal plates and beams to be joined to resist very substantial separating forces. Out of this experience there developed the art of metal bridge construction and the erection of heavy metal frames strong enough to support multi-story buildings.

As has been typical of engineering in general, the practice of civil engineering began to gradually develop into two allied but separate fields of professional endeavor. Civil engineering moved toward the retention of the art of bringing improvements to the outdoors, in such areas as roads, bridges, water distribution, sanitary and storm water management, and, of course, the construction of massive dams to retain and control rivers. The second field of structural engineering began to concentrate on the scientific application of materials, mainly steel, to allow the erection of all manner of structures. The key to this new art form was the use of applied mathematics to predict the load-carrying capacity of a proposed design, building in factors of safety, but using the optimum quantities of material to maintain minimum cost.

It was these two interlocking professions that allowed the city of Washington to plan for ways to cross the Potomac River and other ravines, and bring these plans to fruition.

William Howard Taft Bridge

Heading north up Connecticut Avenue just above Columbia Road, one comes to a ravine several hundred feet deep through which Rock Creek gently flows on its way to the Potomac River. Spanning the ravine is an elegant structure of arches and massive columns, all cast-concrete, done in a soft gray with balusters and what appears to be old gas lamps at each end. This is the William Howard Taft Bridge, better known to the residents of Washington as the Connecticut Avenue Bridge. Until 1907 Connecticut Avenue stopped at the south rim of the ravine, and travelers had to turn off to the right and take Belmont Road down a winding path to the bottom and cross the creek on a wrought-iron truss named Thompson's Bridge, built in 1888. The path then wound up the other side of the ravine to a rural road that headed into the countryside. L'Enfant's original plan had the northern boundary of the city ending at Rock Creek without consideration for the future expansion.

While the truss bridge served the purpose in summer, the often icy and muddy inclines in winter became a hazard, to the point that the District Government in 1895 initiated a competition for designs for a more permanent structure that would avoid the hills and meet the needs of traffic, particularly the recently invented horseless carriage. In 1897 the winner turned out to be a local architect, George Morrison, whose scheme called for five main arches, each with a span of 150 feet, supported on columns that extended down to the creek bottom more than two hundred feet below.

The structural design fell under the supervision of the District Bridge Division, whose chief engineer, Colonel John Biddle, is given credit for the project. Several methods of conforming to the aesthetic design of the spans were examined, including the use of a structural steel frame clad with limestone sheets as one option, and the use of concrete reinforced with steel rods following the curvature of the arches. It was finally decided to use unreinforced concrete poured into wooden molds shaped to produce the gentle arches required by the design.

Lack of sufficient funding caused the construction to drag out from its beginning in 1897 to the completion in 1907. Of some curiosity is the artificial stone facing used to cover and give a finished appearance to the arches and columns. Local granitelike stone, crushed and mixed with cement and cast into preformed molds, yielded slabs of finished stone that could be anchored to the concrete surfaces of the arches and used for corners, moldings and balusters that ran the full length of the 1,300-foot-long span. The Taft Bridge is a good example of the marriage of architecture and structural engineering, each playing their roles to produce a piece of art, attractive, safe and economical.

Today the bridge, like many of today's innovations, has melded into the scenery, and is an attractive emotional connection between "old" Washington of the late 1800s and "new" Washington of the twentieth century. Crossing over, the visitor is aware of the cast bronze light fixtures, the drop to the creek below, the ease of spanning a formidable gorge, the safety of the passage, and the easy acceptance of engineering solutions.

Key Bridge

In an earlier chapter the task of a crossing the Potomac River and extending the C & O Canal to allow barges from Cumberland to avoid the Port of Georgetown was presented. This river crossing was accomplished by constructing an elevated waterway named the Aqueduct Bridge, sized to permit barges to sail across the river.

A 1915 analysis by the Corps of Engineers of the condition of the old Aqueduct Bridge, which spanned the Potomac between Georgetown and Rosslyn, on the Virginia side, revealed its condition to be so poor that further repair would be uneconomical, so its replacement was decided and work on a new span began in 1916.

In keeping with the experiences learned about the potential for serious flooding of the Potomac River basin, the design included raising the roadbed some thirty feet higher than the Aqueduct Bridge, and the construction of novel reinforced concrete arched spans, which made it one of the forerunners of poured-in-place concrete bridges in the country.

The original design consisted of eight massive concrete caissons, or foundations, to be poured in place into the riverbed and onto the shores at either end, followed by seven concrete arches on which columns, supporting the roadway above, were erected. Included in the substructure under the roadway were the wiring and power that fed the electric streetcar tracks of the Capital Transit Company. The Georgetown line terminated in Rosslyn, with a "turn-around" just beyond the end of the bridge.

With connector roads complete, the span opened for traffic in 1923. It was extended with an additional arch twenty years later to accommodate the George Washington Parkway, then under construction on the Virginia side of the river. Further modification occurred in 1949 with the construction of a connector ramp to the Whitehurst Freeway, and the addition of two traffic lanes in 1970, which caused the bridge to be widened. During this renovation the abandoned Capital Transit tracks were removed.

The bridge is named after a young Baltimore lawyer, Francis Scott Key, who represented the new United States in a civil case against the British in the War of 1812 and was held temporarily aboard one of their warships during their assault on Baltimore. On the night of September 13, 1814, standing on the deck of a ship, he watched the bombardment of Fort McHenry, and by the dawn of the next day was filled with emotion and joy to see the American flag still gently blowing in the wind above the fort. The excitement of the moment prompted him to pen the words to a poem titled "The Star Spangled Banner," which, set to music, became the National Anthem of the United States. Congress saw fit to name the new crossing of the Potomac after the young man.

Key Bridge is a good example of the transition of civil engineering from a comprehensive art that included the practice of hydraulics, roads and engineering structures of all types, into the two specialties known today as civil and structural engineering.

Key Bridge is also a piece of dynamic art, pleasant to view, but more fascinating to study as it melds with the varying elevations and curvatures of the roads to which it connects on both sides of the river. The purpose of a bridge, obviously, is to provide for movement of human and animal systems from one side of a barrier to the other. Judged on that basis Key Bridge is a success. But engineering goes beyond the simple solution. Not only must the basic purpose be attained, but the solution must employ the least expensive, safest, most permanent, maintainable materials, arranged to deliver a solution that has the lowest total "life-cycle" cost. The life-cycle cost is the sum of the initial cost of construction added to the annual costs necessary to keep the design in satisfactory working condition beginning in the first year of its use and ending when there is a better solution to the problem, many years away. Judged on the basis of life-cycle cost, Key Bridge is a successful piece of engineering.

Downstream from Key Bridge, the western end of L'Enfant's grand plaza was originally planned to terminate about where the Washington Monument sits today. The Potomac River at that time stretched to the shores of Virginia in a mix of swamps and main streams almost a mile wide. The work of Colonel Haines in the late 1800s reclaimed all of the swamps on both sides of the river and extended the buildable land sufficiently to allow the planning and construction of the Lincoln Memorial and a system of highways to connect the District of Columbia to Virginia.

Arlington Memorial Bridge

Arlington Memorial Bridge was one of the pieces added to Pierre L'Enfant's plan for the city of Washington. The original plan, conceived more than a hundred years before, did not consider the impact of motorized highway traffic and the demands that it would have on the connecting roads leading to Virginia. A bridge across the Potomac in the vicinity of Arlington Cemetery had been the subject of planning for years, and in 1901 the final location was determined to be an extension of L'Enfant's grand plaza, lined up on the axis extending from the Capitol Building to the Washington Monument. One end of the proposed bridge would abut the Lincoln Memorial, and to the west the other end would look toward an historic building, the Lee Mansion, overlooking the Arlington Cemetery. The cemetery, one of the most hallowed cites in the nation's capital, was the final resting place of citizens who had lost their lives in the defense of the United States.

A design for the proposed bridge by architects McKim, Meade and White received approval by Congress in 1924, and with federal funding construction began. Completed in 1932, the structure presented a multi-span, reinforced, concrete arch bridge with granite facing and double bascule spans that permitted light naval vessels, tugs and sand barges to enter Georgetown until the 1970s. Since then the spans have remained closed in deference to the pleadings of motorists attempting to enter the district via the George Washington Parkway. In consideration of the needs for military vehicles to have access from bases in Virginia, the outer lanes have the capability of supporting forty-ton tanks over the maximum arch span of 184 feet. The bridge crosses the Potomac with a length of 2,138 feet.

The concept of the "bascule" allows a roadway or bridge element to be raised and lowered, like a seesaw, with a counter weight at the other end, thereby greatly reducing the force necessary to raise the bridge beam. In the case of the Arlington Memorial Bridge, the counter weights and machinery necessary to enable the spans to be raised and lowered are housed in mechanical equipment rooms fitted into the bases of the main arches, and powered by electric motors served by underwater cables.

The three engineering projects presented in this chapter were not only successful from a technical point of view, they were also constructed without major interference from the public sector and members of elected institutions. Perhaps this was because their presence was obviously in tune with the needs of the majority of users and the legislative bodies overseeing the projects. The same cannot be said about the arrival of commercial aviation to the city.

Since its phenomenal birth in Kitty Hawk, North Carolina in 1903, the development of aircraft had been primarily propelled by its use as a weapon of war between 1914 and 1918, and subsequently funded by the military through the 1920s. Small private companies emerged whose interest lay in the development of two-seater biplanes for recreational and special purposes such as surveying and forest surveillance. It was in this context that the Congress in 1926 passed a prohibition against government involvement in commercial aviation. It was up to cities and the private sector to sponsor and build the necessary infrastructure to support an aviation industry.

In Washington's case, two private entrepreneurs obtained permission to use vacant land on the south bank of the Potomac River as adjacent airports. Hoover Field and Washington Airport operated side by side until their merger in 1930 and remained the only airfield catering to civilian traffic in the region until Washington National Airport emerged ten years later.

Washington National Airport

In the 1920s and '30s the site where the Pentagon now sits was the location of Washington's airport. The south bank of the Potomac had been filled in by the Corps of Engineers in the 1890s, and by the 1920s the flat, grass-covered field provided an airstrip quite suitable for small biplanes to land and take off safely over the river while avoiding the more densely populated portions of the city. The first airport, Hoover Field, opened in 1926, followed in 1927 by the adjacent Washington Airport, and then, in 1930, both facilities merged into the Washington-Hoover Airport. The new entity provided air service through the 1930s, but with the development of larger airplanes specifically designed to haul passengers, it became obvious that the limited runway length precluded the introduction of the newer aircraft, while the passenger terminal facilities were wholly inadequate for commercial purposes.

One of the main curiosities of the airport was the fact that the runway intersected a public roadway, which meant that civilian police had to shut down the roadway with barriers on each side of the runway before every takeoff and landing.

By the mid-1930s the need to consider a national airport worthy of the nation's capital had gained momentum. Many sites were considered, both close to the existing airport and down Route 1 to sites in Virginia and to Camp Springs, Maryland, the present site of a military airport. The science of air traffic control was in its infancy, including the necessity of adequate approach, landing, takeoff and holding patterns. Many studies were performed, and those that suggested the siting of the proposed facility near to Chantilly, Virginia, some twenty-five miles from the Capitol, as an ideal location were summarily rejected by the Congress as being too far to travel. More studies and more rejection and deliberation by Congressional committees finally led to the repeal of the law precluding the federal government from operating commercial airfields.

In 1937 President Roosevelt gave the issue of site selection to the Civil Aeronautics Board, and requested that they take an unbiased look at all the proposed sites based on the best safety and long-range information they could assemble. Surveys by the Corps of Engineers indicated that the quality of materials beneath the silt on the banks of the Potomac were suitable to allow filling in the low-lying areas with crushed stone and gravel.

The sand and gravel lying just below water level had been washed by years of flowing water, which had removed non-compatible organic material and left the easily excavated rock-based strata ideal for the foundation of airport runways. Curiously enough, the site was known as Gravelly Point, probably named by fishermen of a bygone age who trudged over the washed gravel to reach a reasonable casting point. Overlooking the site for the proposed runways was a hill on which, in 1746, the Alexander family had owned a mansion, and years later had donated the land and mansion to the federal government.

With the approval of site selection, construction began in the spring of 1939. The first order of business was to construct a coffer dam, or dike, around the site in order to separate it from the river, and then pump it dry so that machinery and workers could gain access to 600 acres that would be occupied by the airfield. Next, trenches, approximately 200 feet in width, were dug under what would be the future runways, removing all silt and unstable material down to solid subsurface. The site was then filled with stable sand and gravel compacted to the point that it could support the proposed forces of a large aircraft landing and taxiing to the terminal.

Once the filling was at a safe elevation, the dam was opened and the river attempted to reclaim the land, but to no avail, the massive landfill operation was a success and the future runways remained dry. (24)

Next came the terminal building together with the first of eleven hangars, and the airport opened for business in 1942. A central oil-fired heating plant on the hilltop behind the terminal building generated high temperature water, at 350 degrees Fahrenheit, which circulated through underground, insulated steel pipe to the main building and the hangars. Large floor-mounted blower-coil units provided heat for the hangars and kept the "deluge" fire-protection system from freezing. The deluge system, invented to serve facilities like aircraft hangars, consisted of a number of large nozzles high in the roof structure, fed by several vertical water pipes, each six inches in diameter and arranged so that, in the event of a sensor detecting the beginnings of a fire, valves would automatically open and cause a flood of water to rain down from the ceiling and quench the fire below.

The original 1942 Main Terminal Building included air conditioning, with air-handling equipment and distribution ductwork served with chilled water from a local plant. Heating used steam generated by heat exchangers that allowed the 350-degree-high-temperature water to transfer heat and evaporate low-temperature water into steam, which was then used in the heating coils of the air handlers. An interesting aesthetic feature of the terminal building resulted from the use of thirty-foot-high structural glass panels on the airfield side, which afforded the traveler an uninterrupted view of airplanes landing and taking off and of the city of Washington in the background, with the dome of the Capitol dominating the skyline.

After the war, with the rapid growth in commercial air transport, passenger capacity of the facility soon became inadequate. The North Terminal opened in 1958, followed by a new South Terminal in 1966. Then the north hangar was renovated into a new Main Passenger Terminal in the late 1980s, and finally the entire airport received a major renovation in 1996, with the construction of a new main terminal, parking and roadway enhancements.

Plate 13-1
Key Bridge, 1923
Showing the original seven arches and the bridge running straight from
Georgetown to Virginia, with four lanes of traffic; the remains of the Aqueduct
Bridge are just visible above the third arch from the left

Plate 13 -2
Key Bridge, 1975
Showing the bridge expanded to eight arches to allow the George Washington
Parkway to run through below and widened to allow for six lanes of traffic
and sidewalks for pedestrians on both sides

Plate 13 - 3
Arlington Memorial Bridge, circa 1940
Completed in 1932 and erected on a curve connecting the Lincoln Memorial with
the Lee Mansion in the Arlington National Cemetery, the bridge served a dual role
as a memorial to the men and women who had given their lives in service to the
nation and as a piece of engineering art to honor those services; the two massive
piers contain the machinery for opening and closing the bascules and allowing
shipping to enter the Port of Georgetown

Plate 13-4
Chain Bridge, 1938
This continuous steel girder bridge was the seventh to be built across the narrows at Little Falls on the Potomac between 1797 and 1938; it has a length of 1350 feet and clears the normal river surface by forty-five feet

Plate 13 - 5
Washington National Airport, August 1939
Showing the filling operation approximately 60 percent complete; a dredger at the bottom of the photo is pumping fill onto the site from the Potomac River

Plate 13-6
Washington National Airport, October 1940
The runways are complete and the fill has raised the elevation of the site above the
flood level of the Potomac River; main terminal building and adjacent hangars
are under construction

Plate 13-7
Virginia Avenue, 1880
Virginia Ave. heads for Georgetown and the Gas Works; the abandoned Washington
Canal runs by the Van Ness residence, now the clubhouse for a sporting and
athletic club; the gatekeeper's house stands where it does today on 17th Street

Plate 13-8
Virginia Avenue, 1950
Constitution Avenue replaces the Washington Canal; World War temporary buildings
occupy L'Enfant Plaza; Pan American Union building replaces Van Ness residence

Plate 13-9
The Mall looking East, 1950
The Navy and munitions buildings are on the left, with World War II temporary
buildings on the right flanking the reflecting pool and the Lincoln Memorial

14 . . . AIR CONDITIONING THE CAPITOL OF THE UNITED STATES

The Origin of Air Conditioning

Cotton continued to be a major agricultural occupation in the southern states of the Union at the beginning of the twentieth century. From 960,000 tons in 1860 the annual yield ranged slightly above 2.5 million tons in the years before 1910.

Typically handpicked in the fields, it was brought into sheds, thrown on large, flat, wooden tables and cleaned of field debris. The price the grower received depended on several factors, one of which was the moisture content of the fibers. If the cotton tested too dry, the fibers would not hold together and would become brittle, resulting in breakage during the spinning process. To help solve this problem, just before baling the cotton was "conditioned" by spraying it with fine jets of water and simultaneously tossing it up in the air with pitchforks, and in so doing a measure of moisture could be added to the dry cotton. If one was careful to uniformly and lightly spray the cotton and diligently toss it until it was conditioned, all was well. However excess moisture in a bale stored for any length of time would cause decay and the harboring of insects. Too little water or uneven spraying left the product subject to considerable attention in the mills.

In 1906, Stuart Cramer of Charlotte, North Carolina, a mechanical engineer and contractor in the cotton industry, met with a man named Willis Carrier, who worked for the Buffalo Forge Company in Syracuse, New York. Buffalo Forge, an old line company and manufacturer of fans, pumps and air-handling equipment, had hired Willis Carrier some years before, and recognizing his inventive spirit, made him head of the research department of the company. On this occasion, Cramer and Carrier discussed the theory of moisture in air under various temperatures, and Carrier gave details of his findings and equipment.

In 1907 Cramer presented a paper to the National Cotton Manufacturers Association in which he described his success in maintaining the moisture content of the baled cotton in warehouses and mills by controlling and maintaining the humidity of the air in the buildings constant, and at a level that precluded drying. He accomplished the process by circulating warm air through sheetmetal ducts suspended at the ceiling of the mill.

To make the air warm and moist, it was circulated through a large sheetmetal box, fitted with heated water sprays that caused the air to pick up heat and moisture. Then a fan pumped the air into the ductwork, which distributed it throughout the mill. This process, he maintained, eliminated the hit-and-miss process of "conditioning" the cotton with manual sprays. He called the new method *air conditioning*. This event marks the beginning of the recognition of air conditioning as a distinct art in the field of mechanical engineering. (44)

The first years of air conditioning were directed mainly at industry. The printing process was very humidity dependent, and many studies and applications were devised to maintain a more constant interior climate using the Carrier "Apparatus for Treating Air," for which he received a patent in 1906.

Typically in the process of printing, an environment so dry that allowed the fluid in the ink to evaporate too rapidly caused the type to appear to separate and become nonuniform. Conversely, if the printing plant were too humid, the ink evaporation process slowed to the point that the printing speed had to be reduced.

Experience with auditoriums and the Houses of Congress indicated that humans were sensitive to both the temperature and the humidity of the occupied space. To properly control both temperature and the amount of moisture in a given space required a source of heat to raise the space temperature and, if the space humidity were too low, to evaporate water to allow it to turn into a vapor and diffuse with the air.

By contrast, if the space humidity was too high, then a source of cooling was required to reduce the temperature and cause the humidity to "condense," that is turn to water, and be drained off.

Thus, for a year-round air conditioning system to be practical, there had to be reliable sources of both heat and cooling available on demand.

Air Conditioning the Capitol

Mechanical refrigeration was an established industry in the United States at the end of the nineteenth century, employing steam-engine-driven ammonia compressors for the production of ice and for cooling in the food and beverage industry.

The first attempt to provide comfort cooling for the U.S. Capitol was made by Henry Adams, consulting engineer of Baltimore, Maryland. Adams, formerly Chief Mechanical Engineer of the Treasury Department, had opened an engineering firm in Baltimore in 1898, and in 1906 prepared a design for a system of mechanical cooling for the House of Representatives. It included two electric motors with belt drives to two single-cylinder horizontal compressors. The design included a spray-type condenser to convert the high-pressure refrigerant gas to a liquid, and cooling coils where the air was cooled and dehumidified before being pumped back to the House Chamber by a large, motor-driven centrifugal fan. (45)

Typical of designs prepared in that era, the drawings contained notes stipulating that the "Contractor is to check all dimensions at the Building, and to be responsible for all measurements and details." The drawing showed a *design*. In this respect it is remarkable because it shows with clarity what was expected of a professional engineering design in 1906, and by default what was left to the constructor, who was both a builder and an engineer. The "details" referenced in the notes covered those elements, engineering calculations and sizing *required of the contractor's engineers and performed by the installing mechanics.*

As far as is known, Henry Adams's design was never implemented, but it is beyond doubt that in 1906 engineers were capable of designing comfort-cooling systems.

The pressure to improve the indoor conditions at the Capitol continued over the next few years with the invention of better equipment and, in particular, control systems that could do the work of several building operators more accurately and for much less cost. So, in 1918, the Senate of the United States authorized the preparation of a set of specifications and drawings covering an "Air Supply and Exhaust, Air Conditioning, Refrigerating and Ozonating Apparatus" to be bid by selected contractors and equipment suppliers. The specifications ran some fifty-one pages, covering in as few words as possible the minimum provisions on which the offerors should base their bids.

Two compressors of the "double-acting fly-wheel type" were required, each having a cooling capacity of 175 tons of refrigeration, using carbon-dioxide as the refrigerant, and driven by variable-speed electric motors through "leather belts of approved construction." The motors were required to operate at different speeds, from 250 to 500 revolutions per minute, in eight steps, initiated by "field weakening for the first 20 per cent, and armature resistance for the balance."

The system included 40,000-cubic-feet-per-minute supply and exhaust fans, spray washers for cooling the air, and cast-iron "cored extension" heating sections for warming the cold air in the winter, with separate sections for providing heat to each cloak room, corridor, and the chamber. Controls were operated by compressed air provided by two motor-driven air compressors, and included thermostats, air-operated valves for modulating the steam and hot water, and automatic dampers of sheet steel for the control of air.

Quality control was maintained by the liberal use of manufacturers' names; pipe should be A. M. Byers, unions should be Kewanee, valves Lunkenheimer, steam traps Crane, and gaskets Garlock, to name just a few. The project was bid on April 10, 1920, and the W. G. Cornell Company of Washington was the low bidder with a price of $236,730.00. Cornell, as was the custom at that time, offered the owner various alternatives for using products and manufacturers whose prices were higher than those on which the bid was based. The result was that the mix of manufacturers and products selected by the Congress exceeded the available funding, and the project was put on hold.

In the light of the rapid development in the air conditioning industry, the Senate decided to postpone their project and called in the Carrier Air Conditioning Company to investigate the feasibility of providing cooling to both Houses of the Congress.

In 1921 Carrier responded with a design of an air conditioning system for the Houses of Congress, but it was not built because a satisfactory refrigeration machine had not yet been invented. Carrier Air Conditioning Company at that time was working on the design of a centrifugal compressor that used a nontoxic refrigerant, and in 1925 announced that a Centrifugal Refrigerating Machine had been invented and tested. It cooled water to a temperature sufficiently low that it could remove the moisture from air and maintain comfortable conditions in an occupied space, and was considerably smaller than the reciprocating compressors in vogue at that time.

To accomplish satisfactory air motion in the chambers of both the Senate and the House of Representatives, the method of air distribution, which had been such a problem beginning in 1857, had to be revised again. This time the air was to be delivered from above and allowed to mix with the air in the chambers so that the representatives were unaware of the cooling and did not sense drafts. This approach had been successfully used in a movie theater in Los Angeles and became the accepted design for air distribution in an auditorium. Carrier made a proposal to David Lynn, architect of the Capitol in 1926, and a contract to provide air conditioning to the two Houses of Congress was awarded to the Carrier Air Conditioning Company. The completed House system went on line in December 1928, and the Senate in August 1929. (46)

Two of Carrier's new centrifugal refrigeration machines, located in the basement of the Capitol, provided the cooling. The Senate equipment had a capacity of 176 tons of refrigeration when cooling 600 gallons of water per minute. The compressor was rated at 250 horsepower, on 220-volt 3-phase, 25-cycle current, and driven at 1,450 r.p.m. The motor was a variable-speed type, rheostat-controlled and capable of a 25 percent turndown in speed, which in turn reduced the compressor capacity by 60 percent. The operator manually maintained the machine output by watching the temperature of the water leaving the cooler. If the temperature fell a degree or two he knew the cooling load had declined, so he gradually slowed the machine down until the temperature returned to 42 degrees Fahrenheit. If the water temperature went up, he knew the cooling load was increasing, so he speeded the compressor up to bring the water down to its optimum value.

An electric, motor-driven pump circulated the chilled water through the refrigeration cooler and then to the sprays in the air-handling unit.

The heat absorbed by the chilled water in the air-handling unit sprays was removed during the refrigeration process and rejected to the condenser. Here water picked up this heat and conveyed it to a blow-through-type cooling tower with sprays and a large fan, all situated in the basement of the Capitol. The condenser water was cooled by the evaporative cooling process, the same process as was used in the air-handling units, except the temperatures were higher, which allowed outside air at 95 degrees to cool the condenser water to a level suitable for reuse by the chiller plant. The air for the cooling towers was drawn from a courtyard and discharged up an unused chimney shaft.

The air-handling units serving the Senate side of the Capitol included a main unit for the chamber and a unit for the cloakrooms and offices. Each was of the open spray type perfected by Carrier. The air-handling units were of the field-erected type, with sheetmetal casings, insulated on the outside with asbestos sheets, and finished with metal lath and plaster, painted white. Automatic outside air and return dampers were installed to regulate the amount of air passing through the unit, and were adjusted to increase the ventilation to the building during occupied hours, and reduce it to a minimum when the air conditioned spaces were unoccupied. Also installed in the casings were preheat steam coils, filters for the removal of airborne dust and lint, and steam reheat coils controlled by room thermostats for the maintenance of room temperatures.

Injecting more or less chilled water into the sump under the sprays controlled the cooling capacity of the air-handling unit. Under a zero-cooling-load condition the spray pump circulated water from the sump through the spray nozzles and then back to the sump. When the return air from the occupied spaces began to warm up, indicating the presence of heat in the space, a thermostat in the air sensed the slight rise in temperature and opened a valve to allow chilled water to enter the sump and mix with the water in the sump, gradually reducing the mix temperature and thereby the spray temperature, which then cooled the air passing through and sent it to the supply grilles serving the chambers. In this manner the open spray system was able to accurately track the change in cooling requirements and maintain an essentially constant temperature in the summer.

In the winter the thermostat controlled a steam valve, and on a fall in return air temperature gradually heated the spray water, thereby providing not only heat but also moisture in the air to raise the space humidity.

In keeping with the thinking prevailing in 1929, humans did not want a constant space temperature throughout the year, so the system was designed to maintain interior conditions of 80 degrees dry-bulb when the outdoors was 95 dry-bulb and 78 wet-bulb. At 90 degrees outdoors the inside was set for 78 degrees. At 85 degrees outdoors; inside was 75. This gradual reduction followed until at full heating the indoor temperature was maintained at 70. Summer humidities were of the order of 55 percent, while in winter they were 49 to 45 percent.

The system serving the House of Representatives was identical in design to that in the Senate, but the capacity was greater; the chiller was rated for 210 tons of refrigeration and the fan was proportionately larger.

It should be noted here that closed-circuit finned coils, to be used in lieu of open sprays, were in the process of development but emerged on the market in 1940.

The House and the Senate were each served by five air-handling systems. Systems H1 for the House and S1 for the Senate provided air to the floor of the chamber; system 2 served the gallery; system 3 served the cloakrooms; and 5 the press areas. System 4 was a constant-volume unit providing cooling to the attic space above the glass ceilings, and in so doing Carrier separated the units dedicated to offsetting solar and transmission heat gains from those dedicated to providing cooling and ventilation to the occupants of the various spaces. Smoking was allowed in the cloak rooms, so those systems were capable of bringing in almost all outside air to dilute the odor effects.

The units were located in the basement, and sheetmetal ducts conveyed the cooled and dehumidified air across the ceilings to vertical shafts, where the ducts were placed in unused chimneys and shafts and distributed in the attic to a system of ductwork that was required to meet special requirements. Firstly, the appearance of the cast-iron ceilings should be preserved. It was felt that the introduction of grilles or diffusers would change the features of the cast-iron ceiling to a degree that could not be permitted. Secondly, the installation of ducts in the attic above the glass ceiling should not cast shadows on the milk-white glass, either in the daytime when there was bright sun, or at night when the many incandescent lamps were active.

Two fortunate elements solved the first problem. The ceiling height above the floor was thirty-six feet, and with this height it was possible to introduce the cold air in solid streams rather than the trusted method of causing diffusion by the use of high-velocity supply from supply air devices. It was also discovered that the decorative covers and ceiling surrounds were all bolted construction, and that it was possible to loosen the bolts and separate the covers from the base, thereby creating a slot through which air could be discharged. Specially constructed headers were mounted against the slots and connected to the distribution ducts in such a manner that the incandescent light bulbs, exposed in the attic, were not shielded by the headers, nor did they cast a shadow at the edge of the ceiling.

The second problem was solved by using a multiplicity of smaller ducts, white painted, running at the underside of the roof skylight, parallel with the trusses, with vertical drops from time to time down to the headers mentioned before. The new reflective ducts increased the general light level in the attic to a more even level than before, so that the uniformity of light over the lower glass was improved.

Installation of main ducts in the basement to the risers in some cases provided a real challenge. It was found that there was insufficient space at the ceilings, which required the careful removal of old walls and piping and, in one case, the tunneling through an eight-foot-thick blue stone wall, which took two men eighteen days to complete. A duct riser, destined to be run up an abandoned boiler stack, required the removal of two layers of smoke-contaminated brick liner to eliminate the pervasive smell of soot and burned oils, and relining the stack with cement plaster. All ductwork was field measured, piece by piece, and then installed by mechanics suspended in the stack and working from the inside of the duct. A system of new return ducts was installed under the floor of each chamber, with low return grilles, and this, coupled with the slow movement of air down from the ceiling slots, gave the spaces a feeling of freshness even when fully occupied. (47)

Upon completion of construction, the systems were balanced to maintain temperatures of plus or minus one degree Fahrenheit in all parts of both chambers, and the air motion checked with candles mounted on the representatives desks to indicate uniform but draft-free air motion

The balance of the Capitol received air conditioning in 1936, designed by Charles Leopold (1896-1960) of Philadelphia, one of the most prolific and recognized consulting engineers in the heating and cooling industry, and George Weschler of Washington. Carrier Air Conditioning Company was the contractor and furnished equipment similar to that installed in the chambers eight years before. The rotunda, the circular reception area under the dome, was also provided with air conditioning from a unit in the basement. Supply ducts threaded through a maze of abandoned shafts and closets and emerged through the roof beside the original brick wall of the 1819 Bulfinch Dome. They then rose up to the Peristyle Level and penetrated the cast-iron wall to distribute air almost a hundred feet above the floor.

Capitol Central Refrigeration Plant

The House of Representatives was air conditioned in 1926 by Willis Carrier, and the Senate in 1929. Then in 1936 the balance of the Capitol received cooling for the first time, but the 1926 chiller plant was inadequate to serve the entire building, so a decision was made to erect a new cooling plant, adjacent to the Capitol Heating Plant on New Jersey Avenue, which would have sufficient capacity to take care of all the buildings on Capitol Hill.

George Weschler of Washington and Charles Leopold of Philadelphia, both consulting engineers, had been designated to design the air conditioning for the Capitol, and were also retained to prepare a design for the central refrigeration plant. For reasons that are not known, Leopold chose not to use the newly designed Carrier centrifugal machines, but relied instead on the tried and true industrial approach used in large freezer plants, which was multiple reciprocating compressors tied into remote individual condensers and shell-and-tube water coolers. The plant included six 800-ton-capacity reciprocating ammonia compressors manufactured by the York Corporation, housed in a separate building since ammonia is toxic, each one connected to a cooler and condenser. Cooling towers were installed on the roof of the plant.

The system included insulated steel piping laid underground to carry the chilled water to the remote buildings, and a return pipe to bring the water back to the plant. Because of the distances and difference in elevation between the plant and buildings the static pressure in the piping was of the order of 200 pounds per square inch, well above the working pressure of most available refrigeration machines, so specially designed equipment had to be made available. In the spring of 1937 the plant went operational and the Capitol was comfortable for the first time in history. When completed this was the largest air conditioning refrigeration plant in the world.

As part of the continuing expansion of Capitol Hill, in 1949 David Lynn, the superintendent of buildings, retained George Weschler and Burns and Roe, Consulting Engineers to study the existing steam and chilled water plants and prepare a long-range plan for the provision of these utilities to "The Hill" through the year 2000. The existing plant at that time could deliver 5,000 tons of cooling but it was known that on peak days the supply chilled water temperature gradually rose above the design temperature of 40 degrees Fahrenheit, and by 9 p.m. had reached 44 degrees. Comfort was not immediately compromised because of the substantial "fly-wheel," or storage effect, of the massive structures, but it became apparent that the addition of the proposed Rayburn House Office Building would overload the system, and therefore something had to be done.

Leopold and Weschler proposed that the ammonia-reciprocating machines be phased out and a new centrifugal plant be built in the adjacent yard. In 1955 Guy Panero of New York designed the new facility, which contained four 2,200-ton-capacity York centrifugals and associated auxiliaries. The plant, expanded in 1959 with the addition of two 1,100-ton machines and again in 1964 with two more 2,200-ton machines, produced a total capacity of 15,400 tons of refrigeration.

Plate 14-1
Willis Haviland Carrier, 1876 – 1950

Plate 14-2
The Original Carrier Centrifugal Refrigeration Machine
Installed in the basement of the House of Representatives when air conditioning was
first introduced in 1929, the machine produced 210 tons of refrigeration

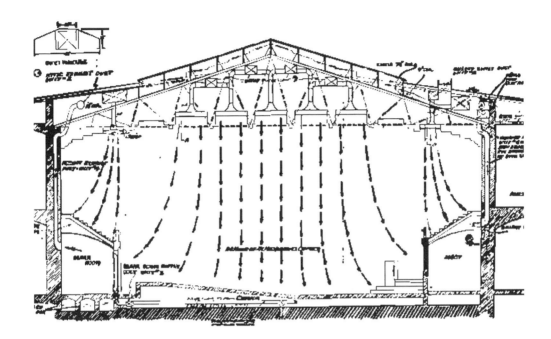

Plate 14 - 3
Section Through the House of Representatives, 1929
This diagram shows the arrangement of the ductwork above the glass ceiling of the House chamber with the supply air slots designed not to interfere with the lighting or natural day-lighting passing through; the return air passes down through the floor to the air handling unit in the basement

15 . . . FEDERAL ENGINEERING SINCE 1925

Public Building Administration

For many years the responsibility for the design and construction of federal facilities was shared between the U.S. Army Corps of Engineers and the Department of the Treasury, with the latter selected by the Congress to take care of civilian projects. Treasury continued to perform this task until the onset, by Congress, of a program to finally implement the L'Enfant Plan.

The plan called for the creation of a 400-foot-wide Grand Avenue flanked by monumental buildings, running from the west front of the Capitol to the Washington Monument. At the turn of the twentieth century much of the proposed avenue was occupied with private housing, a central market and rundown alleys. It was agreed that the development of the avenue and the proposed many federal buildings that would flank the border for almost a mile were beyond the efforts of the Treasury. So, by act of Congress, in 1925 a new agency came into being, named the Public Building Administration, charged with the responsibility of designing and building the Mall.

The design talent and staff who had served the Treasury so well were combined into the new agency, and procurement of additional in-house talent, together with the scrutiny of the resumes of the leading building-design teams in the country, was put into motion.

Apart from the housing, there were numerous roads, a steam plant serving the Agriculture Building, and miscellaneous industrial buildings that used to front on the Washington Canal. The canal was gone, filled in during the renovations of the 1870s. The Washington Gas Company's plants on the Mall had been replaced with others in Georgetown and Anacostia, and Boss Shepherd had summarily removed the railroad station in the 1870s. There was still the old USELCO electric generating plant at 13th and B Streets NW, and all manner of rundown housing in the corridor beginning at 2nd Street SE and running West to the new Tidal Basin.

As part of the act of 1925, the Secretary of the Interior was empowered to condemn and purchase all the property between Pennsylvania Avenue to the north, C Street SE and SW to the south. This constituted a giant triangular piece of land that would become known as the Federal Triangle ten years later. It took three years to buy up the properties, move the ex-owners and begin the demolition process. Then roads and utilities were installed and street names changed. Gradually a partially muddy and grass covered expanse of property began to emerge in the heart of the city, extending from the Washington

Monument to the Capitol. The few selected buildings that were to remain stood like islands in a sea of green. The Smithsonian Castle, the Arts and Industries Building and the Agriculture Administration Building, with its adjacent Boiler Plant, were on the south side of the Mall, while on the north side, Pennsylvania Avenue was a picture of desolation from the Capitol to the Treasury.

Rather than a gradual increase in the local staff, PBA went to work in earnest in 1926, hiring architect-engineering teams, mostly from New York and the West Coast, to begin the planning and design of a number of federal buildings for the Mall. Air conditioning was just around the corner, but was not yet on the palette of the designers of 1925-style buildings, with the result that most of the buildings were laid out to include long wings containing large operable windows, spaced about every ten feet, on the outside walls. The wings were about seventy feet in width, sufficient to allow thirty-foot-deep offices to be partitioned at the outside walls, and a ten-foot-wide center corridor to run the full length of the wing, typically four to five hundred feet.

The design reflected the need to provide some form of cross ventilation in the summer months. Most exterior windows were double hung, single glazed, without screens, and the window stools were fitted with glass "hoppers" to break the down-draft in the winter, and allow it to mingle with the warm air rising from the steam radiator below.

The first group of buildings, each designed with their own coal-fired boiler plant in the basement, provided low-pressure steam to the radiators and central ventilation units, and domestic water heat exchangers for the toilet rooms. Wall construction generally consisted of a four-inch thick limestone exterior, backing on to twelve inches of brick, an air space and interior lath and plaster finish. There was no insulation.

Structural frames were mostly poured concrete with concrete joists and slabs, and in some instances structural steel frames for walls and roofs were included for the upper floors. Recent advances in the art of placing massive monumental structures on the sandy silt that was originally the tidal bank of the Potomac River allowed the structural engineers to build foundations that would not have been feasible some fifty years before. Traditionally, for masonry buildings, laid brick by brick, the mortar was hand- or machine-mixed on site and carried up the ladders by workmen. For the buildings on the Federal Triangle a concrete mixing plant, capable of delivering tons of material per day, was assembled and moved from site to site, ready to feed large buckets of concrete or cement, which were lifted by cranes to the position of the day's pouring.

A lightweight topping or layer of cement mortar, four inches thick on the concrete floor slabs, provided a level surface for the tile finish and allowed the introduction of an electrical in-slab duct through which power wiring and telephone cable could be threaded. This concept proved to be very effective and led to the "under-floor" duct systems used widely thereafter throughout the nation.

The Commerce Building on 14th Street was the first to be constructed. The engineer was Clyde Place of New York. The finished building occupied the block between 14th and 15th Streets and Constitution Avenue and "E" Street N.W., in the course of which Ohio Avenue and "D" Street disappeared. The finished structure had an area just over one million square feet and housed 4,000 persons, making it the largest building in Washington at that time.

With the demolition of the PEPCO power plant at 13th Street, the paving of Constitution could begin, but the planners wisely allowed the brick-lined condenser water conduits (tunnels) that originated at the Tidal Basin to remain. This remarkable or lucky foresight proved to be a real money saver ten years later when air conditioning arrived.

The Federal Triangle then went into full swing with construction on both the north and south boundaries of the Mall all the way from the foot of Capitol Hill to 15th Street.

The Federal Triangle 1926 – 1939

Building Name	Area S.F.	Year
Internal Revenue	688,000	1927
New Post Office	497,000	1935
National Archives	313,000	1931
Interstate Commerce	549,000	1931- 1937
Customs & Labor	296,000	1935
Central Heating Plant	80,000	1932 - 1936
Agriculture South.	1,190,000	1931- 1937
Justice Department	607,000	1932
Federal Trade Commission	164,000	1933
Supreme Court		1934
Interior	750,000	1936
Interior South	68,000	1933
State Department , Old	230,000	1938
Health Education & Welfare North	596,000	1939
Health Education & Welfare South	289,000	1938

Total of Major Buildings Constructed by Public Buildings Administration = 6,317,000 Square Feet

The location chosen for the Internal Revenue Service Building, on the north side of B Street between 10th and 12th Streets NW, was typical of the site preparation that occurred for most of the Federal Triangle. Today "C" Street does not exist in the Federal Triangle, but in 1927 it ran from New Jersey Avenue west to the Ellipse. The new IRS Building was planned to extend from 10th to 12th Streets and from "B" Street (Constitution Ave.) north to Pennsylvania Avenue, which meant that both C Street and 11th Street would disappear, and "Little B" Street, which ran from 10th to 12th just north of "B" Street, would also disappear.

Square 324, between "Little B" and "C" streets, contained twenty-eight dwellings, mostly two- and three-story brick homes, all contiguous, most with a single front entrance and no rear door. All were on grade; there were no cellars. A typical small house was 1,200 square feet in area on two floors; the larger ones were twice that.

To the south of "Little B" Street lay the Washington Market, almost 500 feet in length, consisting of two large iron roofs about forty feet in width supported by steel columns. Granite paving covered the walking areas; the floors under the roofs were unpaved sand. The site plan showed the utility work under the streets. It ranged from a 12-by-12-foot brick trunk sewer on "B" Street, four foot brick sewers on 10th, 11th, and 12th Streets, eight-inch gas mains, six-inch water mains, and all manner of underground electric serving street lights and some of the dwellings.

From an engineering point of view the underground demolition and rerouting of utilities was far more extensive than the removal of the above-ground improvements. This work was accomplished over the entire 150-acre Federal Triangle site, on a piecemeal basis, over ten years to provide water, storm and sanitary sewers, electric power cable, and telephone lines for twelve federal buildings.

The buildings were all furnished with incandescent lighting. Ornate lighting fixtures with multiple lamps were suspended on the center line between the corridor and outside wall and manually switched at each entrance door. Desk-mounted telephones, fed from the under-floor duct, were a status symbol. Managers had them; secretaries and engineers did not. Typewriters were manual. There were, of course, no copiers, computers, fax machines or systems furniture; these would be invented half a century later. Above each office door leading to the center corridor there was a metal grille or operable glass transom to allow air to circulate, and on each side, about seven feet to the floor, provision was made for propeller-type electric fans, manually switched.

Centered over the door at the ceiling, an electric clock was firmly screwed to the wall. It was a special government version that needed 25 volts 25-cycle electric power, so there really was no point in smuggling one home since it would not operate on the standard 100 volts dc that served many homes, or the new 60-cycle power that was coming into use.

The buildings designed before 1935 were not air-conditioned. This was just at the time that Willis Carrier was perfecting a terminal unit that replaced the steam radiator typically installed beneath the exterior windows of all heated buildings since the 1850s. Carrier's new terminal unit, not much larger than a radiator with decorative enclosure, consisted of a chamber into which the cooled air from a central station air handling unit flowed, and then out through a slot at fairly high velocity, discharging through a sill-mounted grille into the occupied space.

A steam-heating coil was mounted on the leaving side of the slot. The high-velocity air caused the pressure on the leaving side of the slot to fall, inducing air from the room to flow over the steam coil, picking up heat that was then mixed with the primary cold air, and both entered the room through the supply grille. A manual damper in the branch duct serving the unit could be opened or closed, thereby varying the quantity of cold air supplied to the space. A manual valve on the steam coil regulated the heat. The device was called a Low Pressure Induction Unit. The big advantage of this design was that it could be applied to a building that was designed to have steam radiators but was not yet built. With the addition of vertical air ducts, called "risers," next to the windows or in the corner at a column, cooling could be added to the building with very little alteration.

The result of Carrier's invention was that several buildings originally slated for heating only were modified to receive air conditioning. These included Federal Trade, Department of the Interior, Health Education and Welfare North and South Buildings, Social Security, Interstate Commerce Commission and Department of Labor. All buildings were provided with central refrigeration plants generating chilled water at 44 degrees Fahrenheit, and steam boilers burning number six fuel oil.

All of the buildings constructed on the Mall in the late 1930s had central station air handling units either in the attic or the basement. These units were equipped with automatic outside and return air dampers, and four-inch-deep metal filters that had to be removed monthly, washed in hot water and sprayed with oil to catch the dust. Cooling coils had not yet been invented, so Carrier's open spray units, developed for humidifying air by passing it through hot sprays, was modified to cool air by passing it through chilled water sprays. The "Open Spray Dehumidifier," as it was named, was extremely effective in cooling the air, thereby removing moisture from the air as well as fine particles of dirt and pollen, which had passed through the inefficient filters.

The unit casings, constructed of galvanized iron sheets, had a cross-sectional area about the size of single-car garage, and a length of fifty feet. Centrifugal supply fans fifteen feet tall and with capacities of the order of 50,000 cubic feet per minute, pumped the air through metal ducts to the low-pressure induction units in each office.

The water tunnels from the Tidal Basin that had provided cooling water to USELCO's steam condensers in 1900 were cleaned and refurbished and became the means for transporting condenser water to the centrifugal refrigeration machines in the buildings along Constitution Avenue. Using the old underground tunnels solved a vexing aesthetic design problem, since the building roofs were not planned with cooling towers in mind to be installed on the sloping red clay tiles.

The growth of the Public Building Administration accelerated in the 1930s in response to the building program of the New Deal. The New Deal included numerous government-sponsored welfare initiatives to help bring employment to the many thousands of workers who had lost their jobs in the Great Depression. For the city of Washington the Depression meant the almost complete shutdown of the building industry. No one could borrow money to fund building programs; the banks had no money to lend. Commercial office buildings stood half-empty so there was no incentive to build.

Private construction was at a standstill; the banks were not helping, so top quality engineers who had been successful in private practice found themselves going bankrupt. One such casualty was William A. Brown, a graduate of Harvard University who had practiced as a consulting engineer in New York in the late 1920s, moved to Washington in 1935 and joined the Public Buildings Administration. Because of his experience in designing air-conditioned buildings, he moved up rapidly through the ranks and became chief mechanical engineer in 1940. He oversaw the design of hospitals, government offices and postal facilities. In those days the PBA did all the design work for the U.S. Post Office throughout the country, and with the growth of the Washington Metropolitan area there was continued demand for their services.

After the war Brown left PBA, and with his contacts and excellent reputation started a consulting engineering practice at 1223 Connecticut Avenue NW. The "Brown University," as it became known, was the starting point for many of Washington's consulting engineers. Typical of design and engineering firms in the district at that time, Brown did not encourage his key employees, all graduate engineers, to get registered under the professional license statute finally enacted by Congress in 1950. In fact, registration was rarely discussed in the office, although, with a staff of thirty, half of whom were graduate engineers, there were only two others who had licenses to practice, and they were both nearing retirement. From time to time someone would resign, and his place taken by another bright young graduate who was only too thankful to be associated with one of the leaders of the industry.

William A. Brown was a man of mathematics and calculations. He reached his recommendations based on the data that the figures spelled out, not from opinions gleaned as a result of similar challenges in the past. For the young engineers who sat in his office to receive instructions for a new project, he often appeared lightly amused to be setting the stage for a play (a design) in which he had been the lead actor years before and now was able to pass on a challenge to an apprentice. He had a dry sense of humor and a deep commitment to telling the story through accurate calculations, which spoke for themselves. He was of medium height, slim, a head of gray hair, sharp features and rimless glasses perched on his nose. He arrived at the office at eight o'clock sharp, clad, as always, in a smart gray suit with topcoat and felt hat. Always pleasant but seldom conversational, he indulged himself and the firm once a year with a trip across Connecticut Avenue to Fan and Bill's, one of few Washington restaurants that could compare with his New York upbringing. The plan for the day included one martini and then lunch, interspersed with a few reminiscences of how the Commodore Hotel on 42nd Street had introduced him to cocktails years before. Bill Brown will long be remembered for an engineering practice that spanned fifty years.

Special mention should also be made of three of Bill Brown's lieutenants, William Stephenson, Oscar Hessler and Robert Von Otto. These three engineers all worked for PBA during the war and became specialists in their fields. Bill Stephenson lived in Baltimore and took the train every day of his thirty-five-year career with the government to Washington station, rode the Capital Transit up to 18th Street and walked down to the headquarters of the General Services Administration at 18th and F Streets NW. Bill specialized in boilers and incinerators. There was very little Bill did not know about the construction, firing, controls, safety, cost and suitability of his specialties as they applied to federal buildings. Bill was sought out by the manufacturers to make speeches at their conventions, meet and discuss refinements and improvements to their products, and instruct the contractors working for the government on their submissions and progress. And all done with a sense of humor and confidence. Bill Stephenson had truly found his identity. He was an expert in his field, and a true professional.

The same can be said for Oscar Hessler. Oscar was to automatic controls what Bill was to boilers. Bob Von Otto was a new breed of federal employee. Registered engineers

Bill and Oscar were not. Bob spent his years learning everything there was to know about air conditioning as it applied to government buildings. Bob left PBA in 1960, opened a consulting firm in Washington and was well-respected for the rest of his career. These are but a glimpse of the talent and engineering expertise that made PBA such a force in Washington.

The Federal District Heating and Cooling System

By 1920 the central "District Heating System" designed by Homer Woodbridge for the buildings on Capitol Hill had been in successful operation for more than ten years, and like its counterparts in New York, had proved to be economical.

Traditionally the heating and cooling plant for a building resided either in the basement or was shared between the basement and the penthouse. This concept prevailed for many years, even in cases where there were groups of buildings situated on the same campus, such a universities or military bases. With the improvement in piping and pump technology, engineers began to consider the feasibility of allowing a single boiler plant to serve not only the building in which it was located, but several adjacent buildings as well. In an earlier chapter the Capitol Power Plant, an innovation by Homer Woodbridge of Boston, presented the concept of a central heating plant remote from the buildings it served. The concept proved to be successful.

So, with the passage of the Public Buildings Act of 1925, came a directive to determine the feasibility of providing central district steam for the Federal Triangle and other nearby government buildings. Neil Thompson, Chief Engineer of the Public Building Administration, spearheaded the study, visiting cities in the United States and Europe that used central steam, and in 1928 concluded that a district heating system would work for the federal government.

The Public Building Administration prepared the procurement documents and the contract was awarded to United Engineers and Constructors of Philadelphia, with Alfred Sadler in charge. The plant, located at 10th and E Streets SW, included four coal-fired boilers, each capable of delivering 80,000 pounds of steam per hour at 250 pounds per square inch pressure to a network of underground piping. The system required the excavation of a trench about twelve feet wide by fifteen feet deep, from beginning to end, and the rerouting of other underground utilities encountered during the digging. First a concrete floor was poured and then the walls and a concrete roof, which provided a fireproof envelope ready to accept the piping. Twenty-four-inch-diameter pipe rated for 400 pounds per square inch pressure was then mounted on rollers in the tunnel, allowing the pipe to expand and contract in response to the heat of the steam. Valve connection points provided branch lines to every building the system was designed to serve.

Midway through the design of the heating piping, consideration was given to the feasibility of constructing a central chilled water plant adjacent to the boiler plant. The thinking was that there were other buildings to be constructed on the Mall, and it would be more economical to operate and maintain a single central plant rather than one in each of the dozen or so possible buildings. The training and expertise of the machine operators proved to be a critical economic factor. Buildings were getting more and more complicated, and the knowledge required to run them efficiently was increasing exponentially. The days when an operator would shovel coal were gone. The age of "mechanization" was on the horizon, and the concept of " central control," where the operator ran the facility from an office in the basement rather than the traditional watch tour with clip board in hand, recording data, had arrived.

The designers finally decided to build a central refrigeration plant in the same building envelope as the boilers plant, and provide for future chilled water mains to the east end of the Mall, where sites for future buildings were already entering the planning stage.

The duplicate insulated supply and return piping, both steam and chilled water, was contained in poured concrete tunnels of sufficient dimensions to provide a walking path next to the piping, which was racked on the walls. At calculated intervals there were access grates to discharge hot air, and at others, supply fans that pumped ventilation air into the tunnel. The initial underground piping originated from the plant on 12th and C Streets SW and extended a mile west to 15th and Constitution Avenue and a mile east to 2nd Street. The plant was designed to have capacity to heat all of the proposed federal buildings destined to front on the Mall.

The Central Heating and Cooling Plant went into operation in 1936, with the Department of Agriculture Buildings as the first customer. As time went by, all of the buildings originally designed with their own boiler plants in the first wave of construction of the Mall from 1926 to 1936 were connected to the District Steam Grid, and the individual building boiler plants were demolished.

The first phase of the district system ended at 15th Street next to the Ellipse. There were plans to construct more federal buildings to the west and to deal with the boiler plants in existing buildings such as the Interior and Public Building Administration buildings. PBA did a study in 1939 and concluded that a new West Boiler Plant in the vicinity of the Bureau of Medicine on 23rd Street would be good place, but objections from citizens in Foggy Bottom caused them to move to a site in Georgetown on 29th Street at K Street.

The West Plant, as it became known, was designed by PBA in 1941 by Neal Melick and N. S. Thompson, put on hold because of the war, and placed under construction in 1946. The contractor for the boilers was J. E. Hurley.

An excavation under Rock Creek, sufficiently large to accommodate the tunnel and two sets of twenty-inch-diameter high-pressure steam pipes insulated with six inches of calcium silicate and wrapped in aluminum, was carried out in 1941. With lighting and ventilation, stairs and drainage, it was now possible to walk underground from Georgetown to within two blocks of the Capitol Building, a distance of three miles.

With the new central steam tunnel passing across the lawn on the south side of the White House it took no time to remove the sixty-year-old boilers from that building, cancel the coal delivery, and turn the basement over to better use. A small steam-pressure reducing station, served from the central system and installed in one corner, provided all the heat needed in a more reliable, much cleaner and safer manner. The same was true of all the older buildings in the vicinity of Lafayette Square. Boilers were removed and in their place small valve stations connected to the federal system. These included the Tayloe House (1828), the Winder Building (1848), Dolley Madison House (1820) and the other buildings on Jackson Place and Madison Place.

The Second World War of 1939 to 1945 essentially shut down the civil building industry in Washington, including the design and construction activities of the Public Building Administration, whose staff either saw service in the military or in the War Department. The war created an expanded view of the needs of the federal government, and many states were now participants in the provision of nationwide services that had been the sole province of the "Feds" before the war.

The Public Building Administration had seldom ventured out of the metropolitan area, but in 1946 representatives in Congress were looking to the federal system to bring much needed office space and building management to their cities, as well as the capital city.

Washington, D.C., in 1946 was still essentially a Southern town greatly impacted by the events of the war, in particular the number of temporary buildings for the departments of an expanded government and housing for the many workers who had migrated to the city to find work as the war effort gradually ended the Great Depression of 1930 to 1940. The business and industry of Washington was government. The war effort included a massive procurement program for all manner of goods and services, mostly acquired on a "sole-source" basis, in which the offeror's ability to deliver on time took precedent to price, which in many cases was settled by negotiation after the delivery was made. The government's needs were advertised on a daily basis, and those willing to furnish the goods or services prepared a preliminary estimate of cost and delivery time, which were then analyzed by government officials, and contracts were awarded to one or more firms to fulfill the requirements. The awards were made, not necessarily to the lowest bidder, but to the firm with the best history of contract performance.

The war had shut down private design and construction in Washington to the point that the only work available was government funded. Many private engineering design firms disappeared with the practitioners, such as Urdahl, Bogan, Brown and Weller joining federal agencies, and others such as Wilberding and Karsunky doing design work on a contract basis for the federal system.

A Federal Reaction to the End of the War

In 1945 everything changed. The war was over and the needs of the federal government were reduced to a trickle for the years 1946 through 1948. The private sector began to recover from five years of inaction, and construction, particularly of private dwellings and a few office buildings in the suburbs of adjacent Maryland, began to pick up.

The traditional method of procuring engineering design services prior to the war, in both the private and government sectors, was by *referral,* in which the owner or the government contracting officer selected a consulting engineer or other professional based on the firm's reputation. The design cost or fee was generally proscribed by a schedule of fees maintained either by the federal or state governments, or by recommended fee schedules published by the National Society of Professional Engineers. Price competition in the establishment of the design fee was considered "unethical" and frowned on by the professional societies.

But unknown to the leaders of the entrenched professions and the professional societies that represented them, the world was changing and a climate of equality and opportunity for all was beginning to pervade society. Special treatment of the old-boy networks was no longer the mainstream of political thinking. The Congress edicted that all federal procurement would be by *competitive bidding*, as the practices used with much success in a wartime economy were swept away.

Based primarily on the appointment of politically active individuals to head up the various agencies of government, the climate of procurement of engineering services moved from the *"referral"* method to the *"competitive price"* method in 1947. Under this method each engineer seeking a particular project would prepare a fixed price proposal, or "bid," to cover all of the design costs anticipated, and the government would award the contract to the lowest bidder. The "competitive bid" process worked in the procurement of construction contractors since they were able to base their bid price on the "bid documents," the drawings and specifications describing the work in detail, prepared by the owner's design team. No such bid documents were available to the engineers bidding on the design work. They had to base their "bids" on a brief written description of the proposed work, prepared by the federal or state government. The method proved to be a disaster because of the impossibility of preparing a fixed price "bid" against a construction scope that had not, and could not, be defined. The definition of the scope of a construction project is one of the primary services performed by the designer in the course of his work for the owner.

After much lobbying by the various associations representing different areas of interest of the design professions, Congress saw fit, under the leadership of Congressman Jack Brooks of Florida, to discard the *competitive bid* method for procurement of professional services, and created the *"competitive negotiation"* method, called the Brooks Bill. Under the Brooks Bill procurement of engineering, architectural, and other services such as surveying, would be conducted in *two phases*.

In the first phase, the government advertised its requirements in short general terms, and any professional who felt qualified could respond by submitting a completed "Form 251," which in twenty or so pages gave information about the firm's technical personnel, their experience and qualifications, success on similar projects, records of the firm's activities in the past ten years, and statements indicating why the firm should be selected for the work.

Each submitting firm's 251 was carefully scrutinized by an impartial selection committee made up of four or five senior technical government personnel. Each submission was then ranked, based on a scoring system, until the top five contestants were determined. These five were then invited to make verbal and visual presentations to the selection committee to further amplify their qualifications and present their proposed key personnel in person to the committee. The presentations were carefully scored by each committee member, the total tallied by the committee chairperson, and the firm with the highest score declared the number one selection. This step ended the first phase of the selection process. The government now had a slate of five interested and qualified design firms, any one of whom was capable of fulfilling the government's needs.

Phase two included a negotiation between the government contracting officer and representatives of the number one ranked firm to reach agreement on a fair and equitable fee. Both sides first met to establish an understanding as to the extent of the scope of the work, and then separately estimated the man hours required to perform that scope, taking into account the special or unique services applicable to the project. Using audited man-hour salary rates for each individual proposed by the designer, and multiplying those rates by the man-hours estimated, yielded a fee for the work.

If the total proposed fee by the engineer was substantially different from that estimated by the government, both sides would attempt to show where the differences lay, and adjust their fee either up or down until agreement was reached, in which case the government would enter into a fixed-price contract with the engineering firm to provide the agreed-upon scope. If the two sides failed to reach an agreement, negotiations with the number one selected firm would be terminated and the number two firm would be called in for negotiations.

In this manner a competitive procurement process, the need for which had been demanded by the Justice Department, was instituted, with the competition primarily falling in the area of competency of the competing parties, with price controlled to a fair value to meet the expectations of both sides. The Brooks Bill proved to be a useful tool since it not only provided a way to eliminate unqualified offerors, but gave the government a detailed look at the components of the price proposed by the engineer *before* entering into a contract. Items that were overpriced could be identified and reduced by negotiation. Items that were underpriced, or omitted from the engineer's pricing altogether, could be discovered and included in the contract amount, thereby removing them from a future claim for "additional services."

In looking back at the history of enactment of the Brooks Bill, it is true to say that the professional societies were *reacting* to a changing national climate, rather than being aware of the impending changes to the profession and then, through national consensus, proposing to *lead the way* to the solution.

With the thorny issue of professional procurement finally out of the way, Congress again took up the need to move federal employees from World War II temporary facilities into permanent buildings of a quality and style set by the Federal Triangle in the 1930s. By an act of Congress in 1948 President Truman signed the bill, creating the General Services Administration, which included the Brooks Bill for the procurement of design services.

General Services Administration (GSA)

The theme of the creation of the new agency allowed for one entity to manage all of the real estate requirements of the federal government, including those of the Public Buildings Administration, which was renamed the Public Building Service and, as a division of GSA, carried on with the tasks of designing and building office space to be occupied by other agencies. With headquarters in an existing building at 18th and F Streets NW, GSA management divided the whole United States into nine "regions," each with a regional director and local staff whose responsibilities covered the full range of providing building management services to other federal agencies in that region.

Washington and the nearby states of Maryland and Virginia, designated *Region 3,* emerged with the largest inventory of existing real estate and the most demand to produce more office space for existing personnel housed in rented or substandard space. One of GSA's first tasks was the renovation of a 600,000-square-foot warehouse at 7th and "D" Streets SW into the Regional Headquarters to house Region 3. The existing building was demolished, with the exception of the structural frame, to reveal concrete columns and floors, which were retained. The modernization then included the provision of new mechanical, electrical and fire protection systems, as well as new exterior walls and windows. Other than its curious plan—the floors changed direction slightly at the midpoint to accommodate a bend in the adjacent railroad track during its career as a warehouse—the renovated seven-story building presented itself as a triumph of the abilities of the designers. Visitors were heard to comment on the geometry of the exterior walls as a model of upscale building design.

Following the directives of Congress, GSA immediately set about developing plans for the construction of eleven major office buildings to be built in the immediate vicinity of the Mall. All would be subcontracted to nationally recognized architect-engineering firms, coordinated with the careful design instructions formulated by the GSA in-house engineers. As a result there were few surprises when the preliminary designs arrived at GSA for review. Generally they reflected a superior level of engineering excellence and reinforced the belief that private contractors, carefully selected and properly charged, were capable of preparing construction documents of a quality equal to those of the historically revered Treasury Department.

It is instructive, however, to compare the fundamental management aims of the old "Treasury" system with those of the postwar GSA. Under Treasury, the long-range development of a team of in-house engineers who would do the actual design and be responsible for the results was a basic goal. And it worked. The results spoke for themselves. One could say that it was a reflection of the "Old English" way of doing engineering. Under the postwar system adopted by GSA, the training and development of engineering talent was not of prime importance. GSA had inherited a staff of competent, experienced engineering talent, but they were not to be used to do the actual design of the projects on hand. Rather they would set the standards and design criteria for the subcontracted private engineering companies who did the actual work. Typically, a design project would incorporate four progress submissions turned in by the designer for review by government engineers. The reviews were meticulous—each detail of the design would be verified against GSA standards, and every sheet of calculations checked for arithmetic errors. The review, when returned to the designer, would include copies of each drawing carefully marked with the government's "comments," and each sheet of calculations inscribed with "recommended" changes. The designer then, equally carefully, responded to the comments and recommendations in writing, a typical response taking fifty to a hundred pages. The prudent engineer accepted the reviews and comments as part of the process, and quickly modified the kind of employee assigned to federal projects. Young persons, in need of guidance and more than willing to accept demotion to a role of trainee, found a place in the system that offered experience on projects of a size and complexity for which they could not qualify in the private market. The result meant that cadres of designers were being trained to conform to the standards of government excellence by following the directions of experienced government engineers. It is not hard to foresee the results of this system. With the government, in effect, training the private sector, while not replacing and training their own in-house designers, the technical quality of government declined while that of the private sector improved, and GSA's role became, to a large degree, a *manager* of the design and construction process.

Design moved apace on ten new buildings, while construction of a new State Department Building on 23rd Street NW moved to final completion ahead of the pack.

The Federal Triangle 1945 – 1975

Building Name	Area S.F.	Year
New State Department	1,600,000	1946
New Executive Office	300,000	1964
Housing & Urban Development	890,000	1965
Department of Labor	1,150,000	1966
Federal Bureau of Investigation	1,500,000	1968
Forrestal Building	1,136,000	1968
Hubert Humphrey	500,000	1970
Tax Court	130,000	1970
Federal Office Bld. 6	420,000	1972
Federal Office Bld. 10A	775,000	1974
Federal Office Bld. 10B	250,000	1975

GSA Construction of Major Buildings In the Federal Triangle to 1975=8,666,000 Square Feet.

In addition to the new buildings under the control of GSA, a massive amount of repair and replacement work, postponed because of the war, moved into the pipeline and was contracted predominantly to local engineering firms. Most of the buildings built in the 1930s did not have air conditioning, and in the postwar world this had to be immediately rectified.

William A. Brown and his firm were given the 1.2 million-square-foot Commerce Department Building on 15th Street, and in eighteen months produced in excess of one hundred drawings covering replacement of the existing heating and electrical system with Carrier's new High Velocity Induction System, plus up-to-date fluorescent lighting.

Of course, all of the post-WWII buildings were connected to the GSA central steam system, and those built in the 1930s, if not already connected, had their boiler plants removed and were fitted with tunnels and piping, tying them into the central steam mains.

16 . . . The 20th Century in the Private Sector

With the end of the Depression of the late 1930s the economy of the United States began to rebound; banks began to make loans, businessmen could get financial credit, small and medium enterprises began to emerge providing products and services to customers who had postponed spending on nonessentials for a number of years. The impact of the Depression on Washington was much less severe than on the rest of the nation because of the influx of money and jobs caused by the massive construction of the Federal Triangle, and the actions of Congress in beginning to fund the defense industry in response to the deteriorating political situation in Europe.

The construction industry, in particular, began to lead the local economy, resulting in an influx of engineering talent from other parts of the nation and the arrival of branch offices of some of the nation's leading building contractors. This was a new experience for Washington. Traditionally, Washingtonians thought of themselves as inhabitants of a medium-sized Southern town, subjected to a lavish overlay of power and greed—the federal government and the Congress—who really didn't belong in the town but ruled it anyway. Apart from the grand buildings of the Federal Triangle, the rest of the city presented a scene of three- and four-story commercial buildings leading out to row upon row of brick town houses, or "brownstones," dating from the 1900 era, or earlier.

In addition to the influx of builders and supporting personnel, there was a whole clan of temporary federal workers moving to the city in response to the availability of work in the federal government. All these people now decided to make Washington their home. One might think of the place as a city of strangers with few roots and connections, imposed on the original inhabitants of a Southern town. Clearly there was pressure and a need for people to communicate and create a homogeneous society. In a like manner there was a need for dialogue between the various branches of the industry, and in response, societies like the Washington Building Congress were formed to fill a void.

Washington Building Congress

Professional and business interests were primarily self-centered and concerned with survival on one hand, yet determined to reach the pinnacle of success and wealth. The average builder, painter, engineer or architect fell somewhere between the two. But it was the age of the Roaring Twenties. It was a time of extremes. Extreme poverty for some and the opposite for a few others.

The "F" Street corridor, Washington's main commercial and professional district, extended between the Capitol and the Treasury, and contained a grand mix of hotels and businesses of all types, housed in four- to five-story brick buildings. With the advent of electricity, the concurrent invention of the elevator and the use of steel and concrete for the structural frames, it was now possible to erect reasonably safe and accessible buildings with many floors. Lighting was basically driven by Edison's electric lamp, while heating relied on a full coal bin in the basement, with manual shoveling to maintain the steam pressure of the boiler between five to ten pounds per square inch.

Business, in the form of design or construction contracts, began with the banks and investors. With the announcement of a new building project, each interested segment of the industry made the necessary overtures in an attempt to secure the work. Once the final team was selected, the project proceeded with almost no communication between the team members, other than what was absolutely necessary. It is fair to say that engineers didn't talk to architects; and architects didn't talk to contractors, who in turn didn't talk to owners, subcontractors and manufacturer's representatives.

It was in such a climate that in 1937 Charles Tompkins and J. R. Skinker, both successful general contractors, met with Tom Marshall, a renowned structural engineer, and architects Ted Coe, Arthur Heaton and Leon Chatelain, to explore the feasibility of starting a dialogue between segments of the construction industry.

Out of these discussions emerged a reality that it was time for the construction industry to move on to the next plateau of cooperation, which, it was believed, would be a benefit to all. It is an interesting fact that the recognition of the benefits of mutual interest and responsibility perceived by those members was the same platform on which the political solution to the Depression was based. This was a time of the merging of individualism into the belief of the public good.

The Washington Building Congress was formed on September 23, 1937, with Charles Tompkins as its first president and the other cofounders on the board. As the years before the war went by, the leading designers and constructors all had a hand in attending the meetings and sharing in the leadership of the Congress. Names familiar to Washington's building industry, such as Howard Foley, an electrical contractor, M. X. Wilberding, Tom Eagan and Waldron Faulkner, all sat on the Board of Governors, and at the annual celebration, held at one of Washington's prestigious hotels, presented engraved plaques of recognition to the selected best designers, contractors and sub-contractors in any year.

There are so many outstanding individuals who contributed to the building of the city of Washington in the years from the end of the First World War to the end of the century that one is hard-pressed to eliminate any from the written history. Perhaps the story of a typical pioneer will help fill the omission of the "many" and provoke those who remember similar stories to reduce them to writing.

Standard Engineering

In 1901 L. F. Gardner came to Washington from Boston as a draftsman in the Treasury Department, where he worked for ten years, producing design drawings of the heating, ventilating and plumbing for buildings like the Agriculture Building on "B" Street SW, the Soldiers Home in 1906, and the City Main Post Office on North Capitol Street. Gardner was sent by Treasury to the construction sites to inspect the work, in the course of which he studied the successful techniques and failing work habits of the contractors doing the mechanical part of the buildings. (41)

Buildings and most other substantial construction projects are built according to an agreement between the owner who wants the work performed and a contractor or builder who has the expertise and knowhow to perform the work required. The final written agreement becomes the "contract." The contractor usually had a staff of experienced inspectors and a few carpenters and other specialized tradesmen who either performed the work or supervised other personnel from separate companies, called subcontractors. The subcontractors, or "subs" as they are referred to, might include plumbers, electricians, pipe fitters, sheetmetal mechanics, elevator mechanics, roofers and many other organizations specializing in a particular part of the project.

The scope of the project was covered by a set of drawings and specifications. Typically, drawings were sheets of paper about thirty-six by forty-eight inches, and each depicted a particular portion of the work, beginning with the general construction, the walls, floors, windows and other miscellaneous details. Then followed the supporting "trades," the structural, mechanical, electrical, fire protection and other specialties depending on the needs of the work. Drawings were prepared to a "scale," for example a quarter inch equals one foot, to allow the preparer of the drawings, the designer, to fit all of the necessary components into the allotted space. The scale also allowed the contractors to "take off," or measure and estimate, the amount of material that they must furnish in order to meet the needs of the contract. It was under these kinds of rules that Gardener represented the Treasury Department in the course of his work.

It is important to understand that until about 1940 the building industry in the United States operated in accordance with a system under which both the designer and the contractor were responsible for preparing a portion of the contract drawings. Designers did not prepare "detailed" or "working" drawings covering every step that a field mechanic needed to do his work. Contractors did not prepare "design drawings;" this was the area of responsibility of the engineer and architect.

The contractor did prepare the working drawings, which, after approval by the owner, became the basis of the agreement between the two parties. It stands to reason then that the contractors and their "subs" had to have a staff of experienced engineers and draftsmen capable of interpreting the design drawings (there might be five or six) and creating the working drawings (there might be forty or fifty).

In 1909 Gardner left Treasury and started Standard Engineering in a row house at 2129 Eye Street NW. Standard Engineering in those days was a typical mechanical contractor, staffed by engineers, draftsman, estimators, and journeymen in their trades. They could take the "concept drawings" done by the owner's consulting engineer and prepare "working drawings" of sufficient detail that they could be followed implicitly by the mechanics in the field. The concept or design drawings outlined in some detail the owner's and his consultant's requirements, and gave sufficient information for a mechanical engineering and contracting firm to prepare the working drawings necessary for the men in the field to know what was required and the extent of the work. Said another way, the owner gave the bidding contractors sufficient information for them to prepare an estimate of what the work should cost to build, and they in turn would do the detail design and make the working drawings. Once the contract to do the work was awarded, sometimes but not usually to the lowest bidder, the successful contractor would go about the task of making the working drawings. These included the drawings prepared by his own staff, in addition to drawings and other data prepared by suppliers and manufacturers, so that the owner knew what he was getting and the men in the field knew what to build.

Typically on a medium-sized building, say the Archives on Pennsylvania Avenue, the owner's engineer would do the calculations to size the main components, and make *design drawings* to show locations and space requirements of the air-handling units, the ductwork, boilers, pumps and other major components of the mechanical system. Typically, on a large project the engineer might produce six or eight drawings. All details and components were not indicated on these design drawings. The purpose of the drawings was to convey to the mechanical contractor the "essence" of the design in sufficient detail to allow a competent builder, familiar with mechanical systems, to fill in the details and submit a set of "*working drawings*" to the engineer for approval.

The mechanical contractor, on the other hand, might produce forty or more drawings, going into much more detail than the consulting engineer. This was the business that Standard Engineering pursued from its inception, and for the next sixty years. Standard gained a reputation for doing outstanding projects with a minimum of legal hassle, with the result that its niche was with sophisticated owners such as the General Services Administration and the C & P Telephone Company.

Standard Engineering installed the mechanical systems on many of Washington's well-known projects, including the Interstate Commerce Commission Building and the Department of Labor Building, both on Constitution Avenue.

The "Competitive Bid" Method

The demand for construction contractors during the war years placed such a heavy load on the industry that many people with a general knowledge of building, but no experience in the preparation of working drawings and no staff to prepare them, approached the government and offered their services on simple projects. The "scope" of the project might be a set of typical "design" drawings or might even be a written document describing the project in general terms but omitting any of the details. These would be worked out with inspectors when the need arose, and billed to the government. In modern parlance these would be called "time and material" (T&M) contracts, in which there was no initial fixed, agreed-upon price, and the owner paid for the work as it was done.

The end of the war saw many construction firms diverting their attention to the civilian market. Some of these firms were headed up by businessmen who had very little knowledge or interest in the detailed building profession, but had made fortunes delivering products under the T&M method. When the building industry began to show strong demand for contractors, these businessmen, lacking engineering staff for the production of working drawings, began to pressure design firms to prepare not only the "design drawings" but the "working drawings" as well. Lacking any leverage to reject the new system, engineers began to comply, thinking, erroneously, that their work effort would be substantially increased along with their fees. The former thought proved to be accurate, the latter did not.

Owners and contractors loved the new method because it reduced their costs (they paid smaller fees), placed the responsibility for the completeness and accuracy of the drawings on one entity (the designer), and owners could now send complete sets of drawings to multiple contractors and obtain competitive prices. Naturally, the owner selected the lowest bid.

The "competitive bid" method quickly became the standard for the industry, not only in the private sector but at all levels of federal , state and local government.

This method of procurement is still widely used throughout the United States. Given competent, ethical and mature parties it is probably the most efficient way of procuring complicated designs at the most competitive price. Its weakness lies in the ability of the successful bidder to allege deficiencies, errors or omissions of vital information, which create unforeseen costs for which he requires additional reimbursement. Unless these allegations can be amicably and quickly settled, the result is the beginning of legal disputes, which are always expensive, time-consuming and affect the expected completion date of the work, which leads to more litigation and loss.

Insurance costs to cover "errors and omissions," the cost of competent inspectors, and the cost of "defensive design," to name just a few, led the federal government in the 1970s to look for alternative methods of procurement. One of the methods was called "design build."

The "Design-Build" Method

This "new" method for the procurement of construction work was tried, and, with minor contractual wrinkles, was the same method offered by standard engineering and many other builders beginning in 1910. The only difference was that *all* the documents and drawings required for the project had to be prepared by the contractor, with the engineer as a subcontractor.

Under the old 1910 method, the engineer produced the design drawings, on which bidding contractors based their estimates, and then the successful bidder, upon receiving the contract award from the owner, prepared the working drawings. The owner paid the engineer.

Under the design-build method the owner solicited proposals from a number of contractors, selected one, who hired an engineer to produce all the working drawings. When they were finished, the contractor and the owner agreed upon a price for the work and entered into a contract. The contractor paid the engineer.

The Washington Building Congress over the years provided a forum for communication between the diverse members of a mammoth segment of Washington's economy—the construction industry. Part of that industry were the consulting engineers in private practice, who prepared the structural, electrical, mechanical and fire-safety designs for private clients and many arms of the public sector, including the federal government.

Concurrent with the organization of the construction industry, as expressed by the formation of the Building Congress, there occurred a similar process by the engineers in private practice, known as "consulting engineers." These individuals, the surviving band from the era of Latrobe and Meigs, found themselves gradually overwhelmed by an expanding industry, with dominant elements such as owners, clients, industrial companies, the government and competing design companies that were part of larger manufacturing entities. Gradually, the need to unite became part of meetings in New York, Chicago and Washington.

Consulting Engineers

The first known history of engineers in private practice deciding to organize, in order to establish standards of service and quality, dates back to 1905, when eight engineers in the building design industry in New York founded the Association of Architectural Engineers. They adopted goals for the new venture, including the principal target, which was "to unite in fellowship the engineers engaged in the structural design of buildings, to promote the science and practical efficiency of the profession, and to foster professional relationships between architect and engineer." (48)

In 1909 the organization changed its name to the American Institute of Consulting Engineers (AICE) and set about the task of developing a schedule of fees to cover various types of service based on a percentage of the construction cost, or hourly rates to be billed to the client. A code of ethics was adopted, very similar to those of lawyers and architects. The codes of all the organizations were to a degree self-serving in that they attempted to deal with other competing institutions that might offer the same services as the "professional," but for substantial less cost or none at all. Particularly vexing to the engineers were the large companies, corporations and bridge builders that performed the necessary design as part of their construction effort, which was deemed to be "free engineering," in direct competition with the private practitioner.

Throughout the years before, during and after World War I, AICE gradually grew in size and continued to do battle with the "free" service providers, in particular the government, which had allowed the Corps of Engineers to take over much of the federal construction program. Also, the Public Building Administration in Washington had assembled an experienced body of designers and draftsmen capable of performing the very work that AICE was attempting to promote. Gradually the AICE became more of a lobbying organization, representing the interests of practitioners before such bodies as the Bureau of Public Roads and the Congress, and was successful in heading off legislation that would have had the effect of diminishing the size of the available market for engineering services.

Fees, however, were still a problem, particularly those with architects, and a study produced in England by the Association of Consulting Engineers confirmed that the 2,000 miles of ocean separating the countries had no effect on the relations between architects and engineers. On both sides of the Atlantic, relations between the two professions were tense. Another study of occupations in 1930 disclosed that the engineering profession was represented by eighty national technical societies, none of which could speak for the engineering profession as a whole.

The Second World War produced masses of engineering work in the defense industry, but very little directly for those in private practice, with the result that many practitioners joined the military in Washington. At war's end the return to a peacetime economy buoyed up the construction industry, and there was an increase in the number of firms in private practice nationwide from 1,280 at the start of the war to 2,750 in the mid 1950s. AICE in 1954 had some 200 members, mostly from New York, whereas it was estimated that the ninety different technical engineering organizations in the United States representing more than 200,000 members.

In 1955 there were nineteen organizations in the United States, all claiming to represent the professional interests of their members, yet no attempt had been made to unify these entities into a truly national organization. The agenda of each group was similar, if not identical, once the local partisanship was weeded out. Each espoused, (1) to promote engineers; (2) to reduce government competition; (3) developing standards of conduct; (4) improving the image; and (5) improving the economic position of engineering.

In 1955 representatives of ten of the ninety organizations met to see if a single, unified national organization of engineers was possible, and after two days of discussion it was concluded that a new entity, welded to the goals of consulting engineers and the high ethics of professionalism, be created and called the Consulting Engineers Council. (CEC). Between 1955 and 1959 CEC founders held many meetings to iron out policy issues and to struggle with a central theme of what is, and what is not, good professional conduct. Budgets were a continual challenge—the activists wanted to expand; conservatives wanted to be cautious. High dues would not be attractive to many of the potential members. But the need for a staff in Washington, the center of the association world and the seat of lobbying power, led the leaders of CEC to make a decision that enabled the organization to increase its budget. The decision, however, was fatal to the future of CEC as a professional society. The decision was that *membership to CEC was open, not to individuals but to firms.*

The logic was that a large firm with, say, sixty engineers and draftsmen should pay greater annual dues than one with a single principal and two draftsmen. While this decision solved the immediate budget plans, it created, forever, the fact that CEC did not represent the professional engineer as an individual, but represented the interests of engineering companies and their relationship to issues, like competitive bidding of federal projects. There was no identity that an individual felt for a Washington lobbying organization. The work that the organization did in those first few years was impressive when viewed from a national perspective.

Included were: improvement of public relations with the Congress and state governments; permitting corporations to practice professional engineering so long as there was a professional license somewhere in the company; generation of articles about engineering in the press; and the release of news stories about the new Consulting Engineers Council.

What this public relations effort did was of great help to the big companies with hundreds of employees. In the 1960s and '70s CEC went on to accumulate a remarkable record of defending private enterprise against the incursion of the government, both federal and state, into all manner of procurement of engineering services, and the effort by public bodies to inject themselves into the private lives of citizens. CEC changed direction, largely because the staff and the governing body of the council saw their priorities in the political battles being waged between activists and conservatives.

Early in the decade CEC had merged with other engineering organizations to form the American Consulting Engineers Council. By 1977 ACEC had enrolled its 3,000th member firm, and thereafter became primarily involved in public affairs, forming committees to attend national and international forums on all manner of legislation, energy policy, mine safety, and the environment. The 1980s saw ACEC involved more than ever before in the legislative process and challenging federal and state agencies on their procurement procedures. The close of the twentieth century bore witness to the success and involvement of ACEC in assisting Congress on many pieces of legislation, covering the full spectrum of issues that impacted the construction industry.

However, CEC never promoted itself as a professional society concerned with the ethics and professionalism of its members. It was a business and lobbying organization. It is logical, therefore, that a movement to bring engineers together would emerge to fill the void. Such a movement resulted in the formation of the National Society of Professional Engineers.

The National Society of Professional Engineers

By 1934 the Great Depression in the United States began to wane, largely because of the efforts of a depleted private sector and the effects that the New Deal was beginning to have on the business sector. Money that had been withdrawn from the economy in the Crash of 1929, and carefully placed in secure banks or foreign holding companies, began to emerge on the premise that there were good investments to be made in a market that had bottomed out three years before. The profession of engineering had been particularly hard hit in the economic downturn since construction all but ceased to exist from 1930 to 1934. No one was building. No one had the financing. And then, in New York City, the Rockerfellers started construction on Rockerfeller Center in the heart of Manhattan, with the largest building program in ten years. This single event became the focus of the building industry, the lending industry and the steel producers, who began to talk in terms of the "future," something that had not happened in years.

The engineers in private practice, mainly structural but with a sprinkling of mechanical and electrical, began to talk to one another about the prospects of making a decent living when the industry finally came back to "normal." The discussion was not about the standards of structural steel or the need to produce a specification for a newly invented non-toxic refrigerant, but about how the design profession could get together and take care of their mutual problems. Problems such as competitive bidding of design contracts that reduced fees below survival levels, or the establishment of a fee schedule that would allow them to fairly compete with large manufacturing corporations that offered design services as part of marketing their products.

The notion of a professional society representing the interests of engineers in private practice had been on the back burner for twenty years. In 1914 the American Association of Engineers (AAE) in New York had proposed a society concerned with the ethics and goals of the engineer in private practice. In 1922 they published a set of principles that included the goal, "To put engineering practice on a higher plane by the passage of engineering registration laws in every state and the enforcement of existing registration laws." (49)

In 1934, D. B. Steinman, who had been president of the AAE in 1925, called a meeting of a number of state societies, and they voted to create the National Society of Professional Engineers. In his acceptance of the presidency of the new organization, Steinman outlined the principles of NSPE, which were, "To protect engineers from competition by unqualified competitors, from unethical practices, from inadequate compensation; and to build public appreciation of engineers." Steinman's view of the future professional society was based on a need to build an organization to which each licensed professional engineer felt an emotional longing to belong and contribute for the greater good. "Through membership and active participation in NSPE, the individual engineer renders his contribution toward making engineering a better and more satisfying profession than he found it," he said. (49)

This was an organization that needed the services of its members. For the engineer who had found his professional identity, probably through a successful private practice, and was financially secure, the new society offered a place for meeting his peers and building the profession of engineering, with all the trappings of welfare, fraternal relations, advancement, legislative enforcement and unity.

The founders prepared a set of objectives to give direction for future action.

OBJECTIVES

1. To promote the public welfare and to advance and protect the economic and professional interests of the engineer, individually and collectively, through united effort, legislation and public relations.
2. To organize, coordinate, unite, and extend the activities of state societies of professional engineers and their country chapters.
3. To strengthen, unify, extend and enforce state legislation protecting the public welfare, the practice of engineering , and the designation "Engineer."
4. To protect the engineer against exploitation, unprofessional competition, unlawful encroachment and restriction of the rights of practice.
5. To improve conditions of employment and methods of engaging engineering services.
6. To wage a militant campaign for more adequate compensation for engineering services.
7. To extend employment services and build up a reserve fund for assisting engineers in distress.

8. To encourage and guide student engineers and engineering assistants.
9. To promote cooperative and fraternal relations within the profession.
10. To conduct a planned campaign for the advancement profession in public recognition, confidence and esteem.

A reading of the objectives discloses the difficult economic climate in which the authors and most other engineers found themselves, and the need to assist the downtrodden practitioner from exploitation and "unlawful" competition. The need to build a "guild" mentality, where you are unwelcome to participate and cannot join until selected under the rules of admission, becomes clear in the light of objectives "protecting against unlawful encroachment." But this was the theme that dominated the politics and social behavior of that time. The crunching reduction of self-esteem that happened, when hard-working persons found themselves destitute and unable to find work to support a family, is not easy to understand in a time of affluence and security.

By 1934 twenty-eight states had enacted registration laws, and this left many engineers ineligible for membership in NSPE since registration was a requirement. The District of Columbia had embraced the concept of registration in 1920, with the formation of a Board of Professional Registration and the issuance of licenses to practice to many engineers. But it was not until 1950 that the Congress finally saw fit to pass an act bringing the practice of engineering under control of the District of Columbia government.

The story of NSPE is the story of an organization composed of a central body in Washington, and many state organizations, each having voting power and influence on the direction of the core. At one time the Board of Directors had a membership of almost 200 persons, each with a vote and an agenda and the perseverance to stay in the board meeting until given the opportunity to say what was on one's mind. There were many long board meetings. From time to time there were movements to allow membership for non-registered graduate engineers and to bring in the majority of technical people in industry and government, both federal and state.

In 1969 the board hired the Opinion Research Corporation of Princeton, New Jersey, to poll nonmembers as to their impressions of the society and what it meant to them. The results indicated that the nontechnical goals were well understood, and the thrust, in areas such as ethics, education, registration, legislative action, public relations, and inter-society coordination, were important, but not relevant to the individual. The society activities were too broad and the programs of little concern. The board responded by increasing publicity and emphasizing state membership.

Throughout its history NSPE promoted the goal of establishing engineers as professionals. The concern persisted about the number of engineering college graduates who seemed to view their employment simply as a means of livelihood. They had little interest in the society's mission. The board recognized that early introduction to the story of the need for professionalism could be delivered by educators during the student's university experience. A program was instituted in the 1960s to encourage college instructors to include the subject in the course of their lectures. A study done a few years after revealed that most deans of engineering believed that the normal contact between student and lecturer was sufficient to begin the growth of professional awareness.

Over the years the society encouraged professionalism and the protection of engineers by supporting a ban on bidding and direct financial competition between firms, and the "raiding" of personnel from one firm by another.

The one-man firm was a thing of the past. As engineering projects and buildings became more complicated, so did the need to have more competent personnel in the various disciplines increase. A typical small consulting engineering firm would consist of a registered principal, two mechanical engineers, an electrical engineer, four graduate engineers, six or seven draftsmen, and two secretaries. It took between six people as a minimum and twelve as an average for a professional engineer to stay in business. These small firms needed the protection offered by NSPE against all manner of regulation and government intrusion.

NSPE was concerned with the differences between members of the engineering profession. NSPE at that time had a membership of 85,000 members. There were in the states of the Union 650,000 registered engineers who were eligible to join the society. In the nation as a whole there were more than 2.7 million engineering graduates, of whom more than two million worked in industry or occupations where a license to practice engineering, issued by one of the states, appeared to be of little or no value.

NSPE looked for ways of creating identity for all. To meet the diverse needs of engineers in different employment fields, "functional sections" were created, which more closely related to the working environment of private practice versus government, industry or education. This was a recognition of the fact that the world of engineering employment in government is very different from that in industry, and to get the industrial employee interested in becoming registered required a whole different set of inducements and information about the advantages of membership. There were also issues like fee schedules, which were desired by those in private practice but opposed by those in government, and of no interest at all to education and industry.

The functional sections served valuable purposes over the years and brought focus and participation to many members. NSPE continues to be a major force in recommending professionalism in engineering. It should also be recognized that parts of society change drastically, and others move on slowly with the changing times. While professions such as law and teaching are still practiced by *individuals,* with the practitioner dealing one-on-one with the client (individually or in groups), the same cannot be said about engineering, with the result that the lawyers and teachers (and many other professionals) can maintain a distinct behavioral pattern with the client because the client is sitting in front of them and is easily identified.

The Ubiquitous Profession

Thinking back to Benjamin Latrobe, Christopher Colles, or the other engineers who practiced in the eighteenth and nineteenth centuries, one can immediately identify their roles in the projects with which they were involved. They were the only technical advisers to many untrained workers who followed instructions in order to execute the project. Not only did they individually conceive the design of the project based on their knowledge of science and engineering, but they transformed their design into nuts and bolts, beams and columns, pumps and engines and other elements with which they were familiar.

While analogies are usually somewhat removed from the issue at hand, one can picture the eighteenth century process by looking at a full glass of water, on the surface of which floats a very thin layer of olive oil. The oil represents the engineers; the rest of the glass of water represents the workers. A ratio of one hundred to one or greater.

In the modern world the simple water has changed into a complicated fluid, such as orange juice. The oil has disappeared; its place has been merged throughout the glass by many special components, such as sugar, calcium, potassium and magnesium—all stand-alone things in their own right, but carefully proportioned together to become orange juice. Each chemical, such as calcium or potassium, represents a special branch of engineering expertise, such as mechanical, electrical, aeronautical or electronic, performed by many different engineers at varying levels of training and responsibility.

This mental picture is the same as what has emerged in the world of engineering. No longer do they float on the top. They are part and parcel of almost everything in society, beginning at the bottom of the heap with the production of the basics, such as sand, gravel and bricks, to the pinnacle of technology in medicine, computers and a host of other ventures. They are part of very nearly everything we do, everything we buy and use, everything that makes us safer, healthier, more informed, more in control of our lives and more able to find time for other interests rather than just survival.

And the concept of being a "professional," standing alone with the client, no longer challenges most engineers because their world is one of team building—working with the financial-, human-, career-, results-building and ladder-climbing people in an organization. Their main product is coordination and technical input to join the many threads comprising any economic effort.

Such is the reality of the field of engineering in the latter part of the twentieth century in Washington. The things that are making headlines in the newspapers, apart from politics, are such ventures as the space program, the Washington Metro, the power outages in winter, and the gridlock of our road transportation system. Most have a distinct connection to technical expertise that has failed or succeeded in some manner.

Certainly one of the unsolved problems of the late-twentieth century is urban transportation. Cities have grown in population and area, with more and more people commuting from home to places of employment using an automobile. This approach gives the individual a degree of freedom, but collectively creates a need for highway capacity that always lags behind the demand. The result is a requirement for alternative methods of transportation based on the notion that it is more efficient to use buses or rail rather than individual automobiles. It was with this thinking that the leaders of metropolitan Washington began to invest in the idea of a system of transportation similar to the New York subway.

Mass Transit: The Washington Metro

One of Washington's successes is its mass transit system known as the Metro. At the close of the twentieth century the city had the dubious distinction of having the third-worst record for commuter travel in the nation, and without the Metro rail system there can be no doubt what position it would occupy.

The first questions as to when Washington would get an "underground subway" system were raised by the *Washington Post* in 1907, and it was not until 1944, toward the end of World War II, that Congress came to the conclusion that the metropolitan region needed more than the existing streetcar system. The electric streetcars, with their concealed underground supply of electricity, presented an aesthetically pleasing alternative to the elevated railways of New York and Chicago, with their steel gantries that turned the roads below into tunnels. But the elevated rail systems did the one thing that the streetcars could not do; and that was carry masses of people quickly and safely through the crowded cities, independent of the ever-increasing congestion of the roads.

The population of the metropolitan region, about 800,000 in 1939, had soured to more than 1.3 million in 1945, with forecasts reaching 2 million by 1965. To plan for this change, the engineering firms of J. E. Greiner and DeLeuw Cather, both of Chicago, were contracted to prepare a study of the future mass-transit needs of the area, and prepare a plan to relieve the growing congestion in the downtown area. Their scheme called for the construction of a seven-mile-long subway system in the center of the city, connecting to above-ground gasoline and diesel-powered buses operating over new freeways connected to the suburbs.

A brief flurry of opposition to the "paving over" of the district caused the plan to be shelved in favor of the creation of the National Capital Regional Planning Council in 1955, representing Maryland, Virginia and the district, and charged with the responsibility of planning a system to meet future forecasts. In 1959 this body produced a plan including a 33-mile rapid-transit arm supported by a 66-mile freeway system of highways and bridges, much to the liking of the highway lobby, but opposed by most of the locals and their planning organizations.

The National Capital Transportation Act of 1960 proved to be the turning point in the commitment of the federal government to a rapid rail system in the region, largely financed by Congress but cost-shared between all jurisdictions as an integral part of the financing plan. The 1962 plan called for an eighty-three-mile-long rail line, nineteen miles underground, connected to an above-ground bus system. With the creation of the Washington Metropolitan Area Transit Authority in February 1967, management and responsibility for mass transit was transferred from the federal government to a regional body with local interest in building and operating a mass-transit system. The previous year DeLeuw, Cather and Co. had been hired to do the final planning. They began the preparation of design drawings for an ultimate 103-mile-long system running underground in the downtown parts of the District of Columbia for about nineteen miles and stretching out into the suburbs, to what were the fringes of the metropolitan region at that time.

The story of the building of the Washington Metro, called the "Largest Public Works project in history," is the story of superb cooperation between the engineering designers, headed by DeLeuw Cather, architect Harry Weese, WMATA management and the project management by the Bechtel Company. It is also the story of the application of the latest technologies in electric and electronic controls, computers, geology, hydrology, structural engineering and construction. Much of the nineteen miles underground required the tunneling through rock.

In a previous chapter the building of a 3,100-foot-long tunnel at Paw Paw Junction on the C & O Canal is described. Actual construction in the 1840s took a little more than four years, or about 1,050 working days, which means the progress was of the order of *three* feet per day. Since then, the development of tunnel-boring machines has been advanced to the point that Metro's builders could drill through *two hundred* feet per day, and remove the bored rock to the surface.

Influenced by improvements in mining engineering gleaned from all parts of the world, the laying of a duplicate rail line and the building of a number of passenger stations, all underground in the heart of an existing city, became a process of development of the best techniques to solve each unique challenge at it confronted the designers and contractors. For example, the early tunnels through solid rock under Dupont Circle were rectangular, almost forty feet wide, which required the insertion of heavy steel beams every eighteen inches at the ceiling of the cut to support the rock overhead.

Developments in the art of rock boring machines in the 1970s led to a change in the approach the contractors used when faced with solid rock. Instead of building a single rectangular tunnel capable of housing two rail lines, they bored twin circular tunnels, side by side, each sized to carry a train. This breakthrough dramatically reduced the cost of rock penetration by increasing the productivity of the builders by a factor of three.

To solve the problem of water leakage into the tunnels and to secure the exposed surface of the rock, a new process named "shotcrete" was developed in which a fast-drying concrete paste, sprayed at high pressure, bonded with the newly drilled surface, sealing the fissures against seepage and providing a solid envelope on the inside of the tunnel.

In the heart of the city the rail lines were installed using the "cut and cover" technique. Here the entire street for one or more blocks was closed and excavated, leaving a massive open trench through which the existing underground utilities, electric cabling, sewers, telephone and water mains threaded like spider webs. The first task therefore was to rework these utilities under, over and around the future concrete envelope that would enclose the rail lines. Generally, the Metro envelope fell well below the existing utilities, which occupied a stratum twenty feet deep, but it required excavating to a depth of fifty to sixty feet as a minimum to allow the bottom foundations to be poured. Many times this requirement set the rail tracks below the elevation of the foundations of the buildings on either side of the street.

To prevent any movement or potential collapse of these foundations they had to be "underpinned." This process required the existing building foundations to be extended down with new concrete foundations. One classic example is the work occurred on F Street NW in front of the original U.S. Patent Office. Here, to support the old historic building, more than 400 seventy-foot-long steel "I" sections, called pilings, were driven into the street just beyond the building property line and bonded together to form a structurally sound wall. This allowed the building of a reinforced concrete arch to take place, the full width of the street, spanning from the face of the Patent Office to the building across the street.

Where stations were planned, the arch dimensions were 600 feet in length by 60 feet in width and 50 feet from track to the peak of the arch. One curious observation is the fact that the street widths in the city were planned by Pierre L'Enfant to be 100 feet minimum, which allowed the engineering of the Metro envelope to take advantage of a condition so deplored by the citizens almost 200 years before.

The *engineering process* is well illustrated by the methods used to cross the Potomac into Virginia. There are two crossings, one between Foggy Bottom and Rosslyn on the Orange Line and the second from L'Enfant Plaza to the Pentagon on the Yellow Line. The first step in the process is to *define the problem*, and for the two projects the definition was the same: "How do we install a rail system under the river in a safe and constructible manner and at the least cost?" The second step is to *determine the facts* that are relevant to the solution, which required the extensive underground survey of the routes and the drilling of hundreds of 2-1/2-inch-diameter earth and rock core samples for laboratory analysis, then determining the characteristics of the material and its ability to be drilled, support load, allow water penetration, allow excavation, strata formation and hosts of other data, from which the engineers began to envisage potential solutions. Having *analyzed the facts* it became possible to *select a solution,* and it became apparent that the best solution for the Rosslyn crossing was an underwater envelope drilled in the solid rock formation that straddles the river at that point.

For the Pentagon crossing, however, the studies showed the presence of a depth of porous earth on the bed of the river to the point that a drilled tunnel would have to be very deep and expensive. The alternative was to use the "sunken tube" method, which consisted of several 340-foot-long, 40-foot-diameter, watertight, steel submarine-like tubes floated from their factory on the Susquehanna River and settled into trenches excavated into the mud at the bottom of the river. The tubes were ballasted on top with tons of rock to keep them from floating, then joined together and pumped dry to form a watertight secure steel envelope sufficiently large to allow the installation of two parallel rail lines inside on a poured concrete base.

No discussion of the building of the Washington Metro would be complete without mention of the enormous impact that electronics and computers had on the success of the system. The digital technology age arrived at just the right time to allow the designers of the system to embrace the power of the computer chip and the efficiencies and safety that it brought to the network. From fare cards to train controls, engineering has allowed management to oversee an enterprise of such complexity and size with reliability and the knowledge that not much is cast in stone: everything can and will be modified as the demands of the future dictate.

Viewed from an engineering perspective the Washington Metro is a grand success. Not only does it meet its goal as a superior people mover, but it has begun to influence the expansion of the city. There has been, and continues to be, substantial economic growth at each of the Metro stations. In the downtown area a number of commercial buildings have appeared within walking distance of stations, while both commercial and residential construction has boomed in the suburbs.

Metro can be judged as an engineering success because of the benefit it brings to its riders and the region as a whole. The alternative modes of transportation in a modern city are severely limited and generally rely on the automobile, which has been unable to provide the flexibility and time saving that it can in small towns and rural settings.

Not all successful engineering endeavors, however, bring a better way of life immediately to the general population. Some are heavy in scientific research that yields knowledge of our universe on a molecular scale, in the case of medicine, or on a universal scale, in the case of space exploration. The history of the National Aeronautics and Space Administration in Washington is such a case.

Exploration of Space

As a fallout of the events between 1941 and 1945, a vast amount of research had been done in areas such as communications and radar. The scientific community was anxious to foster the expansion of these technologies, with further research and the development of useful products for the nation as a whole.

One ideal vehicle to propagate scientific research was the International Council of Scientific Unions, a long-established group of academics that first met in 1882. In 1932 the council's interests were primarily concerned with the accurate measurement of the earth's surfaces. In a meeting held in 1951, the development of rockets, primarily by the Germans during the war, led the scientists to look to space as the next subject to research. The council designated 1957 as the International Geophysical Year (IGY) and issued requests for all countries to attempt to put a satellite in orbit during the IGY. Both the United States and Russia accepted the challenge, which caused President Eisenhower to actively pursue the formation of an arm of government to lead the effort. Various parts of the public sector had been or were involved in the development of rocket science, while others had substantial knowhow in communications and project management, but no single agency possessed all the skills necessary to begin the exploration of the upper atmosphere. The first effort by the United States, beginning in 1956, utilized the Vanguard rocket, developed for the military, but it proved to be unreliable, and several attempts failed to put a small satellite in orbit.

In 1957 the Russians launched their Sputnik satellite, and the entire world was taken by surprise as it orbited the earth issuing a "peeping" signal picked up by normal radio receivers and broadcast by the media to every corner of Earth. This event led to much rhetoric from the Congress and the media as to the failure of our engineering and scientific communities. And what should be done about them to keep pace with, and then overtake our Cold War enemy? We failed to teach our high school students mathematics. We failed to teach our university students science. The state of our national technology was appalling. So said our detractors.

In due course the U.S. did succeed in putting a four-pound stainless steel ball in orbit, launched on March 17, 1958 by a combined Army/NASA team using a modified Vanguard rocket as the launch vehicle. This was followed by the first American satellite, Explorer 1, launched on December 31, 1958, from the newly constructed space facility at Cape Canaveral, Florida, by a Jupiter rocket.

After considerable debate and review of the alternatives by his advisors, President Eisenhower decided that the fastest and most reliable approach to improving the space research effort was to set up a separate agency of government. It would be staffed with scientists and engineers from the various branches of government, industry and academia that had some experience in the scientific measurement of the atmosphere and radio communications. However it soon became apparent that most experienced scientists were already committed to their chosen fields of research and were unwilling to gamble their careers on an untested and novel program with an unknown probability of success. So it fell to young recent science graduates to fill the need. Substantial infrastructure in the way of buildings to house such a research program, and manufacturing capability to construct the research equipment, became an immediate challenge.

So in 1958, with the creation of the National Aeronautics and Space Administration, it was decided to build a laboratory to coordinate all the research and development necessary to begin a space program. A site adjacent to the Agriculture Department in Beltsville, Maryland, a suburb fourteen miles distant from downtown Washington, was chosen and named the Goddard Space Flight Center in honor of one of America's rocket pioneers.

NASA-Goddard

Of all the successes and failures in the engineering industry in Washington, perhaps the story of the Goddard Space Flight Center falls close to the top of the heap when the successes are examined. This is both curious and gratifying because the mission given to the fledgling laboratory was unheard of in the preceding history of man; the mission was to develop a program to explore outer space.

The story of Goddard is a story of people motivated by a narrow mission who worked together with much friction and frustration in the early years, and with a fluent team spirit in the later years. It was the classical conflict between the scientist and engineer—the young scientist slowly developing his theoretical research model, and even more slowly transforming the model into set of requirements that could then be given to an engineer to design the hardware for insertion into space.

Scientists were not used to performing their research to fit with a time table; whereas the engineers, accustomed to planning and managing time-sensitive programs, were unwilling to let schedules slip in order to improve a satellite with the addition of more bells and whistles dreamed up by the scientist. Congress, in providing substantial funding for the new agency, wanted results, and the engineers running the various projects were under considerable pressure to produce not only "on time and in budget," but to have the project deliver results. To have a planned launch of a satellite blow up on the launch pad was an engineering failure, but to have a successful launch of the same project six months late was also an engineering failure.

The rockets, or "launch vehicles" as the parlance quickly developed, would not be Goddard's responsibility; they would be produced in Huntsville, Alabama, and later in Houston, but the "pay-load," or satellite carrying the scientific experiment, would be designed and built at Goddard in Washington.

The solution, after much pain and frustration on the part of all four participants—the scientists, engineers, NASA headquarters and the Congress—proved to be a system of engineering management. It carefully and realistically established research goals for the scientists and then worked closely with them to agree on the experimental requirements so that the engineers could begin to manufacture the hardware, and in conjunction with the scientist, begin pre-flight testing.

In 1959 very little was known about outer space; scientists were waiting to measure its magnetic fields, temperatures, solar winds, gasses, radiation, and a host of other factors. To bring about an orderly process to the planning of future research, a committee in conjunction with the National Academy of Science was set up to screen research requests from all parts of the nation. The committee then prepared a long-range agenda for meeting the requests, based on many factors, not the least of which were the cost of the hardware to meet the requirements and the weight of the final satellite for launch purposes.

A "satellite," as the name implies, is a smaller object in orbit around a larger object. For Goddard the larger object was Earth, and the smaller object was a data collection station, designed to measure the phenomenon that was the subject of the experiment. The early satellites, for example, were concerned with the appearance of Earth, as a whole, when viewed from twenty thousand miles out in space.

These satellites, therefore, were equipped with a *sensor*, in this case a camera, which could gather an image of the earth visually and then transform the visual image into an electrical signal. The devise is named a *transducer.* The transducer then passed the electrical coded image to a *transmitter*, on board the satellite, which sent the coded image to a ground station. The ground station received the radio signal, and a second *transducer* converted the coded signal into a visual image, which could then be displayed on a dynamic visual screen or converted into still pictures.

Thus all satellites concerned with gathering data about our universe had to be fitted with one or more sensors capable of detecting and quantitatively measuring whatever the variable was that the science experiment was designed to explore. Then ways had to be invented to convert the measured variable into electrical (and later digital) signals that could be transmitted, using radio technology, back to Earth.

Viewed from this perspective, it becomes obvious that the satellite is a means to an end to allow the scientist sitting on Earth to conduct the experiment by remote control, rather than in the close environment of the earthbound laboratory. It also becomes clear that there is a massive amount of engineering necessary to allow the scientist to work on a specific piece of research. Beyond the physical construction of the satellite itself, there is the task of the entire launch cycle. Then the data acquisition phase, involving huge antenna dishes, recorders, displays, and imaging systems, and the ground controllers constantly monitoring the performance of the satellite and invoking repair routines built into the system.

In the early 1960s the first order of business was to begin with the basics, the most immediate of which was how to get things to work; in other words, build reliability into everything. In April 1959 the first of thirty buildings destined to serve the Goddard Center came off the drawing boards and went into construction, followed by two buildings dedicated to materials and component testing.

Engineers knew how paint and rubber and a host of other materials performed on Earth. But there was no information on how a painted surface would perform in the vacuum of outer space when subjected to intense radiation of the sun on one side and almost absolute zero of cold on the other. The solution was to build test chambers that simulated the conditions of outer space.

To analyze the performance of various painted and applied surface treatments, a "coating test tank" was designed. It consisted of an L-shaped steel vessel, ten feet in diameter, with each of the two legs of the L twenty-five feet in length. At one end of the L an infrared heat generator, capable of producing radiant heat from a 2,500-degree-temperature element, was mounted. At the opposite end of the L a ten-foot-diameter refrigerated stainless steel plate, capable of being cooled to 100 degrees below zero, was mounted. The entire tank could be evacuated by vacuum pumps to produce the same zero air pressure expected to be encountered in outer space. At the apex of the L, test samples, either fixed or gradually rotating, could be exposed to the burning radiation of the heater in one instant, and then to the freezing cold plate the next. In this manner the samples could be introduced, to a fair degree, to the conditions expected in space.

The coating tank was just one of many pieces of testing gear designed and built at Goddard in the initial planning and setup of the facility. The engineers were well-aware that once a satellite was in space, there would be very little that could be done to repair a broken connection or cool an overheating device. The planning and testing had to be sufficiently rigorous so that most weak links would be uncovered and improved before the experiment left the Earth's surface.

Each scientific experiment was reduced to a set of instruments capable of gathering the necessary data and then transmitting it back to Earth. Generally, two identical satellites were constructed, one as a backup, and both were heated, frozen, vibrated, shaken, rotated and tested in every imaginable way before they were certified ready for launch. Initially the scientists were concerned that their delicate instruments could be damaged by all the rough testing, but it soon became obvious that the vibration, shock and forces generated during launch could not be avoided, so it was better to have the satellite fail during testing rather than during its flight to space.

In its journey through space, the first task of the experiment was to gather data, and the second task was to transmit this data back to Earth. Each satellite, therefore, had to be equipped with a data-transmission system capable of sending whatever it had sensed back to Earth. This requirement meant that Goddard had to develop and build receiving stations and monitoring and control rooms to track the orbit of the satellite and issue commands for the satellite to perform various functions such as "wake-up," "record," "turn-off sensors," "transmit," "repeat," or "charge battery," to name a few. In addition, the ground controller had to be able to fire the small thrusters that were able to rotate or position the satellite or change its attitude to improve performance. The earliest systems were battery powered, but with the invention of the solar-powered electrical generators it became possible to extend the performing life of the satellite.

With power collected from the sun it became possible to consider designs with continuous receive- and transmit-capability, which greatly increased the volume of data picked up by the satellite's sensors and transmitted back to the ground station, where it could be recorded for future analysis by the scientist.

By the middle of the 1970s Goddard's engineers and scientists had developed a system that allowed the complete cycle of research to be conducted by a team of participants, all working to maximize the number of successful experiments conducted in a climate of dwindling research funding. What emerged was the *Integrated Research Cycle,* a management strategy that looked at the previous experiments' strengths and weaknesses, and built the findings into ongoing efforts and into the planning of future experiments, in particular the reuse of devices and efforts to avoid restarting the planning of new ventures from scratch.

This *Integrated Research Cycle* included:
1. Develop the theory of the proposed experiment
2. Reduce the theory to an experiment plan and hardware design with budget costs
3. Review and determine feasibility and probability of success
4. Manufacture the satellite hardware, and later the software
5. Test all the components, before assembly, rebuild as necessary
6. Assemble whole unit, and simulate mission by testing
7. Subject unit to launch simulation by vibration, shock, pressure, solar temperature, freezing, and prove reliability
8. Launch
9. Track, adjust, communicate, simulate test, and approve
10. Collect data, record, encode, transmit to ground station
11. Analyze data, prepare report, plan next cycle, share data with other experiments
12. Start next cycle by developing follow-on theory

Bringing a system of management to the research process not only greatly reduced the cost of personnel and materials to produce the next generation of satellite, but gave a sense of *professional identity* to the team members.

As a direct consequence, professional behavior erased feelings of conflict and allowed all team members to develop mutual respect. Needless to say, the performance of the stream of satellites that were developed, built, launched and monitored by the scientists was outstanding and exceeded all predictions. In its first decade of operations the center produced and launched more than 100 successful experiments, and by May 1998 the count reached 250. (50)

At its inception in 1958 there were 350 personnel assigned to the laboratory, many in rented space in the suburbs of Washington, and others at the Naval Research Center. By the time the facility was in full production, housed in thirty specialized laboratories, offices and test facilities, there were 11,000 employees and contractor personnel employed in the Beltsville Center.

The main story of the Goddard Space Flight Center, from an engineering perspective, has two interlocking but separate fields of success. The first is the unique and powerfully competent management of the diverse scientific and engineering staff, traditionally different in their approach to their professions, which were assembled and motivated to work together toward a common success. The second is the remarkable creativity of the team of mechanical, electrical, industrial, metallurgical, and aeronautical engineers who created the satellites from their imagination, designed and then built them to fly to the edge of our universe.

The feelings that this generation of engineers must have experienced when on April 24, 1990, they confirmed that the Hubble Space Telescope was in orbit were probably similar to those felt by James Watt in 1769 when he realized that he had accomplished something unique and vital to the success of man for the first time in history.

It is also important to put the effort into perspective with regard to the professional performance of the scientists and engineers who worked on the projects that yielded such successes. First and foremost, the teams did their very best; mistakes were made but no professional liability insurance policies were called upon to make a damaged owner whole. The owner in this case was the government acting for the taxpayers. This owner expected some errors on the part of the designers, did not demand perfection, and did not hold the scientists and engineers liable for their mistakes. This owner had expectations not unlike the owners of the eighteenth and nineteenth centuries.

Secondly, the design teams did not practice *defensive engineering*. Defensive engineering is the mode of design in which the designer departs as little as possible from tried and true solutions to any given problem. To try innovative engineering exposes the designer to unforeseen conditions, which in the private sector may lead to allegations of "design error" for which the owner wishes to be compensated. The space program was built around professionals who were able to exercise their best judgment, sometimes opting for untried and risk-prone solutions, with the knowledge that the client, the government, expected some failure as part of the quest for ultimate success.

Thirdly, and most important, the scientists and engineers were dedicated to the immediate solution to the tasks at hand. They, like most engineers, were focused on their jobs, their families, and their immediate surroundings. There was little to distract them.

Goddard Space Flight Center produced the kind of research and used engineering talent in the same way that most of the great industrial organizations do in the United States today. Individuals were not paramount to the success of the enterprise. Individualism was submerged in favor of the team. In some ways it could be said that management is more important to the attainment of a technical goal.

For the Washington Metro and Goddard Space Flight Center there can be little argument that the right mix of engineering talent, motivated and directed by management, was necessary to reach their goals. Fortunately, not all research is confined to reams of engineers and scientists.

The following relates to the practice of professional engineering by an individual working with two medical doctors at the National Institute of Health in the 1960s.

The Sleep and Dream Laboratory

In their quest to understand the human mind and bring relief to those suffering from mental disability, the medical profession is ever seeking new, yet unexplored ways to approach a problem and devise a treatment. With this in mind, a national medical research facility in 1964 approached a firm of consulting engineers to see if it was possible to build a facility that would allow "normal" patients to have their brain activity monitored while they slept, recording and plotting it over time, regardless of the time of day.

By exploring the dream sequences related by the normal patients, and coordinating this with the brain recordings while they slept, it was felt that a baseline of non-problematic behavior could be generated. Those suffering from disability would then be "dreamed and recorded" in the same manner, and the patterns of their brain behavior compared with the established baseline in the hope that the area of defect could be discovered.

Apart from the electronic recording equipment, design of the facility obviously required a quiet set of rooms, with beds, shielded from sunlight (the testing was to be done during normal working hours), appropriately heated, cooled and ventilated, and provided with normal controlled artificial lighting.

The normal patients were local university students who, for a small fee, agreed to be "dreamed" to set up the baseline. To verify that the "dream laboratory" was in no way influencing the baseline, the students were first asked to come in for a few nights, spend the night hooked up to the recording equipment and discuss their remembrances in detail the following morning. The baseline was duly established.

To meet the needs of the medical personnel, who worked a day shift, the students were then asked to come in during the day and be monitored. This was when the fun began.

Quite apart from the fact that some of the students had great difficulty getting off to sleep, while it was almost impossible to keep others awake, the results of the monitoring were not consistent. There was something about the physical makeup of the laboratory that had a direct bearing on the brain waves. The designers were perplexed. The rooms were soundproof, quiet and carefully temperature-controlled. It was then that they began to think what variables that occur at night they had failed to incorporate into the facility.

The first thing they tested was the sound spectrum. A sound test of the bedrooms revealed a spectrum with heavy emphasis on the low frequency, typical of day noise, whereas typical night sounds contains a predominance of high frequency: wind and the rustle of leaves. So night sounds were recorded, a high fidelity sound system installed, and when switched on, test results improved at once. They were better, but not satisfactory.

The designers then decided to look at the full set of senses typical of most people and see if they had met emotional needs of the "dreamers."

The sense of *touch* in the sheets and surfaces had been met.

The sense of *taste* in the air was not obvious.

The sense of *hearing* had been met with the hi-fi.

The sense of *sight* had been met with adjustable light levels.

The one issue that had not been met was the sense of smell. Was it possible that the odors in the air are different between day and night. Odor was thought to be electrical in character. Minute particles of substance containing odor in the form of an electrical charge float through the air and are drawn in through the nose and impinge in the follicles at the rear of the mouth, and deposit their charge, which is transmitted to the brain, where it is interpreted as a particular odor.

To test this theory, large direct-current electrical coils were installed in all the air-supply registers to the rooms to neutralize any charged particles, and the carpets on the floor replaced with electrical conducting carpets that were attached to a good electrical ground; the theory being that the airborne particles containing the odor would be given a massive positive charge by the electrical coils and, upon entering the space, would be immediately drawn to the grounded carpet and captured.

When the coils were turned on the rooms immediately gave up a most peculiar odor, like mild onions. That was the bad news. The good news was that it was mild onions day and night. After a few minutes in the spaces one immediately became accustomed to the odor and it became irrelevant. When tested the students showed the same data regardless of the time of day. The research could proceed.

Engineering projects like Sleep and Dream occur daily in the United States. They involve an engineer facing a problem whose solution will bring success to another field of endeavor, or the development of a product that in some small way will bring a safer, more enjoyable, more productive experience to someone. This is what engineering is all about.

References

1. "Elegy Written in a Country Churchyard," Thomas Gray. London, England. 1751

2. "History of Technology," Donald Cardwell. Fontana Press. 1994.

3. "Precis de Lecons d'Architecture Donne a l''Ecole Polytechnique," by Jean-Nicholas-Louis Durand. Paris 1802.

4. "Lectures on the Industrial Revolution," by Arthur Toynbee. 1884. Encyclopedia Britannica.

5. "Cast and Wrought Iron for Building Purposes." William Fairburn. London, England. 1854.

6. "Heat and Cold". A Selective History of Heating, Ventilation, Air-Conditioning and Refrigeration from the Ancients to the 1930's," by Barry Donaldson et al. ASHRAE. 1994.

7. "The Beginning of a Century of Steam and Water Heating," by The H.B.Smith Company. Westfield, Massachusetts. 1960.

8. Appleton's "Dictionary of Machines,Mechanics, Enginework and Engineering." New York. 1857.

9. "Old Virginia and Her Neighbours," by John Fiske. Houghton Mifflin and Company. Boston. 1898.

10. "The Pursuit of Science in Revolutionary America, 1735-1789," by Brooke Hindle. The University of North Carolina Press. 1956

11. "Washington," by Douglas Southall Freeman. Collier Books, New York. 1992.

12. "The U.S. Army Engineers Fighting Elite." Edited by Col. Franklin M. Davis, Jr. Franklin Watts, Inc. New York. 1967.

13. "The Engineer in America." Terry S. Reynolds. Editor. The University of Chicago Press. 1991.

14. "The Mid-Atlantic Engineers: A History of the Baltimore District," U.S. Army Corps of Engineers. 1976.

15. "Contemporary Modern America." Volume 4. Ballinger Publishing Company, Cambridge, Massachusetts. 1976.

16. Records of the Columbia Historical Society of Washington, D.C. 1948-1950. Volume 50. Page 308.

17. "Washington on View: The Nation's Capital Since 1790," by John W. Reps. University of North Carolina Press. 1991.

18. "Plan of the City Intended for the Permanent Seat of the Government of the United States," by Peter Charles L'Enfant Library of Congress. U.S Coast and Geodetic Survey. 1887.

19. "Growing with Washington." Robert R. Hershman, et al. Washington Gas Light Company. 1948.

20. Records of the Columbia Historical Society of Washington, D.C. 1953-1956 Volume 53.

21. "Our Capitol." 89th Congress. U.S. Government Printing Office. Washington D.C. 1966.

22. The Engineering Drawings of Benjamin Henry Latrobe. Edited by Darwin Stapleton for the Maryland Historical Society by Yale University Press. 1980.

23. "The Presidents," by Frank Freidel. White House Historic Association. 1964.

24. "Civil Engineering Landmarks of the Nation's Capital." National Capital Section of the American Society of Civil Engineers. Washington. D.C. 1982.

25. "Chesapeake and Ohio Canal." U.S. Department of the Interior. Washington. D.C. 1991.

26. Engraving on a Monument at Wisconsin Avenue and the C. & O. Canal in Georgetown. 1998.

27. "A Short Course in Plumbing History," by Jim Olsztynski, Editor, PMEngineer. July/August. 1998.

28.   *The Washington Post*. November 28, 2000.

29.   "The Federal City: Plans and Realities." By Frederick Gutheim. The Smithsonian Institute Press. 1976.

30.   "Ventilation Problems in the Halls of the Senate and House of Representatives." by G.W.Calver, Commander, Medical Corps. U.S. Navy. U.S.Government Printing Office. 1930.

31.   "Specifications for Materials and Labor to be Performed in the Construction of Eight Boilers for Heating and Ventilating the United States Capitol Extension." By Nason and Dodge, Contractors. New York. Architect of the Capitol. 1857.

32.   Correspondence Files of the Architect of the Capitol. 1863-1869.

33.   "History of the United States Capitol." Glen Brown. 1900.

34.   Report to the Secretary of the Interior by the Architect of the Capitol and Appendix by Professor S.H.Woodbridge Government Printing Office. Washington D.C. 1896.

35.   "Temple of Liberty," by Pamela Scott. Library of Congress, Washington D.C., and Oxford University Press, 1995.

36.   "Washington's Telephone History and Growth." Bell Atlantic Telephone Company. Washington D.C. 1976.

37.   Report of the Board of Public Works of the District of Columbia. November 1, 1873.

38.   "Political and Social Growth of the United States: 1852-1933," by Arthur Meier Schlesinger. The Macmillan Company. New York. 1933.

39.   "The Mechanical Engineer in America : 1830-1910," by Monte A. Calvert. Johns Hopkins Press. Baltimore.

40.   Records of the Washington Historical Society.

41.   Records of the Washington Building Congress.

42.   J.G.White Company to Elliott Woods, Superintendent of Buildings. U.S.Capitol. July 14, 1906.

43. Memorandum from Mr.L.Laser to Mr. Walter Rubel, Office of the Architect of the Capitol. January 11, 1963.

44. "Progress in Air Conditioning in the Last Quarter Century," by Willis H.Carrier. 1936. Transactions of the American Society of Heating and Ventilating Engineers. Vol. 42.

45. Drawing Number 3028, "Ventilating Apparatus Etc. – for House of Representatives." Elliott Woods, Superintendent of Buildings. U.S.Capitol. and Henry Adams, Consulting Engineer. Baltimore, Maryland.

46. "Willis Haviland Carrier – Father of Air Conditioning," by Margaret Ingels. 1952. Carrier Corporation.

47. "Air Conditioning the Halls of Congress." L.L.Lewis, Member. A.S.H.V.E. Journal. 1929.

48. "Engineering the Future." A History of the American Consulting Engineers Council. Washington DC. 1993.

49. "Building for Professional Growth." A History of the National Society of Professional Engineers by Paul H. Robbins, P.E. Washington D.C. 1984.

50. "Dreams, Hopes, Realities." NASA's Goddard Space Flight Center: The First Forty Years. By Lane E. Wallace. 1999.

Plates

Index

Y